The early twenty first century has been defined by a rise in Islamist

war with the West' – comprement ... the latest date stamped below.
two extremes rhetorical allies and building a spira...
hatred: 'The Rage'. By looking at extremist movements both on
and offline, she shows how far-right and Islamist extremists have
succeeded in penetrating each other's echo chambers as a result of
their mutually useful messages. Based on first-hand interviews, this
book introduces readers to the world of reciprocal radicalisation
and the hotbeds of extremism that have developed, with potentially
disastrous consequences, in the UK, Europe and the US.

Julia Ebner is a terrorism and extremism researcher based in
London. She is Research Fellow at the Institute for Strategic
Dialogue and Global Fellow at the Project for the Study of the 21st
Century. She spent two years working for the world's first counter-
extremism organisation Quilliam, where she led research projects
on terrorism prevention for the European Commission and the Kofi
Annan Foundation, and gave evidence to the Home Affairs Select
Committee on far-right extremism. In her role as coordinator of the
pan-European network Families Against Terrorism and Extremism
(FATE), she carried out radicalisation-prevention projects across
Europe and North Africa. On the basis of her research, Julia
advises parliamentary working groups, frontline workers and tech
firms, speaks at international conferences and delivers workshops
in schools and universities. She regularly writes for the *Guardian*
and the *Independent*, and gives interviews in English, German and
French on the BBC, CNN, ZDF, ARD, France24, Al Jazeera, LBC
and others.

'Julia Ebner shows how Islamist and right-wing extremism are two sides of the same coin. Her analysis is compelling, insightful, and highly readable.'

– Peter R. Neumann, author of *Radicalized*

'*The Rage* reads like a novel but unfortunately its story is non-fiction: Islamist hotheads and those on the far-right polarise our societies and the moderates in the middle lose ground to populists who play politics with extremism.'

– Alex P. Schmid, Editor-in-Chief, *Perspectives on Terrorism*

'An original and highly informative book on one of the core security issues of our time. *The Rage* demonstrates powerfully how apparently opposite strands of extremism feed so readily off each other and, in doing so, it illuminates the extent of the problems facing us. Essential reading.'

– Paul Rogers, Emeritus Professor of Peace Studies, Bradford University and author of *Irregular War*

'An excellent debut: informed, well-researched and thoughtful. Ebner traces the increasingly important interdependency of far-right and Islamist movements, and offers humane, smart ways through the impasse.'

– Jamie Bartlett, author of *Radicals*

'This book brings alive the causes and consequences of far-right extremism and Islamist radicalism in our midst. These two forms of rising bigotry threaten to tear our societies apart. Ebner exposes them both and powerfully calls on us to defend liberal tolerance. *The Rage* is an excellent master course for those seeking to understand the growth of fanaticism.'

– Ed Husain, author of *The Islamist*

'Julia Ebner has written a fine book, approaching the vexing topic of "reciprocal radicalisation" with admirable ethnographic empathy. Crisply written, *The Rage* journeys through the leading and often intertwined forms of extremism today: jihadi Islamists and the far-right. The mirroring of these violent narratives is striking, and is revealed here through both eye-opening vignettes and wide-ranging empirical data. Without doubt, *The Rage* is *the* most important contribution to this burgeoning subject to date, and surely will be of use to scholars, policy-makers and the wider public alike.'

– **Matthew Feldman, Professor of Contemporary History,
Teesside University**

'Julia Ebner draws on the very latest evidence to deliver important new analysis of two seemingly opposing forms of extremism and their mutually reinforcing worldviews. The perpetrators of most terrorist and violent extremist acts committed in recent years have followed some form of radicalisation process; Ebner's book makes an important contribution to our understanding of the circumstances in which such radicalisation can take place.'

– **Rob Wainwright, Director of Europol**

'There couldn't be a more appropriately timed book than *The Rage* by Julia Ebner. With an up close and personal view of two sides of the extremist coin, Ebner lays out the nearly identical narratives between the extreme right wing and Islamists who align with Al Qaeda and ISIS. Locked at the hip, these two groups are in a perpetual battle to destroy anyone who gets in the way of their ideology. Both groups use remarkably similar techniques to radicalise recruits, preying upon a need for identity, belonging and purpose. The personal narrative breathes life into the voices of those who believe they are on a just cause even as that cause ends in terror for others. *The Rage* is a must-read for anyone who wants to understand the interconnected nature of extremism.'

– **Chris Sampson, co-author of *Hacking ISIS***

To Hilde,
my great-grandmother, who has always
been a source of inspiration and strength

&

In memory of Jo Cox,
who fought for breaking the vicious circle

THE RAGE

THE VICIOUS CIRCLE OF
ISLAMIST AND FAR-RIGHT EXTREMISM

JULIA EBNER

I.B. TAURIS

LONDON · NEW YORK

Published in 2017 by
I.B.Tauris & Co. Ltd
London • New York
www.ibtauris.com

ISBN: 978 1 78831 032 1
eISBN: 978 1 78672 289 8
ePDF: 978 1 78673 289 7

A full CIP record for this book is available from the British Library
A full CIP record is available from the Library of Congress

Library of Congress Catalog Card Number: available

Printed and bound by CPI Group (UK) Ltd, Croydon, CR0 4YY

Contents

Abbreviations

AfD	Alternative für Deutschland
Alt-Right	Alternative Right
BNP	British National Party
CIA	Central Intelligence Agency
DGSE	General Directorate for External Security
DGSI	General Directorate for Internal Security
EDL	English Defence League
EU	European Union
FBI	Federal Bureau of Investigation
FPÖ	Freedom Party of Austria
GDP	Gross Domestic Product
GTD	Global Terrorism Database
Hogesa	Hooligans Against Salafists
IIE	Institute of Islamic Education
ISIS	Islamic State of Iraq and Syria (alternatively ISIL, IS or Daesh)
KKK	Ku Klux Klan
KRG	Kurdistan Regional Government
LIFG	Libyan Islamic Fighting Group
NATO	North Atlantic Treaty Organization
OECD	Organisation for Economic Co-operation and Development
PEGIDA	Patriotic Europeans Against the Islamisation of the West
RUSI	Royal United Services Institute
SIS	Secret Intelligence Service
UKIP	UK Independence Party

Acknowledgements

'YOU GOTTA BE CRAZY' IS PROBABLY THE SENTENCE THAT I'VE HEARD THE most over the past few months. I admit, I have done some peculiar things to complete this book. I went undercover to far-right and Islamist extremist events, had drinks with EDL marchers, chats with ISIS supporters, neo-Nazis, would-be terrorists and internet trolls, clashes with PEGIDA supporters and strolled around in the Parisian suburb of Sevran, which ranks high on the list of foreign fighter hotbeds. I interviewed homeless people, refugees, hackers, intelligence officers, former jihadists and far-right militants, had my avatar Twitter accounts shut down countless times, got held up in security checks for carrying inflammatory literature and internal teaching materials of extremist groups with me, and spent the US elections night monitoring the social media feed of extremists. All this would have been neither possible nor safe without the support, help and protection of people from all over the world. Throughout the entire research and writing process I have enjoyed the support of my family, friends, colleagues, as well as strangers. Every single one of them has made a substantial contribution to this book – from its first lines that were drafted in a remote Zen military academy on a mountain in China, to interviews on planes, in hotel lobbies and at the busy Medina market in Tunis, to the last few edits made while café crawling in London.

First of all, I express my gratitude to I.B.Tauris's founding chairman and publisher Iradj Bagherzade for the faith he put in my project and the thought-provoking conversations we've had. A very special thanks to my brilliant editor Joanna Godfrey, who challenged and inspired me, hammered every section of this book into shape, and significantly improved its final outcome. I would also like to thank my outstanding copy-editor Nick Fawcett, who seemed to be reading my thoughts whenever my wording was clumsy or my sentences were incomplete. I admire his British politeness that showed in his way of saying 'the current wording doesn't quite make sense' even when 'this sentence is rubbish' or 'were you drunk when you wrote this?!' would have been just as legitimate. I equally thank my excellent production editors Sophie Campbell and Paul Tompsett, as well as my great publicity managers Ash Khan, Tia Ali, Clare Kathleen Bogen and Rory Gormley.

Then there is my supervisor and friend J.R., who was a constant source of support, guidance and advice. I cannot thank him enough for trusting me and putting up with me at work after sleepless nights of writing and editing. I am infinitely grateful for all the support from Leah Selig Chauhan, Adam Lomax and Difaf Sharba, who have been driving forces behind the background research, databases and case study analyses. I would also like to express my deep gratitude to M. R. Bech, J. Stewart, Cecile Guerin, Peter Apps, Chris Sampson, Tom Neugebauer, John Kirbow and several other people who I cannot name here for their invaluable feedback, advice and contacts. A special thank you also goes to A. Faissal for her help with Arabic primary sources; Didier Serre and Rabia Nasimi for their input on statistical analysis; and Carl Miller, Louis Reynolds and Kier Eliot for their insights on social media monitoring and analysis.

I would not have started this book without the inspiration provided by Jamie Bartlett, who was a great mentor and role model for me. A special mention also goes to my former professor at the London School of Economics, Dr Kirsten Schulze, whose engaging teaching and formidable supervision first sparked my interest in the topic of extremism.

I would not have finished this book without the support and encouragement of Lena Schmidtkunz, Jade Zhao, Alessa Lux, Frederick Ladbury and Arthur Vetu; for their patience, honest feedback and constructive criticism, and most of all, their invaluable friendship, thank you.

I am furthermore grateful for the time and insights provided by all of the interviewees, especially Mohammed Chirani, Richard Barrett, Sajjan Gohel, Daniel Heinke, Daniel Köhler, Götz Nordbruch, Ahmad Mansour, Seyran Ates, Usama Hasan, Noman Benotman, Salah Ansari, Adam Deen, Fiyaz Mughal, Alexander Ritzmann, Charlie Beckett, Rashad Ali, Tahar Akermi, Kenza Isnasni, Bjorn Ihler, Matthew Feldman, Abdelghani Merah, André

Oboler, Ivan Humble, Nigel Bromage, Michael Fellner, Tommy Robinson and the various other interviewees, including intelligence officers, counter-terrorism experts and policy makers who either preferred to remain anonymous or were given pseudonyms for privacy protection reasons. I am very grateful for the support and insights provided by The Families against Terrorism and Extremism network, the TEDxVienna team, the Radicalisation Awareness Network and the Nordic Safe Cities network.

Finally, I would like to thank my entire family, in particular Lisbeth Ebner-Haid, Heinz Ebner, Barbara Haas, Gilbert Petutschnig, Ulrike Ebner-Stella and Elisabeth Haid, for supporting and motivating me throughout the entire writing process. Without their patience and love I would have most likely lost my mind during this project.

Preface

THURSDAY 16 JUNE 2016 BEGAN AS A NORMAL, MILD SPRING DAY IN THE WEST Yorkshire town of Birstall. The newspaper headlines that day were dominated by the upcoming Brexit referendum and the aftermath of the Orlando shooting. Hundreds of families were still mourning the victims killed four days earlier in the deadliest mass shooting in US history, committed by Islamist extremist Omar Mateen. At around 1 p.m., outside Birstall town library, far-right extremist Thomas Mair shot and stabbed MP Jo Cox as she was on her way to a constituency meeting.[1] Cox died of her injuries later that day. She left behind her loving husband Brendan Cox and two small children. This book has its origins in this sombre June week that illustrated the simultaneous surge of far-right and Islamist extremism.

The place where Jo Cox died is 15 minutes away from Dewsbury. The ringleader of the 2005 London tube bombings Mohammad Sidique Khan lived there, as did Britain's youngest suicide bomber Talha Asmal.[2] Dewsbury and its neighbouring towns have gained notoriety in the tabloid and broadsheet press for its thriving Islamist extremist scene. Its far-right activities are less widely known to the public. Yet, at least seven far-right groups who share anti-Muslim or xenophobic ideologies are active in West Yorkshire. White supremacist and patriotic parties that have turned the area into one of Britain's primary far-right strongholds include: Britain First, the National Front (NF) Party, anti-Islamisation street protest movement the English Defence League (EDL), and ultra-violent group The British Movement (BM).[3] Jo Cox's death brought the threat posed by far-right radicalism back to public conscience.

In the past, the media has given disproportionate attention to Islamist extremist attacks but has been reluctant to label violence motivated by right-wing ideologies as terrorism. The Norwegian far-right extremist Anders Breivik shot dead 77 civilians in 2011. Headlines described him as a 'murderer' and 'killer'.[4] Omar

Mateen, who killed 49 civilians in Orlando's Pulse Nightclub, was immediately called a terrorist. The Munich shooting of July 2016, the Quebec City mosque shooting of January 2017, the Portland train stabbing of May 2017, vehicle attacks in Finsbury Park in June 2017 and in Charlottesville in august 2017 were all far-right-inspired incidents. Although there is enough evidence concerning their perpetrators' political and ideological motivations, they are not often referred to as 'terrorist attacks' by politicians and the media. As a result, few people today know that attacks motivated by anti-Muslim or xenophobic sentiments take place 50 per cent more often in Western countries than those inspired by Islamist extremist ideologies. While 130 violent far-right incidents occurred across the US, Australia, the UK, France and Germany between January 2012 and September 2016, only 84 such attacks were staged by Islamist extremists.[5] The distorted depiction of today's terrorist threat landscape has not only led to a perceptual gap among the general public; could it also be responsible for the lack of academic research on the increasingly concerning dynamics between far-right and Islamist extremists?

This book stems from my desire to gain a better understanding of the vicious circle of spiralling extremism known as 'reciprocal radicalisation'. Comprehending the drivers and dynamics behind mutual breeding grounds for radicalisation is a crucial step to preventing future terrorist attacks. The murder of Jo Cox not only deeply moved me; it also motivated me to keep defending her belief that we are 'far more united and have far more in common than that which divides us'.[6] Building on these common grounds, I will try to trace back the sources of today's widening divisions in this book.

Introduction

DRINKING STRONGBOW WITH FAR-RIGHT MILITANTS IS NOT MY NORMAL idea of a casual Saturday morning. Discussing a caliphate in the UK with Islamist extremists is also not a normal Saturday evening. Nevertheless, on 5 November 2016, I broke my routine and, within a mere 20 hours, plunged into two radically opposed extremist worlds that I would soon realise are two sides of the same coin.

When I began my research on extremism, I did not realise how biased I was. I grew up without material worries in Austria, attended university abroad and read the *New York Times*. I never questioned the universality of human rights, the indispensability of democracy and the benefits of cultural diversity. As a former researcher at the London-based counter-extremism organisation Quilliam I spent my days studying radicalisation. And yet, when I first tried to put myself into the shoes of extremists – whether far-right or Islamist – I failed miserably. Throughout this research I was exposed to people I would never normally have talked to and heard stories I would have never heard otherwise. My research made me realise that had I been taught a different narrative, I would have thought, acted and reacted differently. The stories we are told determine how we construct our worldviews.

The first step in tackling extremism is to listen to extremists' stories. This is, of course, best done from within – where the unfiltered conversations happen. It was for this reason that I decided to go undercover to infiltrate both far-right and Islamist extremist groups. Coincidentally, both the EDL and Hizb ut-Tahrir happened to organise events on Saturday 5 November 2016.

Inside Extremist Groups

Infiltration of the EDL

The EDL's Facebook page had announced a national protest against 'Muslim grooming gangs' in the English town of Telford. When the *Sunday Mirror*[1] dubbed the town the 'child sex abuse capital', it did far-right groups a favour. As the rape gang members were of Pakistani descent, the EDL was quick in adding an 'Islamic' to the label. The protest was not just against the 'Telford child rape gang', it was also against 'the cover-up by officials and churches' and 'Islamification in the UK'.[2]

I am not the only one to get off at Telford railway station on that chilly Guy Fawkes morning. Many of the disembarking passengers wear remembrance poppy flowers on top of their EDL-branded jumpers. St George flags and beers change hands and there is an agitated atmosphere in the air. 'Welcome to the Islamic child rape capital,' says a man in a grim voice. They all seem to know each other and immediately identify me as an outsider. But they are curious enough to enquire. 'Are you also here for the protest?' one of the men asks. He is probably in his late forties and has tattoos inked across every inch of his skin not covered by his jeans, T-shirt and leather jacket. I nod. Technically I'm not lying; I have come here for the protest. He gives me an odd look.

'Are you surprised?' I ask.

'You're not English, are you?' he responds. His alcoholic breath momentarily stuns me; it's only 11 a.m. after all.

'No: Austrian.' His forced smile indicates he is not convinced.

'Where do you live?'

'London,' I reply.

'You came all the way up for this?'

'It's a national protest, Danny,' his friend interjects.

'Is this your first one?'

'Yes.'

Danny seems amused. 'Oh don't worry darling – we'll take care of you then.' As long as I am not exposed as a spy, I assume.

'How often have you been to these ... protests?' I am careful to use their vocabulary.

'Oh, I stopped counting.'

We walk up to the town centre, which obviously has heightened security. Police officers from all over the country are deployed; one of them tells me later he came all the way from South Wales.

Danny tells me about the early times of the EDL. He was one of its first followers, when the membership numbers were still in the tens of thousands.[3] He takes out his mobile and starts playing an EDL song. 'I'm here to protest, right, 'cos I'm going on a march 'cos I want Britain to be about British. I want Britain to be about British.'

I breathe deeply. Is he really playing this song to an Austrian living in the UK?

'We've got inter-racial law, and the Muslamic infidel; they're trying to get their law over our country.' He waits for my reaction.

'Ah,' I respond, not sure what to do or say. 'Will you be playing this at the march?'

'Yes.' He closes his eyes in what seems to be a melancholic daydream. 'You know, it has changed a lot over the years. In the beginning there used to be many more but now not so much.' I am not sure if he means events or people. Probably both.

The police are still following us – on horses, in cars, by foot.

'You know these things can turn violent.' It was more of an observation than a threat, though it did nothing to lessen my fear of that violence. I believe him. He has deep bruises below his eyes and some of his teeth are missing.

We stop in front of a café. At first I assume that we are going to have breakfast and I feel my mood brighten; at least a morning cappuccino would feel normal. But the cans of beer being swigged by the EDL members quickly puts a stop to that prospect. Danny greets several men, who seem to be friends that he hasn't seen in a while. 'Did you hear, George is in prison?' he asks them. Some are too busy staring at me to hear what he says. 'Oh, this is Julia.' He gives me a pat on the shoulder. 'It's her first time. Let's look after her.' We have one hour left before the march starts. 'Want to join us at the pub?' Danny asks. 'Your drink is on me!' I decline politely and instead take a seat on a bench outside next to a young woman who looks slightly bored.

Sarah has a slim face with a slim nose and even slimmer eyebrows. Her hair is dyed red but her hairline reveals that her natural colour is a light brown. 'Strongbow?' she offers.

'Sure,' I say. Somehow a cider first thing in the morning with a woman unimpressed by this motley gathering of men seems to fit. I help myself to a can.

'The police made us rip off the question marks.' She points to a small pile of paper. Indeed, every single one of the flyers has a torn-off edge. The question on top of the paper, 'Islam a peaceful religion?', now reads like a statement. But below this the paper quotes 12 Qur'anic verses that contain calls for violent action. These are, however, incomplete verses quoted out of context. Even the most hard-core Salafi English translations of the Qur'an do not contain passages such as 'Terrorize and behead those who believe in scriptures other than the Koran' or 'The unbelievers are stupid'.

'You can keep one,' she says. I take a flyer, hoping that no one will look into my bag later.

'How did you get involved?' I ask Sarah. She admits that at first she didn't know how to go about it, though she had been following the EDL on social media for a long time. 'And then my boyfriend met Luke, who introduced us to all the others.' She gets up. 'Paul!' An attractive man in what looks like EDL-branded pyjamas turns around, walks over to us and gives her a kiss on the cheek. 'We have a six-month-old baby girl. We are here because we want our Mia to grow up in a better world, right Paul? I don't want to be scared for her to be raped in the street. I don't want her to end up jobless one day.' For lack of comforting words, I resort to downing my cider. 'We can't continue to pretend all is fine, when it's so obviously not. Now we have to be careful, though. The police know Paul.' Most of their friends are involved with the EDL too. 'It's like a family – we protect each other,' she says.

'Protect from …?' I ask.

'Well, it's not us who are the aggressive ones but the left and the Muslims – they always start the fighting.' In the background, I hear them chanting: 'Muslim penises – get out of our streets.'

'I'll take another one, yeah?' A middle-aged guy sits down on the opposite side of our table and opens his Strongbow. 'Hi, I'm Sam.' He leans over the table to shake my hand. Sam has a friendly smile, even if some of his teeth are missing. It doesn't take long until he tells me his story. 'I used to be a security guard at Gatwick Airport, so I couldn't tell anyone at first about my joining the League because they might think you are racist. You have to be careful with who you are seen.' He unfolds an EDL flag with pride, revelling in the moment.

It is Sam's firm belief that 'there is no such thing as a moderate Muslim'. To him, all Muslims are the same. He thinks that it is only a question of time until the moderates turn to extremism. His conclusion is that 'you cannot trust anyone who subscribes to that religion because they wouldn't say "no", if an extremist asks them for help'. In the same way you would do anything for your militant mates here, if they ask you to? I don't ask that question however; the cider hasn't given me quite enough courage. Instead, I listen to his analysis of the political dynamics in the Middle East. His detailed historical knowledge surprises me. How naive was I to assume that all EDLers were ignorant, uninformed thugs?

When one of his friends takes a seat next to him, Sam has a sudden shift of inspiration and starts talking about a halal butcher in Bradford: 'and he doesn't serve non-Muslims'. That was not his only concern: 'they live in our houses, rape our women, it's gradual but they are slowly taking over everything that is precious to us'. I can sense his desperation; he feels powerless. 'The politicians don't listen; they think we are extreme and call us racist.'

'So what's the solution?' I ask without having an answer myself. 'Maybe we need to nuclear bomb everything and start from scratch.'

His friend laughs. I cough, and spill cider over my trousers. Sam instantly gets up to fetch a napkin and offers to lend me his scarf in case I get cold.

'Liberalism and tolerance don't work, we have seen that. The only solution is war,' he adds as he sits back down. Apparently he shares an apocalyptic world vision with the very people he blames for every failure in British society. As I raise a cynical eyebrow he is overcome by a moment of weakness. 'Maybe it needs extremism to fight extremism,' he utters almost under his breath.

The rally starts and, with every metre it moves forward, the crowd's angry chants grow louder. The friendly chats and warm smiles in front of the café almost feel surreal now; it is as though rage has erased all other emotions. I stay in the background, away from the cameras. A Quilliam staff member caught in the midst of anti-Islamic banners, crosses and British flags would make for a good headline. As I mingle with the journalists instead, my eyes meet Sam's disappointed gaze. 'Come on, she's one of them,' I hear one of his friends say before he shoots me a dirty look. To avoid sharing a train compartment with them, I leave the rally early. I feel guilty and confused: I had not been prepared to meet a protective drinking buddy, a caring mother and a well-read gentleman at the rally. What led them to support one of Britain's most extreme anti-Muslim hate groups? How did they accumulate so much rage?

On the train I start reading Hizb ut-Tahrir's political handbook *From Darkness into Light*,[4] trying to make sense of Chapter 4, 'The Enemies of Islam', while my head is still filled with EDL chants. As I get off the train, the Qur'anic verse, 'Mocked were (many) apostles before thee; but their scoffers were hemmed in by the thing that they mocked', echoes in my head.

Infiltration of Hizb ut-Tahrir

I arrive at Mile End Road just before 7 p.m. The street is barely lit, which plays to my advantage, as the two men standing in front of the entrance won't be able to make out my face. 'I'm here for the Kashmir event.' They immediately let me in. I climb up the stairs to the second floor where I find a large conference room that can host roughly 300 people with a speaker's podium in the front. A man stands at the door to welcome the audience. As he looks at me, I can sense a touch of suspicion. Luckily, he does not realise that I worked for someone he considers a traitor. My boss, Maajid Nawaz, was a leading recruiter for Hizb ut-Tahrir. Now he runs Quilliam. 'You have to go over there,' he finally tells me and points to the very back of the room: the segregated women's section.

I sit down next to a group of women with colourful hijabs because they look friendly. A woman called Sana immediately starts talking to me. Sana is eloquent, well-read and holds a degree from Westminster University. At least in the women's section she appears to know everyone. 'I often come to these events,' she tells me. 'What are you doing in London? Are you a student?'

I decide not to lie. 'No, I finished my studies not so long ago. Now I'm doing research on the rise of the far-right and anti-Muslim hate crimes. I actually just came from an anti-EDL demo in Telford.' I go on before she can ask me more about my research affiliation.

It works; Sana picks up on the EDL topic. 'Oh, what's their leader called again … Tom … Tommy …'

I decide to help her. 'Tommy Robinson? He's no longer their leader but—'

'Oh right, he's with Quilliam now', she interrupts. Quilliam's engagement with Tommy in 2013 sparked a national controversy and generated a creative set of rumours. To put it simply, Quilliam succeeded in decapitating the EDL, resulting in a membership drop from over 25,000 to only a few hundred. But it failed to deradicalise Tommy, who would later return to his anti-Muslim rhetoric after having served time in prison.

I can't afford to put Sana off, so I stay in character.

'Interesting,' I mumble.

But the girl next to me is curious. 'What's Quilliam?' It is obvious that she was dragged along to this event – she fits in as little as I do, with her strong eye make-up and long, loose hair.

'The bigoted advocacy group that this traitor Maajid Nawaz heads.' Sana is now almost shouting. I keep my head down as more and more people are arriving. Most of the around-300 seats are filled up by now. I am glad when she returns to the EDL topic. 'Far-right groups like the EDL are just manifestations of the evil that exists within our society. In a way, I actually pity them.' For her, EDL's actions are the product of larger ideas that are circulated by the media and politicians. They are representative of all the evil in Western societies. 'We have to ask where they get their ideas from. Islamophobic hate crimes are rising,' she says; 'incidents on public transport have become more frequent especially. But we just have to be patient; eventually it will be those who mock the Prophet who will be hemmed in,' she says, pursing her lips.

When the UK chairman of Hizb ut-Tahrir, Dr Abdul Wahid, begins his speech, the room immediately falls silent; only a baby is crying in the back. After welcoming everyone, Dr Wahid starts talking about the oppression of Muslims in Kashmir. I'm having a *déjà vu* moment. When he speaks of the rape of Kashmiri women by Indians I am reminded of the speeches that I heard earlier in the day. The wording he uses is similar to that used by the EDL leaders: 'rape epidemic' and 'no respect for women' are recurring terms. Dr Wahid thinks of Kashmir as just one example of the worldwide oppression of Muslims. He lets the next speaker shed light on what he means by that. Mohammad Atif explicitly addresses the rise of the far right across Europe, the US and Australia. 'Western countries all across the world are voting for anti-Muslim politicians,' he says. His voice is calm but I can sense his agitation as he talks about what he calls 'the global discrimination against Muslims'.

'France banned students from wearing the hijab, Germany recently banned the niqab in schools, in the Netherlands Geert Wilders wants to ban the Qur'an (his party ironically calls itself The Freedom Party), in Australia the One Nation Party called for a ban on Muslim migration, and, of course, let's not forget about the circus we see in the US right now.'

In the same breath, he also refers to former British Prime Minister David Cameron's extremism-prevention strategy, the Prevent programme, which he believes is merely a tool to spy on Muslims. 'All the liberalism and tolerance that they talk about seems insecure and fragile. We have seen that democracy doesn't manage to secure the rights of minorities. Muslims are literally bullied in the West, all under the guise of freedom. Western politicians have let this happen. What happened 70 years ago is happening again today. Muslims are today's Jews.'

'Are we dreaming?' the next speaker, Rizwan Sheikh, asks. 'Liberation, jihad – in fact, defensive jihad – is the only solution.' He explains that jihad means fighting against the *kufr* occupation and liberating the world from capitalism and colonialism. 'There is no greater evil than these twin sisters.' This required jihad, according to Rizwan, was exemplified by tribal militias who liberated areas of Kashmir during the Indo-Pakistani war of 1947–8. 'The very same people are being bombed now in the War on Terror, which we now know is war on Islam.' In the light of what he calls 'the global war on Islam' it is necessary for all Muslims to return to their true identity and to unite 'as a brotherhood' to confront all enemies. Liberation, however, will only solve half of the problem, according to Hizb ut-Tahrir. Once the lands are liberated, one must give them a system. Their proposition for a post-liberation system is a *khilafah*, which will unlock the potential of all these lands.

'Now we will take questions from the audience,' the chairman concludes. He explicitly invites women to submit questions in writing, if they prefer not to speak out in front of everyone. The woman beside me looks at me in anticipation. 'Do you want to ask a question?'

I hesitate. But she takes my silence as a 'yes' and gives me a piece of paper. I write down my question and hand it back to her.

'You don't want to stand up and ask it yourself?'

'I'm shy.'

She nods, walks up to the barriers that separate us from the men's section and submits my paper to the front. The chair clears his throat as if to gain time to make out my sloppy handwriting. I instantly regret not having written more legibly; what if he calls me to the front to help him decipher my letters? 'What can be done against the rise of right-wing parties and anti-Muslim hatred across the world?' he finally says, addressing the question to Mohammad Atif.

It's impressive to watch Mohammad skilfully link the grievances resulting from anti-Muslim incidents to the wider failure of democratic and liberal systems and to the conclusion that the only alternative solution is to establish a caliphate. 'Whether it is Modi, Trump, Wilders – these people have a free run. There are about 60 Muslim leaders worldwide, yet none of them has spoken up against these bigots. There is complete silence because they don't actually represent Muslims. The War on Terror, the financial crash and the serious economic problems unleashed in the West all derived from the capitalist system.' This will only be resolved if the *ummah* has its own state, media and foreign policy,' Mohammad explains.

'I have to go,' I whisper in Sana's ear.

'Okay, you should come to our other events. And … don't get too involved with the EDL,' she adds, winking.

As I leave the conference, my head becomes a peculiar meeting point for EDL rally chants, Qur'anic lines and Guy Fawkes fireworks. The two 5 November excursions into the mindsets of far-right and Islamist extremists are a good starting point for exploring the parallels and dynamics between them.

You Hate Me and I Hate You

On the next morning, I find a little note in my bag: 'Stay safe as we are approaching the final battle.' The ink is purple, the handwriting shaky. While speculating about the originator of the note, I realise that it could be from a member of either the EDL or Hizb ut-Tahrir. In many ways the rhetoric and *modus operandi* of the EDL and Hizb ut-Tahrir are strikingly similar. Both are inciting hatred against the other, which is presented as representative of society as a whole. Both sides feel under attack in their collective identity and dignity. Both accuse the other side of lacking respect for their women. At the same time, misogyny and outdated gender perceptions are central to both Islamist and far-right ideologies. American white supremacists have dipped into the vast pool of anti-feminist memes and sexist jokes of the so-called 'Manosphere'. Meanwhile, ISIS criticised Hillary Clinton for being 'a female feminist', warning that the Prophet had said: 'Never shall a people who give their leadership to a woman be successful.'[5] They also share a call for action against the 'idle, corrupt or incompetent politicians' and the 'rigged media'. They are two sides of the same coin.

While EDL members protest against 'the Islamisation of the West', Hizb ut-Tahrir sees itself as in the vanguard against the 'Westernisation of Islam'. The former dreams of a Great Britain without Muslims, whereas the latter's goal is to purify Islam from all Western influences and to re-establish a caliphate. As a result of their shared pessimism about the status quo, both groups adopt apocalyptic visions of the future – visions that will allow them to press 'reset'. Because victimisation and demonisation work well together, extremists are in a mutually beneficial relationship. To tell a coherent story, the victim needs a perpetrator as much as the perpetrator needs a victim. In extremism, this leads to an effect called reciprocal radicalisation.

Reciprocal radicalisation is a vastly underexplored phenomenon. A 2014 Royal United Services Institute (RUSI) report concluded that more research is needed to understand how 'extreme narratives at both ends of the spectrum feed into one another'.[6] In 2006, the British academic Roger Eatwell[7] was the first to introduce the concept of 'cumulative extremism', which he defined as 'the way in which one form of extremism can feed off and magnify other forms [of extremism]'. Far-right expert Matthew Feldman coined the term 'tit-for-tat extremism' soon after a jihadist gang plotted to bomb an EDL demonstration in Dewsbury in 2012. 'It may just turn out that extremists need each other to fuel their own hatred and natural inclinations to violence', he wrote.[8] Although the connectivity between extremisms is a rather new field of research, it has increasingly attracted attention from academics and politicians in recent years.[9]

Much of the existing research[10] has highlighted commonalities in the narrative and communication strategy of far-right and Islamist extremists. Most scholars agree that far-right and Islamist extremist groups share a common enemy, the 'establishment', as well as a common target audience, disenfranchised youth. Most recently, a study released by the Program on Extremism[11] compared the ways in which white nationalists and ISIS supporters used Twitter. It demonstrated that extremists on both sides use sophisticated communication strategies and experience rapid growth rates of their support networks on social media.

While parallels between far-right and Islamist extremists' propaganda and mobilisation strategies have been extensively explored, little research has been done on their interaction.[12] Academics and think tanks[13] agree that we need to understand reciprocal radicalisation and its concrete manifestations and conditions better to derive practical implications and policy recommendations. This book will therefore give firsthand insights into online and offline interactions of far-right and Islamist extremists, illustrating the accelerated reciprocal radicalisation dynamics.

The Age of Rage

The past few years saw one momentous news event after another in the West: terrorist attacks in Paris; San Bernandino; Brussels; Orlando; Nice; Munich; Berlin; Quebec City; London Westminster; Manchester; Portland; London Bridge; Finsbury Park; Charlottesville; Barcelona. In between, there was Brexit; a coup attempt in Turkey; burkini bans in France; an anti-Muslim president in the Oval Office; 46 per cent support for a right-wing gun enthusiast in Austria; a defeated prime minister in Italy; the new US administration banning immigrants from several Muslim-majority countries; and the rise of nationalism in Europe. These events were tremors that healthy societies could have coped with. Yet, all in all, they have widened the fissures within our societies and brought to where we are now, in 2017.

By the end of 2017, most of the major Western heads of state who had shaped the post-financial-crisis world order will have left office: David Cameron, Barack Obama, Matteo Renzi, François Hollande and, potentially, Angela Merkel. A new era has begun – *The New Statesman* referred to it as 'the Age of Putinism'; the *Guardian* called it 'the Era of Trumpism'. I call it 'the Age of Rage'.

This era is characterised by a vicious circle of emotionally driven actions and reactions. Whether on social media or in the streets, anger and fear are omnipresent: online and offline hate crimes are at an all-time high. Brexit and Trump are among the products of this global rise of rage. So are terrorist attacks.

In the Age of Rage, an unsecure future of the EU and NATO lies in front of us. Tensions between their most powerful members are increasing, levels of trust decreasing. The timing is bad. In the words of NATO's Secretary General Jens Stoltenberg, the West currently faces 'the biggest security challenges in a generation'. Heavily armed soldiers patrol tourist hotspots in Paris, Brussels, Nice and other European cities. The German government is lifting the last taboos left from World War II and the Cold War by militarising its streets and stepping up state surveillance. Meanwhile the UK is detaching itself from Europe, and may stop sharing both growing economic burdens and increasingly critical intelligence with its neighbours. Only rapidly rising hate-crime rates will likely remain a common feature that outlives the single market.

The wave of terrorist attacks in the heart of Europe was a powerful reminder that Western democracies are not immune to conflict and violence. The shock that has ended our generation's illusion of eternal peace has left many looking for someone to blame. Everyone has identified their own scapegoats: Muslims, idle politicians and incompetent police are all near the top of the list. Further down we come across capitalism, Eurocrats, globalisation, Putin and many others. But all the scapegoating, finger pointing and scaremongering exercises come at a high cost. As fringe narratives are becoming mainstream in Europe and the US, extremists see their binary worldviews turn into reality. Terrorism thrives in divided societies. How many more tremors and ruptures can our societies take before extremists' apocalyptic visions of a confrontation between 'the West and Islam' become a self-fulfilling prophecy?

Exploring Rage with Empathy

This book explores the dynamics between the 'new' far-right and Islamist extremists, and its effect on the global terrorism threat. In the light of the global rise of both far-right and Islamist extremism it is crucial to enhance our understanding of the interaction of the two threats that have mostly been treated as isolated by both commentators and politicians. The elections in the US, France, Germany and other countries where the far right is currently thriving have made a debate on reciprocal radicalisation more important than ever. The following chapters seek to provide answers to questions such as: how do far-right and Islamist extremist narratives amplify each other? How can we break apart both binary worldviews? What do victories for far-right leaders across the Western world mean for the global jihadist insurgency? Do we need to combat far-right extremism to fight Islamist extremism?

To make progress on these questions this book uses conversations with far-right militants, Islamist extremists, hackers, intelligence officers, psychologists, former jihadists, terrorism victims and policy makers. It analyses numbers, people and their behaviour to provide insights into both online and offline dynamics between far-right and Islamist extremists. Findings are based on a mixture of interviews, field trips, statistical analyses and social media monitoring. None of the explored numbers, people or contexts are invented. However, as this book deals with highly sensitive topics, some of the interviewees' names have been altered to protect the privacy of those individuals who preferred to stay anonymous or who did not know that they were being interviewed. I have also used pseudonyms for all online accounts that were monitored without the account-holder's knowledge.

Extremism in all its shapes and forms is a highly controversial topic. There is no universal definition of the term, which itself has been abused for extremist purposes: some oppressive regimes use the fight against extremism as a pretext to introduce draconian measures against entire minority communities The British government defines extremism as 'vocal or active opposition to fundamental British values, including democracy, the rule of law, individual liberty and mutual respect and tolerance of different faiths and beliefs'.[14] In this book, anyone who deliberately incites hatred and fears to exploit existing or provoked tensions for their political agenda will be labelled 'extremist'. There are extremist politicians, activists, even journalists – far right, far left, Islamist, Christian and atheist. My intention is not to use the term 'extremist' as an insult or a permanent label. An extremist is defined as such merely by his/her actions, not by their nature. In fact, some of the extremists that I talked to were friendlier and more welcoming than the average person I might encounter in daily life. Because extremism always starts with the dehumanisation of humans, I will do my very best to avoid falling into the same trap and will aim instead to present every single person as a human being with good qualities and bad. The goal of this book is not to add fuel to the fire but to show that extremists' actions exacerbate one of the most pressing problems of our time – growing rage – and thereby make our planet an increasingly dangerous place. It also attempts to show that the dynamic is not irreversible and that there are ways out of this vicious circle.

The book takes the reader on a journey with eight different stops. Each chapter will look at the problem of extremism from a different angle in an attempt to add a missing piece to the puzzle. Starting with an exploration of the sources of extremism, Chapter 1 shows how both far-right and Islamist extremists have been good at exploiting modern-day problems and opportunities to turn their black-and-white stories into realities. While Chapter 2 dissects the ideas, motivations and manifestations of the global jihadist insurgency, Chapter 3 examines the ideas and drivers behind the burgeoning 'new' far right. To show how the rise of identity politics has helped extremists, Chapter 4 traces back the breakdown of the political centre ground in Western nation states. In Chapter 5, the media's role in amplifying extremist stories is assessed, looking at new dynamics of i-propaganda, sensationalism, alternative facts and fake news. Chapter 6 takes the reader into the dark online spaces of ISIS and far-right militants to explore the interplay of the stories they tell. Based on a number of field trips, Chapter 7 gives insights into the world's most dangerous reciprocal radicalisation hotbeds across Europe and the US, where tit-for-tat laws apply. Finally, Chapter 8 provides ideas for the way ahead and tells the stories of individuals who have made tangible contributions to breaking the new vicious circle of fear and hatred. While this book does not claim to offer ready-made solutions to one of the world's most complex problems, it will hopefully make a small contribution to raising awareness, clarity and, above all, empathy.

1

The End of a Collective Illusion

WE LIVE IN BETTER CONDITIONS TODAY THAN ANY GENERATION BEFORE US. On a global level, we are wealthier, healthier and more educated than ever before. Despite the 2008 financial crisis, the subsequent European debt crisis and the current migration crisis, worldwide life expectations, living standards and literacy rates are at a record high.[1]

Every day we are moving one step closer to reaching the Millennium Development Goals. Poverty, hunger and child mortality are lower than ever before.[2] 'The end of extreme poverty is in reach', Oxfam enthusiastically claimed in 2015.[3] Half a billion people escaped extreme poverty between 1990 and 2011.[4] Over the past 25 years the child mortality rate has gone down by 53 per cent[5] and the conquering of major communicable diseases such as malaria, HIV and tuberculosis is in sight.[6] For millions of people in developing and emerging countries we live in a golden age.

Yet, despite all the achieved progress, growth and prosperity, it feels as if we are only one step away from descending into complete chaos. 'I've witnessed the years that led up to Hitler's rise. Today, we live in troubling times again,' my great-grandmother told me in October 2016. One month later Trump was elected US president. Born in 1921, my great-grandmother has lived through almost a whole century. She grew up in the golden 1920s, experienced the Great Recession, saw Nazi Germany rise and fall, fled the Czech Republic as a Sudeten German, raised three children as a single mum in post-war Austria and became one of the country's first councilwomen during the tense Cold War years. At the age of 80, she completed a university degree in history. 'We are moving away from tackling problems together and turning our backs on the achievements of international cooperation. This return to isolationism and nationalism is alarming. America first, Britain first, Austria first. I have seen the harm that this uncompromising focus on national interests can cause.' She leans over to me, now almost whispering. 'I'm afraid humans will never be capable of learning from history, not even from one of the darkest chapters that hit the whole world not too long ago.'

The Leaning Tower of Jenga

The world we live in today seems to be more divided than ever before. Wherever we look, we can find deep rifts that divide our societies in left and right, Muslim and non-Muslim, Remain and Leave camps, Republicans and Democrats. 'In many ways, the years to come could be among the most dangerous in recent human history, particularly with the risk of both outright collapse and great power conflict higher than they've ever been', my friend Peter Apps wrote for Reuters during the turbulent 2015 summer.[7] The tensions are palpable across the world: a fractured and war-torn Middle East, escalating territorial disputes in the East and South China Seas, resurgent Russian nationalism, an unstable, rogue Turkey that is just a glimpse away from civil war, an increasingly divided and xenophobic Europe, and, of course, we should not forget to mention that the United States elected an openly anti-Muslim bigot for president.

The current political situation reminds one of the final rounds in a Jenga game, where the tower is already leaning so badly that removing one more block will most likely lead to its collapse. Is it too late to intervene? Many of the bricks that have provided a stable foundation – international consensus, economic integration, a strong political centre – have been removed or are in the process of being removed. There is even a sense that old disputes between East and West, Left and Right, and North and South had never truly vanished and are now coming back to the surface again: a dangerous cocktail of neo-Cold War tensions and neo-fascism. Did we carry all the ingredients in our backpacks over the past decades? Was one stimulus enough to bring back all collectively repressed memories and traumata?

In an attempt to predict how prone a society is to polarisation and conflict, political scientists have come up with a political instability index, which calculates the sum of change in vote totals per party from election to election divided by two. According to this metric, political instability has been rising among various EU members over the last decade.[8] Yet there are, of course, no reliable indicators to measure the likelihood of war in a society. It is only with hindsight that history books can tell the full story of what led to the escalation of a conflict. Sometimes the dynamics appear so complex and the events so intertwined that even a retrospective description of what happened becomes a challenge. Even today, you can get into a passionate argument with historians when speculating about the developments that led to World War I. Yet one thing is almost undisputed: once the shot aimed at Archduke Franz Ferdinand was fired, there was no going back. The first brick had fallen, causing a chain reaction that brought all the others down. One event led directly into the next and it was too late for any single state to halt the collapse.

In the aftermath of World War I, the tower was rebuilt. Yet its foundations remained fragile. In the Paris Peace Conference, the Allies accepted most of President Wilson's ambitious peace programme put forward in his so-called Fourteen Points. It was the birth of The League of Nations – the collective will to ensure a peaceful future was there. But so was self-interest. Germany was declared solely responsible for the war; the Treaty of Versailles and its harsh punitive implications left the German population suffering. Unbearable reparation payments, painful territorial losses and escalating tensions with the French nourished German post-war grievances, effectively turning the country into a ticking time bomb.

Eventually, the tower collapsed under the weight of the Versailles Treaty's war-guilt clause and the Great Recession. Hitler's promise of a glorious future that would expand the German *Lebensraum* and make Germany great again was appealing to the German people, who were desperate for change. This time it was not only the politicians who wanted war; it was the masses' desire – at least in the beginning. '*Wollt ihr den totalen Krieg?*' German Propaganda Minister Joseph Goebbels asked in 1943 at the Berlin Sportpalast. After half a decade of war, millions of extinguished Jewish lives and major defeats on all fronts, Goebbels had to select his audience carefully to make it appear as if the public still cheered at the idea of war. The total war brought about the total destruction of the tower. This time, the bricks did not simply fall; they were shattered.

Again Europe rebuilt the tower – this time on a more solid basis, so its architects thought. Everyone joined in. Everyone wanted to avoid another war, at any cost. The Americans pumped $12 billion into rebuilding the foundation for a stable continent. Nations came together, leaving behind their enmities and hostilities to create the United Nations (UN) and to set up the predecessors of the European Union (EU) and the World Trade Organisation (WTO). Increasing economic interdependency was seen as a tool to secure peace. They had learnt from the past, European leaders thought. They believed in the virtue of supra-national organisations and multi-lateral trading as a prophylactic treatment against war. No one would be able to attack an economic partner without harming their own interests. Trade disputes would no longer escalate into armed conflict. This could have been the end of patriotic and nationalist narratives and the beginning of a stable world order.

Unfortunately, it wasn't. 'The cold wind of intolerance, authoritarianism, and nationalism is blowing across America and Europe', a post-Brexit *Huffington Post* article reads.[9] The tower appears shaky again. On 23 June 2016 more than 17 million Brits[10] voted to remove a major brick of its foundation by leaving the EU. Britain's independent anti-terrorism watchdog Lord Carlile argues that the EU has been one of the most important guarantors of a peaceful Europe. 'If you compare that period since the Second World War, which is now 70 years, to the previous 70 years, it's game, set and match for the EU. The EU has meant peace in Europe,' he told me a few weeks before the referendum.

The fear that Brexit might cause a chain reaction among other European countries is real. Post-Brexit polling results published by the London-based think tank Demos give a gloomy outlook of the future of Europe. Their polling project 'Nothing to Fear but Fear Itself' revealed that a 'widespread sense of precariousness, uncertainty and pessimism is sweeping the continent – presenting an unprecedented social and political challenge to the future of the Union'. It demonstrated that Euroscepticism is no longer a phenomenon that is exclusive to the UK but is increasingly becoming commonplace all across Europe.[11]

Meanwhile, far-right leaders across the US and Europe have been gaining support, mainly playing on people's fear of Muslims and benefiting from their lack of understanding of the distinction between

Islam as an individual faith and Islamist extremism as a political ideology that exploits religion. This has led to a stark rise in political radicalisation and violent extremism. Growing support for both far-right and Islamist extremist militant groups has manifested itself in a surge in terrorist attacks and hate crimes throughout the world.

While World War I was provoked by a chain reaction, World War II can be seen as the product of the ticking German time bomb. Today, there is reason to be worried about a repetition of both effects. As the Arab Spring demonstrated, increasing interconnectivity and modern communication tools can easily spark chain reactions not just on a political level but also on a civil society level. At the same time, one glimpse at the world map is enough to see that there is more than a handful of ticking time bombs akin to interwar Germany. Even more concerning, however, is the non-linear nature of today's threat. The extremes are increasingly feeding off and escalating one other, effectively creating a vicious circle. Consequently, our democratic societies' natural resilience to polarisation and, in its extension, radicalisation has vanished. Or was our perceived post-war immunity against conflict never more than a collective illusion?

'You have no idea how lucky your generation is,' my history teacher told our class of 13-year-olds in 2003. We had just finished discussing *Schindler's List* and were about to start another group exercise on World War II. I remember exchanging looks with my classmate, who was busy finishing her Viennese croissant under the desk. At the time, neither of us understood what she meant. We didn't care too much about the past, saw little connection to the present and were even less concerned about the future.

In 1942, the Austrian-Jewish writer Stefan Zweig published his memoirs in *The World of Yesterday*. He described the pre-World War I period as the Golden Age of Security:

> There was as little belief in the possibility of such barbaric declines as wars between the peoples of Europe as there was in witches and ghosts. Our fathers were comfortably saturated with confidence in the unfailing and binding power of tolerance and conciliation. They honestly believed that the divergences and the boundaries between nations and sects would gradually melt away into a common humanity, and that peace and security, the highest of treasures, would be shared by all mankind.[12]

We had another Golden Age of Security. 'But history tends to repeat itself, in a circle,' my great-grandmother cautions. Stefan Zweig's *The World of Yesterday* is timeless precisely because today's yesterday is similar to Stefan Zweig's yesterday: after the end of the Cold War, European stability appeared staunch, the idea of another war distant. Generations X and Y have grown up in the illusion of timeless peace and prosperity. Today's only generation to have experienced what war feels like – the wartime generation – is dying out. The Baby Boomers were raised in the bitter post-war atmosphere; they instinctively understood their parents' pain, though it was not treated in school. Generations X and Y learnt about it in school but had no emotional connection to the topic. The Boomers understood it without talking about it, while my generation talked about it without understanding it.

The Yugoslavia War weighed heavily on my parents' generation's shoulders, but it was the war of a different world: the ex-communist world. We, in the West, were deemed immune to war. After all, we've had the pre-emptive vaccination of the UN, the WTO, the EU and even NATO. Yet this past decade has exposed the powerlessness of those international organisations and bodies that we had considered to be our invincible vanguards of peace, human rights, democracy and prosperity. In the light of the global financial crisis, the migration crisis and the rising threat of terrorism, they all look ridiculously toothless.

'*Cette fois, c'est la guerre*' ('This time it's war'), the French daily newspaper *Le Parisien* announced after the terrorist attacks in the French capital that killed over 130 innocent civilians in November 2015. It was the first time a French president had officially used the word *war* since the Algerian war. 'It felt like I had fallen into a nightmare,' a Parisian friend recalls. Mattheu was having a glass of wine a few streets from Bataclan when the first shots were fired. The political science major thinks about it for a few seconds as we walk through the militarised streets of Paris. 'Or rather woken up from a dream. All of a sudden war seemed possible again.' Even the French, of all people, were shocked to hear the word *war* and see policemen standing in front of the Louis Vuitton shop on the Champs-Élysées – one would think the revolutionary spirit is encoded in their genes and the preparedness for confrontation runs through their veins. Yet we had all been part of the collective delusion of eternal peace;

France was not exempt. Losing this feeling of absolute security and protection almost feels like we have been betrayed, like a broken promise.

Needless to say, the Jenga tower looks shaky: trust in international institutions and national constitutions is dissolving, the viability of democracy is under scrutiny. It is against this background that a global jihadist insurgency and an international renaissance of the far right are looming upon us. Extremists have been good at using the arising insecurity and fears to their advantage, because they thrive in uncertain environments, where their apocalyptic stories find wide resonance.

Extremist Storytellers

Studying extremism without studying stories is like studying the brain without studying the neurons. 'We used stories to transmit our extreme ideologies,' Ivan Humble tells me over the phone. The ex-EDL community manager used to recruit people into the group's East Anglian Division. For the Scottish philosopher Alasdair MacIntyre,[13] 'man is in his actions and practices, as well as in his fictions, essentially a story-telling animal'. The narrative is what ties it all together: it is the connecting element between non-violent and violent extremism as well as between far-right and Islamist extremism. 'Radicalising people was easy; I just had to tell better stories than the Establishment,' Ivan notes. 'Most people I talked to already had their views; all I had to do was to reinforce them by linking their existing prejudice to current events and convincing them of the EDL's narrative.'

Stories have implications both for reality and fiction.[14] The creation of common myths has enabled human beings to cooperate in large numbers and to live together in bigger communities.[15] Israeli historian Yuval Noah Harari[16] even argued that any kind of human cooperation and power structures is rooted in shared myths and stories. We were only able to form political institutions, trade networks, religious communities and social movements thanks to our collective idea of states, money, gods and rights. Today, the World Bank would be powerless if we could not imagine currencies, exchange rates and derivatives. The UN would be pointless if we could not collectively understand concepts such as democracy, equality or freedom of speech. Today's world order – including its intellectual foundations provided by the Washington consensus, the idea of a free market, the concept of the nation state – is no more than collective fiction aimed at creating stability. In contrast to natural laws, this fictive order is dependent on people's faith in it.[17] Even if half of the world's population stopped believing in gravity, apples wouldn't stop falling from trees. But democracy, the rule of law and press freedom are likely to collapse once people stop believing in them. As extremists have been good at telling stories about corrupted political institutions, rigged democratic systems and 'fake' media, today's world order is in danger of crashing.

The power of imagination combined with the ability to communicate its products effectively to wide audiences can be an important driver of change. Any imagined order is inter-subjective, which means that it can only be challenged by convincing, persuading or manipulating 'millions of strangers' into believing in a new order.[18] Change in the social, political or economic order is therefore provoked by influencing the collective consciousness. A power struggle is nothing else than a competition for who tells the better story, because the best story will mobilise and control the masses.

Lasting change in social structures cannot be achieved by force and coercion alone; it also requires a support base of 'true believers' who share an objective based on a common story.[19] The French Revolution would most likely not have succeeded without the pioneering work of ideologues such as Montesquieu, Mirabeau and Rousseau, who provided the intellectual backbone for the tens of thousands of fighters descending onto the streets. Today, new narratives and identity can be created, expressed and influenced in a variety of ways, ranging from print media to visual illustrations in the arts.[20] It is no coincidence that media and arts professionals are the first to be silenced, suppressed and persecuted. Hundreds or even thousands of journalists, writers and artists are currently in exile, according to PEN International.[21]

The imagined order shapes our desires by creating value systems[22] but our desires can also be used against us to shape the imagined order. As our emotions, habits and objectives can now easily be tracked back because of the digital footprint our actions leave behind, our future choices can be determined in market studies and manipulated through targeted communication campaigns. This has been abused and exploited by those who want to achieve, consolidate or maintain power. Politicians, car sellers and journalists all use our desires to pursue their agendas – be it to win an election, to hit their sales targets or to expand their readership numbers. In the age of consumerism we are used to ready-to-use solutions – the *homo consumericus* takes whatever the best storyteller sells him or her. We are more prone to manipulation than ever before.

Both far-right and Islamist extremists have been extraordinarily good at manipulating us into believing their stories and therefore acting in accordance with the rules of their fictive world order. Let's lift their glossy magazine covers and shed light on the communication strategies that lie behind their propaganda. The success recipe of extremists' stories has five basic ingredients, sometimes supplemented with additional seasoning, depending on the taste of their target audience.

Simplicity: The Star Wars *Effect*

The first ingredient is simplicity. 'Good and Evil are the Ying and Yang of human nature', said the famous American psychologist Philip Zimbardo.[23] In an increasingly complex world, black-and-white narratives that eliminate all confusing grey zones can be comforting.

'Extremists provide an answer to people's desire for simplicity within our immensely complex global environment,' Arab–Israeli psychologist Ahmad Mansour tells me. He himself was radicalised by Islamist extremists in his teenage years. 'From now they will fight you,' the Muslim Brotherhood leader of his village Tira told him when he noticed that Ahmad regularly joined their gatherings. He was given brochures and cassettes that built on a global Muslim victimhood narrative. 'I started to believe that the entire non-Muslim world was at war with Islam,' he recalls. 'For years this worldview determined my thoughts and actions.'

A look at the most popular movies in history is enough to see that we love binary worldviews: for example, the *Star Wars* cosmos divides the world into the light and the dark side of the force. *James Bond, Indiana Jones, American Sniper*, and even *Kung Fu Panda*, do nothing else. In a way they all tell the same story based on different characters and embedded in different contexts. One could replace Daniel Craig with Bradley Cooper or Harrison Ford and move the shooting location from US casinos to Iraqi battlefield zones or the Temple of Doom without making substantial changes to the core story. This is what I will call 'the *Star Wars* effect'.

Consistency: The Burkini Effect

Even more important than simplicity is consistency – this means not only consistency in the narrative itself but also consistency between narration and action. Even in literature, telling a consistent story isn't enough: 'good stories don't tell; they show' is the first rule in writing. Whether we read a book or listen to politicians – words that are not mirrored in action are frustrating.

Extremists have been good at delivering consistent narratives – simplicity of their story forms helps. In fact, their stories do not just make sense in themselves; they are also consistent with the other extreme's worldview. There is therefore an intra-extremist narrative compatibility that creates a bizarre symbiosis between opposing extremes. Whether you are on the side of the light or the dark side in *Star Wars* does not really change the story; the only thing that does change is the perspective. The same is true for the far-right and Islamist extremists – they are in the same movie, reinforcing the same story and thus helping each other as storytellers. While Islamist extremists tell us that the 'West is at war with Islam', the far right tells us 'Islam is at War with the West'. While far-right groups tend to see Islam as the only problem, Islamist extremists view Islam as the only solution. One only needs to reverse protagonist and antagonist or exchange problem and solution to see that their narratives are perfectly complementary, if not identical.

The narratives of the establishment, on the other hand, are far from consistent. The gap between its words and its actions has become increasingly wide in Western countries, as it is clamping down on civic rights in response to today's terrorism threats. In the light of a recent series of intrusive counter-terrorism policies, including measures that disproportionately target Muslims such as the controversial burkini bans,[24] France's principles of *liberté*, *égalité* and *fraternité* start to sound like a bad joke. This 'Burkini Effect' has become more commonplace as European governments struggle to strike the balance between the strategically best and politically most convenient solution. To stay in power they have to address their population's concerns while, however, not sacrificing the very principles they seek to defend from extremism: democracy, human rights and pluralism. In short, consistency matters.

Responsiveness: The FPÖ Effect

Responding to the population's grievances and desires matters too. In many ways, Martha – a student at Vienna University of Economics and Business Administration – is a prototype undergraduate student. She is good-looking and popular, wears expensive designer shoes and a Tommy Hilfiger jacket. Martha comes from a small town in Upper Austria but has enjoyed her student life in Vienna for several years now. In the summer she meets friends for an Aperol-Spritz along the Danube canal; in the winter she has Glühwein on campus after (or during) her accounting classes. One would think her life is free from worries. Yet she is deeply concerned. A few weeks prior to the 2016 Austrian presidential elections, I meet her in a small café not far from the new university campus. She tells me about her fears that Austria will be overrun by immigrants and ruled by Sharia one day. 'They are everywhere. When I walk around in the district of Ottakring, all I see is veiled faces, all I hear is foreign languages. I can feel their stares when I wear a skirt. I don't want to make a detour just because our politicians are incapable of keeping our country safe.' She believes Austria's mainstream politicians fail to listen and respond to the public's concerns. 'Why should we listen to them [the politicians in power], if they don't listen to us?'

One of the top five motives for Austrians who gave their vote to far-right presidential candidate Norbert Hofer in March 2016 was that they felt that he addressed the right topics.[25] 'At least the FPÖ (Freedom Party of Austria) addressed my concerns,' Martha confirms. To make sure young people feel heard, it is necessary to address those debates that matter to them. Appealing to an audience means taking its grievances and desires seriously. The establishment has become an easy target for criticism from the fringes because of its failure to do so. For example, the Srebrenica massacre that killed over 8,000 Muslim Bosniaks in the summer of 1995 is on the minds of the close-to-170,000 Slavic Muslims living in Germany today.[26] Nevertheless, it is a topic that has been largely absent in the political debate. On the other hand, many native Germans felt that their concerns over national identity and multi-culturalism were not addressed adequately in mainstream politicians' discourse on immigration.

Far-right and Islamist extremists have exploited these gaps, picking their target audience up where they are coming from. They respond to common concerns by offering simple answers to complex questions. Politicians in positions of power are too busy telling their own stories to address the stories that really matter to their audience. As a result, far from being on the same page as their audience, dominating parties were not even in the same book. In order for individuals to listen to a story, they first have to be interested in its content. Second, they need to empathise with its protagonists.

Identification: The Tinder Effect

Pictures of handsome men posing with kittens are not exclusive to dating apps such as Tinder. Extremists have picked up on the trend: in 2014, a UN report warned that ISIS's social media photos of jihadists holding kittens and AK-47s were turning into a successful recruiting strategy.[27] The July 2016 issue of ISIS's propaganda magazine *Dabiq*[28] shows a foreign fighter cuddling a cat, next to a photo of a romantic sunset. Similarly, French far-right politician Marine Le Pen rarely misses an opportunity for a fluffy selfie, hugging horses or pet cats. The goal of this is obvious in the cases of Tinder, *Dabiq* and Le Pen: generating empathy from the target audience. Good stories stir up emotions. Whether in marketing, literature or politics, the chances of breaking through to a wider audience are much higher when appealing to emotions. On social media, emotion – positive or negative – is among the most important factors that drive the sharing of contents.[29] The most straightforward way of appealing to an audience's emotions is by evoking empathy for the protagonists and their supporters.

Most stories use protagonists and antagonists with recurring characteristics. These are called archetypes. 'Archetypes are the psychic instincts of the human species',[30] the motivating dynamics in the collective unconscious. There are a variety of archetypes: the innocent, the hero, the rebel, the ruler, the creator, the caregiver – among others. Islamist extremists rely heavily on the use of archetypes: the figures of the hero, the Prophet and the Crusaders are recurring motifs in their narratives.[31] Archetypes of contemporary far-right extremists include 'backward' Muslims, 'evil' Jews and 'innocent' Caucasian girls.

Extremists' simplistic and static understanding of identity places their archetypes in binary opposition. The 'other' is summed up under one big archetype: while ISIS implies that Trump is representative of the entire West, far-right supporters often suggest that Al Baghdadi is representative of all Muslims.[32] In ISIS's world, anyone who does not side with its fighters is lumped into one big Islamophobic monolith that wears the label 'The West' or 'The Crusaders'. Similarly, the far right conveniently conflates immigrants and Muslims with terrorists, even labelling mainstream politicians as terrorist supporters. While American far-right politician Sarah Palin accused President Obama of having 'terrorist' connections,[33] Trump referred to him as the 'founder of ISIS'.[34] Both the victimisation of the 'us' and the demonisation of the 'other' is facilitated by the use of archetypes.

An additional appeal of radical groups lies in the strong sense of belonging they create for their members. They foster homogeneity among in-groups through the use of common language, symbols and customs.[35] This allows them to exploit vulnerable individuals' identity crises. For example, Islamic State's propaganda pictures display the values of team spirit, brotherhood and loyalty.[36] Likewise, the (now archived) Facebook page of German neo-Nazi terrorist group Oldschool Society shows pictures of its members hugging each other and celebrating together.[37] Provoking empathy for its story's protagonists and inducing hatred against the antagonists is the basis of both extremes' strategies.

Inspiration: The Final Battle Effect

Stories are about creating the desire to resolve a real or perceived conflict between protagonists and antagonists.[38] In that sense they can be used to bring about change by inspiring action on a desired trajectory. Extremists share a common story form that builds on the idea of victimhood and implies that solving the conflict is only possible by eliminating 'the other', metaphorically or literally.[39] For example, their 'happy end' may be achieved through the annihilation of a race, a religion or a social class. Extremists may refer to this as the 'final battle', 'the inevitable war' or 'the final solution'.

Their stories tend to rely on the following pattern: the integrity, if not survival, of a protagonist P is threatened by the actions of an antagonist A. In order to restore the security or lost dignity of P it is necessary to free the world of all evil caused by A. An excerpt from Hitler's *Mein Kampf* illustrates this: 'The world is undoubtedly going through great changes. The only question is whether the outcome will be the good of Aryan humanity or profits for the eternal Jew. The task of the national State will, therefore, be to preserve the race.'[40]

Islamist extremist propaganda follows the same pattern. An extract from the Islamic State's *Dabiq* magazine demonstrates this: 'We target the crusaders, and we will eradicate and distinguish them, for there are only two camps: the camp of truth and its followers, and the camp of falsehood and its factions.'[41]

The Islamist extremist organisation Hizb ut-Tahrir would phrase it similarly:

It is Islam they (the Kafir nations) want to extinguish. They have not forgotten our dominance for over 1000 years and fight it to ensure that it will not return and end their domination of the world. All Muslims, do we not feel the burden of the women and the children that are suffering and crying out for help? Is inaction an option?[42]

The rhetoric of the Germany-based far-right group PEGIDA offers another example of such a story form. Even spelling out the full name that is behind the acronym of the group, the Patriotic Europeans against the Islamisation of the Occident, points to the simplistic pattern that underlies its story. It divides the world into 'bad' Muslims that seek to impose Sharia law over 'good' Western countries, whose – ideally homogeneous – population needs to defend itself by joining the PEGIDA movement and fighting the common enemy.

Extremists' narratives all share the same characteristic in regards to their conflict resolution: they are built on zero-sum games and call for 'absolute' solutions. It is the nature of their stories that unites jihadist and neo-Nazi groups as well as their non-violent counterparts.

Stories of Wars

Stories allow storytellers to shape the perception of the audience by presenting events and their actors in a certain light. In order to make sense of any event, our brain needs to contextualise it by linking it to other events. A series of events, true or imagined, can be described in the form of a story. It is thanks to narration that we can attribute meaning and validity to both abstract concepts and tangible things.[43] By telling appealing stories and skilfully linking current events to historical grievances, extremists have been able to reinforce their binary worldviews. They have all hijacked stories that are deeply enshrined in our cultural DNA, so-called master narratives, to push their extremist ideologies.

'History is a fable often told,' said Napoleon. The same series of events may be linked together through entirely different stories, changing the overall narrative. The vast differences in history education demonstrate how much the narrative can vary: 'The sons of this nation stood up in front of the tripartite invasion of the Suez Canal, they had patience, a strong will and a faith in the victory', standard Egyptian textbooks teach the country's young generations. Until President el-Sisi changed the curriculum after taking power in 2014, Egyptian schoolbooks had a tendency to overemphasise Gamal Abdel Nasser's successful resistance to British imperialism and glorify him as a national hero without presenting his darker sides. Today's textbooks, on the other hand, manage to talk about the Egyptian revolution he led in 1952, his nationalisation of the Suez Canal and the subsequent Suez Crisis for over 20 pages without even mentioning his name a single time.[44]

Meanwhile, British course materials have reduced their discourse about the humiliating experience of the Suez Crisis that significantly undermined British influence in the region to a minimum. In fact, the course that deals with the history of colonisation and decolonisation is not even a mandatory part of the British A-level curriculum.[45] Neil MacGregor, former Director of the British Museum, criticised Britain for focusing almost exclusively on the sunnier sides of its history. 'In Britain we use our history in order to comfort us to make us feel stronger,' he said.[46]

The origins of some of the ugliest intra-Muslim conflicts are found in irreconcilable narration. For example, the Sunni–Shia divide can be traced back to right after the Prophet Muhammad's death 1,400 years ago, when his followers could not agree on his successor. With every new adversarial incident, the rift between the two got deeper and their narratives more irreconcilable. Today, this Sunni–Shia narrative dispute manifests itself in power struggles between Saudi Arabia and Iran as well as in the multiple conflicts and proxy wars fuelled by sectarian rivalries in countries with significant Sunni and Shia populations such as Yemen, Bahrain, Lebanon, Iraq and Syria.[47] Likewise, the Turkish–Kurdish conflict boils down to the contradictions between the Kurdish nationalism narrative and the diametrically opposed discourse promoted by the Turkish state, which seeks to eliminate the Kurdish identity.[48]

Over time, stories can turn into narratives, and narratives into master narratives through the repetition of their patterns. A master narrative can also be described as a grand story that helps to make sense of the cosmos of little stories, often deeply embedded in culture.[49] For instance, the global War on Terror started as a series of connected events but soon turned into a narrative of 'the West is at war with Islam', which was exploited by Islamist extremists who linked it to a master narrative of the Crusaders and the End Times myth.[50]

Often a reference to a single story or even a single event within a story is enough to stir up collective grievances attached to a master narrative. For example, simply saying '1967' – the year of the Six-Day War in which Israel captured the West Bank, the Gaza Strip, and the Sinai Peninsula – or writing the hashtags #Chechnya, #Kashmir or '#Srebrenica' can be enough to incite outrage and hatred among an entire Muslim community. These grievances increase susceptibility to myths and conspiracies built on a group's victimhood. It is therefore not surprising that Islamist extremists have a long history of distributing DVDs, cassette videos and other evidence of the worst atrocities committed against them by the West.[51] They have used the reference to collective trauma of entire ethnic, cultural or religious communities to reinforce collective identity and to remind or convince them of their collective duty to defend their lands. On social media this strategy resonates with calls for #Jihad or calls to #BanIslam.[52]

On 27 February 2017, news broke that German hostage Jürgen Kantner had been beheaded by Islamist militants of the ISIS-linked

Abu Sayyaf group in the Philippines after the deadline for his $10m ransom passed. Using two separate avatar accounts on Twitter and Telegram, I chatted with a far-right and an Islamist extremist supporter. I asked both the same question: 'Have you heard of Jürgen Kantner's beheading?'

Catha, a woman in her mid-thirties and vocal supporter of far-right PEGIDA and Alternative für Deutschland (AfD), told me that 'this was another piece of evidence that Muslims are vile monsters who want to wipe out the West. Even on the other side of the world that doesn't change.' The Islamist extremist wrote that Abu Sayyaf was acting 'in the service of Allah' and that the hostage was 'an old infidel who deserved to die' in revenge for all the atrocities committed by the West.

The way far-right and Islamist extremists connect events is different. They tell their stories from the opposite perspective, creating diametrically opposed narratives. Victim and perpetrator are reversed. But the end product is the same: both narratives eventually feed into the same master narrative of an inevitable war between Muslims and non-Muslims.

	Islamist Extremist	Far-Right Extremist
Event	A beheads B.	A beheads B.
Story	Brave soldier of Allah beheads infidel.	Vile Muslim terrorist beheads Western hostage.
Narrative	Islam fights back against imperialist West.	Evil Islam attacks West, seeking to extinguish it.
Master Narrative	Islam vs. Crusaders: war between Muslims and non-Muslims is inevitable.	Islam vs. Crusaders: war between Muslims and non-Muslims is inevitable.

Telling stories is a powerful tool for controlling public recollection and interpretation of events. By forming a story around new strings of events, one can create an inter-subjective system for making sense of the world and determine the way new stories will be told. In that sense, it defines the boundaries of collective imagination. Change happens when fictive constructs start falling apart – when the unimaginable becomes imaginable.

The creation of the Kurdistan Regional Government (KRG) in 2005 is an example of an event whose high symbolic significance had real consequences – not just for the Kurds but for many people living in the Middle East. It marked the first fracture in the colonial borders drawn almost a century earlier, demonstrating that the borders were artificial and thus reversible. The realisation that nation states were mere products of our imagination aroused hopes that the lines in the Middle East could be redrawn and the myth of the nation state challenged.

The removal of Saddam Hussein in the spring of 2003 had a similar effect: the fact that a seemingly unchangeable order under a seemingly incontestable leader could actually be challenged sparked hope among Iraqis.[53] Both events were therefore pivotal in inspiring change – whether in the form of the Arab Spring or in the creation of an Islamic state.

While a population's lack of imagination can be a major stabilising factor in national politics, it can also be a source of inter-state and inter-sectarian conflict. If the way we learn to frame our past has an impact on the way we will interpret future events, we are all prisoners to our own history. Master narratives shape our desires and our identity, and limit our ideological flexibility, because we can only imagine a certain trajectory within the boundaries of our imagined order.

Many of today's most complex and concerning conflicts are rooted in conflicting stories about the past. They appear unresolvable because both sides are prisoners to their own history, or rather their own interpretations of history. In the case of far-right and Islamist extremists, the myth of a clash of civilisations has become so strong that it seems insurmountable and the 'West versus Islam' narrative is in effect turning into a reality. What starts as an interpretation of history becomes an identity-defining reality. Stories of war turn into wars of stories.

Wars of Stories

This competition between antagonistic, but mutually reinforcing, ideologies is not new. It has existed since civilisations started to organise themselves in communities built on commonly shared stories, myths and narratives. British historian Norman Cohn wrote in his book *The Pursuit of the Millennium* that these behavioural patterns resurfaced in different environments, epochs and geographic zones.[54]

From the first crusade in the eleventh century to the end of the Ottoman–Habsburg wars in the eighteenth century, there were repeated conflicts between political Christianity and political Islam. The end of this period of holy wars coincided with the Age of the Enlightenment, which brought about a new diversity of ideas and thus ideologies. Religiously centred ideologies were replaced by secular ones that put the emphasis on reason. Although the Enlightenment was a European intellectual movement, it also impacted on Muslim-majority countries in the Middle East, North Africa and beyond. The eventual defeat and dissolution of the Ottoman Empire following World War I meant that both political Christianity and political Islam had been pushed into the background. New political ideologies such as liberalism, communism, capitalism, nationalism and Nazism gained ground.

The early twentieth century witnessed new conflicts between far-left and far-right ideologies. The most obvious example is the violent confrontation between fascists and communists in 1920s Italy. World War II exposed the dangers of fascism, and led to its temporary defeat and a growing call for moderate voices. Yet it immediately transitioned into a new intellectual power struggle: the Cold War. On the one side was the atheist far left, the communist East; on the other side was the capitalist West, which instrumentalised Christianity for its aims.[55] The continued confrontations between the two during the Cold War led to the decline of both ideological forces. The defeat of the global far-left movement was more obvious with the dissolution of the Soviet Union in 1991. Yet the post-1989 secular consensus also led to the weakening of Christian parties across Europe,[56] dropping membership and the declining influence of US Protestant churches.[57]

The Cold War period also saw the far left clash with political Islam, climaxing in the Soviet–Afghan war during the 1980s. *Mujahedeen* from all across the world came to Afghanistan to join the ongoing guerrilla resistance against the Soviet occupation. This major confrontation between the far left and political Islam left the former humiliated and the latter strengthened. It was this confrontation that accelerated the revival of political Islam that had been taking place in the shadow of the Cold War tensions, giving birth to the concept of international jihad. In the meantime, the far right also had time to slowly recover from its blowback in 1945. The millennial turn saw its definitive comeback, as it found a new antagonist: political Islam. Since 9/11 and the War on Terror, rising anti-Muslim sentiments have translated into a rapidly growing support base for far-right parties across Europe and the US. The early twenty-first century is therefore characterised by an open conflict between the far right and political Islam.

On 20 December 2016, I find myself in an empty Christmas market in Vienna. The Glühwein stands are abandoned, the shop-keepers are shivering. 'I haven't sold a single Pretzel today,' one tells me. He looks at me in expectation. 'In solidarity with the victims of yesterday's truck attack in Berlin?' he says, pointing towards one of his Pretzels that is topped with a tiny German flag and the words '*Ich bin ein Berliner*'. His phone beeps. 'They have the wrong man,' he says, after opening a push notification with shaky hands. 'The real perpetrator is still on the run ... I can't believe it. If you ask me, we should lock them all up.'

His voice is calm but his eyes are fearful. 'Merkel should never have let all these Muslims in. They are at war with us.' He echoes the posts that are flooding my Twitter feed. 'These are Merkel's dead' and 'Vote for AfD' write high-ranking politicians of the German anti-immigration party. They have hijacked the news story for their agenda, with more success than the poor Pretzel vendor. Meanwhile, ISIS supporters tell a different story: in chatrooms of the encrypted messaging app Telegram they praise the ISIS 'soldier' who drove the truck into the pedestrian crowd. 'So who continues [the terror] and drives into the next Christmas market. Don't let the kufr [infidels] ever forget this Christmas market', one German-speaking ISIS-supporter writes.

The little note from the extremist of unknown origin is still in my bag: 'Stay safe as we are approaching the final battle.' We have entered a new vicious circle of extremism. But the circle starts in our heads with the birth of a black-and-white illusion. The clash of civilisations is only happening if enough people turn colour-blind. In reality, the borders between competing ideologies are fluid. To varying degrees extremist movements borrow elements from other ideologies, depending on their context and subculture.

For example, some European populist far-right movements hijack Christian fundamentalist values, such as the return to the family unit and the focus on occidental identity. Others borrow anti-globalisation and anti-elite elements of the far left. Politicised Islam and the far left share an anti-imperialist and anti-capitalist rhetoric, whereas politicised Islam and Christianity overlap in their socially regressive tendencies.

Ironically, one finds striking similarities between the BNP and Hizb ut-Tahrir in the UK, Les Identitaires and Muslim identity movements in France, or PEGIDA and Islamisches Erwachen in Germany. Often those organisations that are most vehemently opposed to each other are the best mirrors of each other's ideologies and narratives.

The reflections of this chapter open up many questions. Does a multi-cultural society automatically imply a multi-narrative society? How can black-and-white stories be prevented from taking shape? What could alternative stories that do not pit one group against another look like? How can the desire for simplicity in today's increasingly complex environments be addressed? Before answering these questions it is necessary to gain a better understanding of the nature of those narratives that are responsible for some of today's most irritating and significant societal changes.

Taking a closer look at the anatomy of the stories spread by far-right and Islamist extremists is the first step to finding ways to break apart the vicious circle of extremism.

2

The Global Jihadist Insurgency

ON THE EVENING OF 2 MAY 2011, OBAMA ANNOUNCED THAT OSAMA BIN Laden had been killed in an early-morning operation by US Special Forces in the Pakistani city of Abbottabad. Millions of Americans had waited for this moment. It ended a 13-year-long manhunt, which had started three years prior to the attacks on the World Trade Center's twin towers. For then-British Prime Minister David Cameron it was clear that bin Laden's death would 'bring great relief around the world' and for Obama it meant that the world would be 'a safer place'.[1] Millions gathered all across the US, including on New York's Ground Zero, to celebrate bin Laden's death, setting off fireworks, carrying American flags, yelling national anthem chants and playing drinking games – for Al Qaeda the epitome of Western perversion. Students at Ohio State University even jumped into Mirror Lake, something they would usually do only on the occasion of the annual football game between the Ohio State Buckeyes and the Michigan Wolverines.

The idea of celebrating a human being's death – even if this human being happened to be the world's most wanted terrorist – is macabre enough *per se*. But that was not the only thing that was disturbing about the celebrations. They were also fundamentally misleading. At the end of 2011 Osama bin Laden was dead, Al Qaeda paralysed and the Taliban weakened. The US withdrew its last troops from Iraq in December 2011. Counter-terrorism experts were speaking of the decline of Islamist terrorist groups.[2] Yet it wasn't over. Less than three years later, ISIS announced the establishment of its caliphate and the US was back in Iraq. By the summer of 2014, ISIS territory equalled the size of Britain, its population that of Denmark. In 2016, the United States' National Counterterrorism Center estimated that ISIS comprised over 30,000 foreign fighters and generated an annual revenue of roughly $500 million. The threat from Islamist extremism had never been truly suffocated.

There was a profound misunderstanding that Al Qaeda had inspired Islamist extremism, in fact Islamist extremism had inspired Al Qaeda. Osama bin Laden's death may have meant the end of Al Qaeda as we knew it but it did not mean the end of Islamist terrorism. Likewise, the end of ISIS won't be the end of jihadism. The fall of Mosul would spell the end of ISIS's 'caliphate', American ground force commander in Iraq Major General Gary Volesky claimed in October 2016. But the underestimated jihadist group, Jabhat Al Nusra (the Al Nusra Front), has built up an impressive network of loyal allies in the region and is already consolidating power and ready to benefit from future power vacuums in the Middle East and North Africa.[3]

History has taught us that jihadism is too often reduced to one group. Defeating a terrorist group and cutting off the head of one organisation may temporarily stabilise a region or halt terror attacks but it does not eliminate the long-term threat posed by the global jihadist insurgency.[4] 'While I was in Iraq, the approach we took to fighting terrorism felt to me too much like catching drops of water from a leaky faucet', former CIA analyst Janessa Gans Wilder, who founded the Euphrates Institute, wrote about her 21-month assignment in Iraq.[5] The heads of the hydra are re-growing faster than they can be cut off.

Jihadism is not a new phenomenon. Modern-day jihadists draw on a history of political Islam that goes back to at least the fourteenth century. United in their rejection of modernity, liberalism, secularism and capitalism, their stories all build on similar interpretations of the Qur'an and the hadith. To comprehend today's violent manifestations of these ideas it is crucial to understand the long history of political Islam and its ideological architects.

'Often the doctrine of one ideologue provided a train of thought that was then utilised, developed and orientated by another,' terrorism expert Dr Sajjan Gohel explains. 'What makes young people embrace these old ideas?' I ask him. 'The younger generation will read the books of the ideologues and take snippets of their texts to use in tweets or other forms of social media.' He explains that their understanding of the ideologues has been watered down. 'It's almost on a soundbite basis but nevertheless the use of the ideologues' quotations still carries relevance.' An exploration of the roots of Islamist extremist ideas takes us back in history as far as the Middle Ages.

A Brief History of Islamist Extremist Ideas

Jihad Against Ignorance

Ibn Taymiyyah is the ideological godfather of modern-day Islamist extremism. The Hanbali scholar was born in Harras, Mesopotamia, in the late thirteenth century. Over 700 years later, the 9/11 Commission report cited him as one of the key influencers of bin Laden's beliefs.[6] Ibn Taymiyyah spent most of his career in Damascus during the invasion of the Mongols, who had taken Baghdad in 1258. Although the Mongol invaders had converted to Islam, Ibn Taymiyyah issued a fatwa against them because they failed to implement Sharia. To him, anyone who adhered to man-made law could not be a true Muslim. His fatwa claimed that jihad was obligatory to all Muslims to rescue Islam from the confines of *jahiliyya*, meaning 'ignorance'.[7] This was groundbreaking within Islamic law, as no jurist had ever before mandated the use of lethal force against Muslims in battle.

Ibn Taymiyya's rejection of all *bidah* (innovation) in Islam has inspired modern-day Salafists, who call for a return to 'true Islam', which only existed during the time of the Prophet Muhammad and the first caliphs (*salaf* means forebears in Arabic).[8] In particular, Ibn Taymiyya's legacy has remained influential in Saudi Arabia's Wahhabist ideology. Founded by Muhammad ibn 'Abd Al Wahhab in the eighteenth century, Wahhabism rejects all forms of *bidah* and *shirk* (polytheism). As a close advisor to Saudi Arabia's founder Ibn Saud, Al Wahhab laid the basis for the country's religious ideology. The uncompromising Wahhabi interpretation of *tawhid* (Islam's concept of the oneness of God) has ever since inspired both mainstream Salafists and Salafi-jihadists.[9]

Since the 1970s, Riyadh has exported not just its petroleum but also its puritanical religious doctrines, mostly through investments in madrassas and mosques across the world. European intelligence estimates that Saudi Arabia has invested over $10 billion to promote its heavily politicised version of Islam through charitable foundations – 15 to 20 per cent of this amount may have been diverted to fund violent extremism.[10] In fact, a secret 2009 memo of the US State Department published by WikiLeaks warned that terrorist groups such as Al Qaeda, the Taliban and Hamas have raised millions of dollars annually from Saudi sources.[11] The European Parliament identified Wahhabism as the main source of international terrorism in 2013.[12]

Modern-day terrorists also draw on Ibn Taymiyya's war tactic of Inghimas (*to plunge into*). 'An Inghimas attack's goal is to kill as many people as possible by plunging into them, whilst eventually being killed in a hail of bullets,' explains Sajjan. The Paris attacks of November 2015 are an example of an Inghimas attack against soft targets: suicide bombers shooting as many civilians as they are able before detonating their explosives.[13] According to Sajjan, ISIS has even listed Inghimas in their registration forms when finding out what role their recruits want to serve.

Westoxification

The twentieth century saw a revival of political Islam that planted the seeds for modern Islamist extremism. From the late nineteenth century onwards, France and Britain had been spreading Enlightenment values to their colonies, to the horror of many Muslims who feared that their culture would be eroded. Calls for a return to 'true Islam' by purifying it of all Western influences turned louder in reaction to European imperialism. Egypt was at the heart of emerging protests against Western hegemony. Even after formally gaining independence in 1922, it experienced continuous Western interference. No one was more influential in the resistance to foreign cultural domination than the Egyptian imam Hassan Al Banna. In 1928, he founded the Muslim Brotherhood in opposition to what he called the 'devil of colonialism'.[14] He believed that it was necessary to gradually establish an Islamic state and introduce Sharia to fight Western immorality and the perceived decline of Islam. Al Banna's Muslim Brotherhood would soon become the most powerful transnational movement for the popularisation of political Islam.

The Muslim Brotherhood was influenced by an Indian cleric called Abul Ala Maududi,[15] who is remembered for his jihad against modern-day *jahiliyya*. He argued that Muslims had to reject all man-made law to return to the glorious time of the first generations of Islam. Jihad, according to him, was obligatory to rescue Islam from secularism, nationalism and liberal democracy. In 1941 he founded Jamaat e Islami, one of the largest Islamist movements in Asia. Despite claiming that violence was permitted in jihad, he believed the best way to Islamise society was to change hearts and minds through a top-bottom education process of *dawah* (proselytising). His advocacy of an Islamic state later influenced Pakistani president General Zia-ul-Haq, who introduced *Shariaisation* to Pakistani politics. For Maududi, the ideal Islamic state would not be ruled by a theocracy (i.e. by an individual caliph) but by a 'theodemocracy', whereby the local Muslim community acts as a form of vice-regency that governs by *ijma* (consensus).[16]

Maududi inspired Sayyid Qutb, another prominent Muslim Brotherhood member who is hailed as a martyr for jihad by modern-day terrorist leaders. During his two-year stay in the US, the Egyptian writer developed a profound hatred of American, hedonistic culture. He resented the West for its alleged desire to eradicate Islam – as demonstrated by the Crusades and more recently by colonialism – and predicted a clash between Islam and the West. In his book *Milestones*[17] Qutb argues that a violent jihad is justified to destroy Western *jahiliyya* and to liberate humanity from servitude to man-made laws. As those who have usurped the authority of God will not concede it without a fight, Muslims must prepare for death and torture. For Qutb, modern Muslim leaders who followed man-made ideals such as socialism and nationalism, as Nasser's Arab Socialist Union had done, were not real Muslims. Qutb was arrested in 1964 for allegedly plotting to overthrow the Nasser regime and was hanged in 1966. Following the ideologue's death, his brother Muhammad was exiled to Saudi Arabia, where King Faisal welcomed many conservative preachers and gave them roles as university lecturers. Both bin Laden and Al Qaeda's current leader, Ayman Al Zawahiri, were students of Muhammad Qutb at King Abdulaziz University in Jeddah.[18]

It did not take long until Sayyid Qutb's prediction of a clash of civilisations between Islam and the West materialised. A decade after Qutb's execution, 'Death to America' was heard outside the US Embassy in Tehran. On 4 November 1979, members of the student group Muslim Students of the Imam Khomeini Line seized 52 American diplomats, resulting in the longest hostage crisis in standing history. For half a century Iran had lived under a pro-American de facto dictatorship. Iranian resistance to 'Westoxification' – a phrase coined by the Iranian thinker Jalal Al e Ahmed – climaxed in the Revolution of 1979. Nationalists, Leftists and Islamists all came together under the leadership of the cleric Ruhollah Khomeini, who skilfully combined right-wing nationalistic language, leftist economic provisions and Shia symbols.[19] After the revolutionaries had toppled the US-backed Shah, they transformed the Pahlavi monarchy into an Islamic Republic under Ayatollah Khomeini. Across the entire Middle East the demise of Reza Shah was interpreted as a major strike against Western imperialism and a crucial step in ending decades-long oppression of the *ummah*.

Islamist groups have always followed a similar narrative: they oppose the Muslim leaders who have succumbed to opportunism, Western influence and the neglect of Sharia in favour of man-made legislation. With the 1979 Revolution, Islam had finally achieved a monumental victory against such corruption. Although Khomeini based his Islamic government on the Shia concept of Guardianship (*Velayat*), his successful creation of the world's first modern theocracy was just as inspirational for Sunni Islamists across the globe. This rise in popularity for Islamist parties forced many avowedly secular Muslim rulers to endorse a brand of conservative Islam that would appease such increasingly influential groups.

The Afghan Jihad

The year 1979 was also that in which the Soviet Union invaded Afghanistan. This is where the Sunni Islamic scholar Abdullah Azzam made himself a name as 'the founder of global jihad'. Some even call him the 'father of modern Islamic terrorism'.[20] Born in Palestine, Azzam joined the Muslim Brotherhood in the 1950s and became interested in the works of Al Banna. After the Six-Day War in 1967, Azzam fled to Jordan to join the PLO but became disillusioned with their secular, Marxist, nationalist ideas, which he considered man-made and therefore un-Islamic. Like many radicals he was welcomed into Saudi Arabia to preach orthodox Islamic values. This is where he first crossed paths with Al Zawahiri and bin Laden, with whom he would later co-found Al Qaeda.

When the Soviet troops arrived in Afghanistan, Azzam instigated a fatwa entitled 'Defence of the Muslim Lands, the First Obligation after Faith'. It urged all Muslims worldwide to defend their lands in Afghanistan and Pakistan against non-Muslim occupiers.[21] Azzam's use of insurgency and guerrilla warfare to defeat a militarily superior enemy helped to popularise 'asymmetric warfare'.[22] His ideas lived on after his death, and remain an inspiration for jihadist groups, including ISIS. The 'godfather of internet jihad' Barbar Ahmad made sure Azzam's publications were accessible to everyone on the online platform azzam.com.[23]

'He was probably the most influential recruiter of the Afghan war, especially for the Arab world,' Sheikh Dr Usama Hasan, who himself fought the jihad against Soviet forces in Afghanistan, tells me. There are few people who can claim to be Cambridge graduates, former extremists, astronomers, senior university lecturers, Islamic reformers and radicalisation intervention providers all at the same time. In fact, Usama is probably the only one in the world. By the age of 11 he could recite the entire Qur'an. In his teenage years, he was one of the first British jihadists. Today, he devotes most of his time to challenging the very ideologies that he once subscribed to. He refutes extremist interpretations of the Holy Qur'an and discourages young people from taking the same path that he had once taken.

As we talk about his time in Afghanistan over lunch, Usama's sandwich remains largely untouched. He was only 19 years old when he was trained with Kalashnikovs but his memories remain vivid. 'I would have loved to try one of those anti-aircraft guns we had,' he recalls. His Salafist organisation JIMAS – today a well-integrated charity organisation – had made contact with the *mujahedeen* in Afghanistan before sending the first fighters there between 1990 and 1991. 'I didn't know what to expect, I just went with the flow. So whatever I saw I thought "okay, that must be normal".' His parents were fully supportive of the cause but Usama recalls that his mother had tears in her eyes when he came back. 'It only hit me later that my parents must have gone through terrible times. My mum only told me a quarter of a century later that there were days she couldn't eat or sleep.' By the time he and his friends arrived in Afghanistan, the tide had turned and the Soviets had left. 'It was no longer a defensive jihad, we wanted to establish a caliphate,' Usama says. They were planning to merge Afghanistan with the Islamic Republics of Pakistan and Iran and then expand the Islamic State to

Egypt, Saudi Arabia and other countries in the region. 'That's how you build a caliphate,' Usama says.

'How would you have dealt with the Shia in Iran?' I ask.

'Oh,' he grins, as if amused by the naivety of his 19-year-old self. 'Actually, to be honest, we would have tried to take over.'

In many ways, the grounds of justification for the *mujahedeen* in Afghanistan (such as Usama) were similar to those of today's jihadists in Syria and Iraq. So were the war dynamics after Kabul fell in 1992 and the fighting turned into a vicious civil war. 'It was disillusioning.' Usama's left eye flashes. 'Most people didn't stay true to the cause or their beliefs, as everyone started fighting for power. Maybe fewer youngsters would want to go to Syria today if they could see how history repeats itself.'

The New Islamist Extremist Wave

Even though jihadism is not new, the scale of the problem is unprecedented. In June 2014, Sunni rebels in Syria announced the establishment of a caliphate in Iraq and the Levant. Within 18 months, ISIS conducted or inspired at least 50 terrorist attacks in 18 countries, killing 1,000 people and injuring over 1,700. A record number of countries experienced their highest levels of terrorism in any year in the past 16 years. OECD countries saw the strongest increase in terrorism casualties ever recorded: between 2014 and 2015 deaths there from terrorism increased by 650 per cent. More than half of the recorded deaths were connected to ISIS activity.[24]

Islamist extremists remain a small minority within Western Muslim communities but their numbers have surged rapidly in every European country over the past five years.[25] Not all Islamist extremists are jihadists. There is a wide range of Islamist extremist groups who apply or advocate the use of violence to varying degrees. The continuum ranges from extremely violent terrorist groups such as ISIS and Al Qaeda all the way to non-violent Islamist extremists who confine themselves to propagating extreme interpretations of Islamic scripture without actively engaging in violent activities. Whether violent or not, most of these extremist organisations can be traced back to the same ideological roots.

While they share the same objective of establishing a caliphate and imposing their version of Sharia law, their approaches to achieving this overarching goal vary.

Members of these groups spread their extremist thoughts in the form of a politicised version of Islam: Islamism. This is what distinguishes them from mainstream Muslims who practise Islam as an individual faith. Although it may seem self-evident, it is important to emphasise that most Muslims are not Islamists and most Islamists are not jihadists. This crucial distinction is often ignored by far-right sympathisers, who use the terms Islam, Islamism and jihadism interchangeably to propagate the view that Islam is inherently violent.

Tweets by PEGIDA UK leader Anne Marie Waters demonstrate this conflation of Islam with jihadism. On 7 December 2016, she tweeted: 'People often criticise my language. Here's why: I believe that because people are killed for insulting Islam, everyone should insult Islam.'[26] ISIS is there to back Anne Marie Waters' undifferentiated rhetoric: Abu Bakr Al Baghdadi labelled himself 'the caliph' and claimed to be the 'leader of all Muslims'.

The Jihadist Threat Landscape

Most terrorism victims are Muslim, and the vast majority of jihadist attacks take place in the Middle East and Africa. In 2015, 75 per cent of worldwide terrorism deaths occurred in Iraq, Afghanistan, Nigeria, Syria and Pakistan.[27] But Europe has also experienced a strong surge in jihadist incidents. On 7 January 2015, the brothers Said and Chérif Kouachi stormed the office of the French satirical magazine *Charlie Hebdo*, shooting dead 12 cartoonists and injuring 11 others. Their 'Allahu Akbar' cries announced the beginning of a wave of terrorist attacks that would sweep Europe. In 2015, terrorists killed 151 people and injured 360 across the EU, according to the EU's central police body Europol. Within one year, over 100 attacks were foiled in the UK alone.[28] With attacks in France, Belgium, Germany, the UK and other countries, the 2015–17 period witnessed the highest concentration of Europe-based terrorist incidents in the twenty-first century. Most jihadist attacks in the EU were plotted in the name of ISIS.[29] ISIS's transnational network coupled with the self-starter attacks drove Islamist extremist terrorism in Europe to its highest levels ever.[30]

Security experts are concerned that armed assaults, hostage takings and livestreaming of attacks are becoming increasingly likely scenarios for terrorist atrocities across Europe.[31] In particular, Europol warned of future attacks by returning fighters and local ISIS recruits in the Iberian Peninsula and European countries that are part of the anti-ISIS coalition.[32] When given the choice, ISIS prefers to hit soft targets: that can be anything from tourists strolling a Christmas market, students dancing to live music or families enjoying dinner on a restaurant terrace. Civilian targets make for better headlines and cause higher levels of terror than attacks on security forces or critical infrastructure. ISIS has been successful in rendering their fighters immune to compassion and pity. European intelligence found that 'the nature and structure of IS training apparently enables its operatives (including returnees) to execute terrorist acts in an emotionally detached manner'.[33]

But ISIS is just the tip of the iceberg of the global jihadist insurgency. Although ISIS has claimed the international media spotlight mostly for itself, it does not hold a monopoly on violence. Like ISIS, the Taliban and Boko Haram are both responsible for several thousands of deaths each year.[34] The United States Department of State lists over 40 foreign Islamist terrorist organisations that are a threat to its national security or to American nationals.[35] The United Nations Security Council keeps its own list of over 150 groups affiliated to ISIS and Al Qaeda.[36] Al Qaeda has not carried out any large-scale plots in Europe since the attack on *Charlie Hebdo* in January 2015. In line with its strategy of 'controlled pragmatism', it concentrates on areas outside of Europe, rebuilding its capacity in South Asia, the Caucasus and West Africa.[37] Although Al Qaeda tries to stay out of the spotlight, its gives the EU enough reason 'to focus on a broader range of jihadist terrorist groups'. Especially, Al Qaeda in the Arabian Peninsula (AQAP) still poses a significant danger to the West, according to Europol.[38]

I am at a Christmas party with the former leader of the Libyan Islamic Fighting Group (LIFG), Noman Benotman, who was once an associate of bin Laden and Al Zawahiri. A former jihadist dressed in a Christmas jumper is something you don't see every day. 'Al Qaeda is here to stay. Even when ISIS is defeated they will remain a threat', Noman tells me. One could say he has a classical 'jihadist career' behind him. From a wealthy Libyan family background, he embraced Islamist extremist ideas after reading Sayyid Qutb's works in the mid-1980s. Subsequently joining the jihad in Afghanistan in 1989, Noman helped to found LIFG with the aim of overthrowing Colonel Gaddafi and establishing an Islamic state in Libya. The knowledge and contacts Noman had gained during his time in Afghanistan helped him to establish a network that spread over 17 countries. Today, his understanding of the inside of terrorist organisations has made him one of the most in-demand counter-terrorism consultants. Most people who know Noman would agree that he is as close to James Bond as it gets.

'Jabhat Al Nusra is a dangerously underestimated group,' he warns, vigilance returning to his eyes. This is turning into quite a serious conversation for a Christmas party. Formed in 2012, Al Nusra used to operate as the Syrian branch of Al Qaeda. After its split in July 2016, the group assumed the name Jabhat Fateh Al Sham. 'Western focus on ISIS has enabled it to conduct its activities in Syria relatively unhindered,' according to Noman. By gaining a strong support base and developing strong connections with other opposition groups, Al Nusra has successfully become a dominant force within the Syrian chaos. While it does hold Sharia courts and governance in the areas that it controls, the group deliberately avoids owning territory and prefers to live among other rebel groups so that it is harder to target them. 'Many of ISIS's fighters who grew disillusioned with the realities in the caliphate have defected to Al Nusra,' Noman says. The *Mission Impossible* soundtrack interrupts our conversation. Noman grabs his phone; the ringtone could hardly be more suitable: whenever Noman Benotman receives a call, the chances are high that it is for a new 'mission impossible'.

While Al Qaeda was a product of the Afghan jihad, ISIS was an outgrowth of Al Qaeda. The remnants of ISIS may well see the emergence of entirely new organisations. Ultimately, most jihadist groups share the same goal: to overthrow 'apostate states' to create caliphates and practise Sharia law based on their own interpretation of it. But often they have different ideas of how and when to achieve this. Bin Laden saw jihad as a prologue to a caliphate and accepted that he would probably not see this in his own lifetime.[39] ISIS's approach was the opposite: they announced the caliphate as soon as they controlled significant land and then waged jihad to reconquer the territory that once formed part of the Ottoman Empire.

ISIS has relied heavily on territorial control in order for its caliphate to maintain legitimacy and popularity. As its territory is shrinking, the organisation increasingly shifts to Al Qaeda's mode of operating underground as a geographically diffuse network of autonomous cells. Like Al Qaeda, it can rely on a vast network of affiliates across the globe, including in Europe. But 'Al Qaeda used a top-down approach, tightly managing its plots,' Sajjan explains. 'ISIS's attacks range from lone-actor incidents to large-scale plots coordinated through online communication.'

'Osama bin Laden's focus was on the far enemy – that is, the West,' Noman tells me. 'ISIS, on the other hand, combines jihad against the near and far enemy.' Noman knows Al Qaeda's approach to the far enemy; it was precisely on this topic that he picked a fight with bin Laden. In 2000, Noman had breakfast at bin Laden's mud house in Kandahar and tried to dissuade the Al Qaeda leader from using violence outside Afghanistan. Without success, as it turned out one year later. 'After 9/11, I distanced myself from bin Laden,' Noman says. In 2010 he wrote an open letter to bin Laden,[40] reminding him that his actions have harmed millions of innocent Muslims and non-Muslims. 'How is this Islam or jihad?' he asks.

Who could have anticipated that Al Qaeda's levels of violence would soon be exceeded? Even Al Zawahiri agrees that 'ISIS are exceeding the limits of extremism'.[41] In what can be interpreted as a competition for influence, he accused ISIS of opportunism, cowardice and 'madness'. Al Qaeda did not deliberately target Muslim civilians; if they died in an attack it was seen as collateral damage. ISIS, on the other hand, does not stop short of killing Muslim civilians, including women and children. ISIS fighters justify violence by so-called 'Prophetic Methodology': every decision is supposedly based on an action or saying of Muhammad. But in Al Zawahiri's view, 'they make takfir on the basis of lies'. According to Sajjan, 'Al Qaeda tried to avoid entering into criminal enterprise, whereas ISIS embraces it'. Many extremists grew disillusioned with Al Zawahiri on the grounds that he is not extreme enough. ISIS has repeatedly cited the founder of Al Qaeda in Iraq Abu Musab Al Zarqawi's words as an inspiration for their use of extreme violence.

Islamist Extremists' Inevitable War

Chaos and instability are Islamist extremists' best friends. Their goal is to provoke civil wars that destabilise the current world order and make a reshuffling possible. Asymmetric warfare only works this way. The motto is therefore: the more lethal and vile the terrorist attacks, the better. By creating more fear and outrage they can drive societies apart and exacerbate existing tensions. This will, so the Islamist extremist logic goes, bring about the desired final confrontation between Muslims and non-Muslims. 'ISIS seeks not to spark a World War, but to ignite a World *Civil* War', wrote Maajid Nawaz in his Daily Beast column[42] in the fraught summer of 2016.

Management of Savagery: The Most Critical Stage Through Which the Islamic Nation Will Pass is the title of the online book that Al Qaeda's propaganda head Abu Bakr Al Naji published in 2004.[43] This book is essentially a work on jihadist war theory. It provides a strategy for the formation and expansion of a caliphate based on the considered use of violence to provoke the collapse of the structures that hold together societies. The logic is that in a state of chaos and savagery even the strongest militaries can be defeated. 'Overwhelming military power (weapons, technology, fighters) has no value without the cohesion of society' and may in fact 'become a curse to the great superpower', Naji writes.[44]

Part of the strategy is to provoke military responses from superpowers and local regimes to attract recruits to help defend Islam against its secular enemies. A constant onslaught of violence will eventually exhaust the authority of these regimes, which will in turn lose their ability to maintain control over their respective region. Jihadists can then exploit this ensuing chaos by implementing social services into local communities, thereby expanding jihadist territorial control as well as developing local support.[45]

Another strategic feature of the *Management of Savagery* is its deliberate vilification, isolation and polarisation of Sunni Muslims so that they will suffer local discrimination and be forced to take refuge among their coreligionists. 'I mean dragging the masses into the battle such that polarization is created between all of the people,' Naji explains. This tactic has proven especially successful against the predominantly Shia Iraqi government of Nouri Al Maliki and the Alawite (Shia) government of Syrian President

Bashar Al Assad. A world that is partitioned on sectarian lines is the perfect climate for an Islamic caliphate.

Both Al Qaeda and ISIS have followed Naji's recommendations.

The Jordanian journalist Fouad Hussein spent time in prison with Al Zarqawi and interviewed a range of Al Qaeda members on how they would see the war between Islam and the West develop. In 2005, Hussein explained in his Arab-language book *Al-Zarqawi: The Second Generation of Al Qaeda* that the group's activity was not random or chaotic. Attacks against the West were merely considered the means to an end. Al Qaeda had a clearly structured 20-year master plan in mind:[46]

1. 2000–03: Deal the first blow to the enemy (i.e. the US).
2. 2003–07: Perpetually engage the enemy while simultaneously expanding into other countries with Iraq as the main base.
3. 2007–10: Expand into Greater Syria where the lands of Jordan, Lebanon and Syria will be partitioned into sectarian states. From there Al Qaeda will begin plans to expand into Palestine and the Israeli border.
4. 2010–13: Concentrate on toppling regimes through insurgency. Eventually the constant terrorist activity will exhaust the military resources of the regime until it begins to lose authority in its respective region, which Al Qaeda will then be able to usurp (*Management of Savagery*).
5. 2013–16: Declaration of a new Islamic Caliphate as well as the development of world powers with whom Al Qaeda has no antagonisms (e.g. China).
6. 2016–20: Total war between the believers and the infidel.
7. 2020: Total victory.

'That blueprint has gone according to plan so far', wrote The Washington Institute's Aaron Zelin when he assessed Al Qaeda's 2020 plan in 2013 on the twelfth 9/11 anniversary.[47] His conclusion: total victory remains far-fetched but the threat from jihadist terrorists will not disappear any time soon.

ISIS has been instrumental in polarising communities along religious lines to ignite a global civil war. As Romanian-American journalist Rukmini Callimachi's 2016 interview with German returning fighter Harry Sarfo revealed,[48] ISIS has established an external operations branch called Emni. The primary purpose of this special unit is to terrorise and destabilise Western democracies, what they call the *Dar al-harb* (Land of war). There were numerous reports that Emni had been planning to stage simultaneous attacks across Europe. According to Harry Sarfo, the agency has a good network of fighters who are willing to martyr themselves across Europe, especially in France and Belgium.

Emni was initially led by ISIS spokesman and propaganda chief Abu Mohammad Al Adnani, who was killed by airstrikes in Aleppo in August 2016. The charismatic orator was best known for his convincing rhetoric that inspired ISIS sympathisers across the world to launch attacks. In an audio message Adnani called on Muslims to stay in their home countries and carry out terrorist acts there. 'The smallest action you do in their heartland is better and more enduring to us than what you would do if you were with us.' This resulted in one of the bloodiest Ramadans in history: terrorist attacks were carried out in Bangladesh, Iraq, Jordan, Lebanon, Malaysia, Turkey, Saudi Arabia, the US and Yemen, costing thousands of lives all across the world during the holy month.

Ramadan was followed by an unprecedented wave of ISIS-inspired self-starter attacks in Germany and France, which exposed the powerlessness of intelligence and security services to prevent these kinds of attacks. The perpetrators' remote radicalisation, operational independence and random choice of targets and weapons rendered conventional intelligence and counter-terrorism unfit for the challenge.

ISIS's strategy of psychological warfare appears to work. The fact that any everyday object can become a weapon and anyone a target has sparked fears across Europe. In the immediate aftermath of attacks, it provoked a series of false alarms, scenes of mass panic and led to the cancellation of events such as Europe's biggest flea market 'la Braderie' in the northern French city of Lille. Fear met ignorance and fuelled hatred against Muslims. In the long-term, this has meant rising far-right support, which puts those in power increasingly under pressure. Governments have responded by opting for visible policies such as public security measures and bans on religious clothing. Often these policies mean cutting down on civil rights and sacrificing the liberal values that form the basis of our modern democracies.

Much more dangerous than the terrorist attacks *per se*, or the hysteria immediately afterwards, is the profound fears they instil in the long-term. These are capable of altering and jeopardising the political landscape of liberal, democratic societies. When governments are forced to exchange the strategically best answer for the politically most favourable, the vicious circle that Islamist extremists want us to enter is complete. It is precisely this vicious circle that Al Qaeda wanted to see.

Young, Educated and Online

Sixteen-year-old Kadiza Sultana exchanged her life as a straight-A student for a life as a jihadi bride. In February 2015, she and two friends from Bethnal Green Academy in East London departed on a 17-hour journey to the Syrian border. They had planned and packed together for the trip – with make-up and epilators on their shopping list. The girls' parents and siblings were clueless about their motives, according to the families' lawyer.[49] The Bethnal Green girls were just 3 of over 5,000 Europeans who left their safe homes to travel to war-torn Syria since ISIS announced its caliphate. Eighty per cent of them came from six countries: France, the UK, Germany, Belgium, the Netherlands and Denmark.[50] Like Kadiza, they were prepared to abandon their Western lifestyle in the hope of playing a more fulfilling role in the utopian project of the Islamic State.

There is no typical profile for Islamist extremists. ISIS recruits have different ethnic, religious, social and education backgrounds. But the statistics show that recruits are often young, educated and online. World Bank statistics show that most ISIS foreign fighters were between 20 and 35 years old. The average Western European fighter was 25. The World Bank also concluded that ISIS recruits 'are far from being uneducated or illiterate'. Globally, over 43 per cent of the fighters had gone through secondary school and 13.5 per cent had attended university. Those who had not been working or were in the military before joining were most likely to select 'suicide bomber' as desired occupation in the Islamic State.[51]

The glorification of violent jihad and martyrdom by terrorist organisations is not new: during the Second Intifada in the early 2000s, groups like Hamas and Palestinian Islamic Jihad made heroes of suicide attackers. Yet no group has ever produced more convincing materials to manipulate young people into believing that jihad is cool. ISIS's use of Hollywood-style videos and pop culture references has been a successful tool in galvanising teens into embracing violent extremism. Spanish researcher Javier Lesaca even found stunning parallels between ISIS videos and scenes from *The Hunger Games*, *American Sniper* or the video game *Call of Duty*. He estimated that over 15 per cent of ISIS communications output was directly inspired by Western movies, video games and music clips.[52]

Did thousands of well-educated youngsters believe these glossy propaganda pictures of a utopian Islamic State? The answer is: probably not but they went anyway.

Pathways into extremism vary but there are clear patterns of vulnerability. One characteristic that individuals who join extremist groups have in common is a lack of perspective. Only the lack of hope is worse than the loss of trust. 'He thought he had nothing to lose. To him there were no perspectives. I should have listened more carefully to what he said but how could I have known?' the mother of a foreign fighter who went to Syria in 2014 recalls.[53] It is like playing roulette: *faites vos jeux*. Young people no longer place their bets on idle politicians and corrupt elites.

Extremist groups thrive in such climates where societies can no longer provide meaningful reference points for individuals to establish an identity. They are founded on strict guidelines that can be used to fill identity vacuums. By providing a comfortable mould for individuals suffering from identity crises to fit in, they offer relief from their emotional turmoil and the uncertainty that results from the need to make a decision on conflicting identities.[54] Individuals who lack a sense of belonging are the first recruits for extremist organisations.[55] Identity crises are enhanced in groups with growing grievances such as perceived unfairness, discrimination and oppression.

Next comes the charismatic recruiter and alluring propaganda. Islamist extremists have done a good job in cultivating these grievances and channelling resulting rage into one common cause: jihad. ISIS gives you two choices to take part in their jihad: perform migration in the cause of Allah (*hijrah*) or commit an attack against the unbelievers (*kufr*) in your own country. In other words: come to the utopian state or take the shortcut to paradise. The enemies of ISIS come in many forms: the Crusaders; capitalism; the Zionists; globalisation; the establishment; the media; Trump. This list could go on over several pages. It doesn't really matter – to them they all mean the same. All of it is conveniently subsumed under 'The West'. In ISIS's words: 'cross worshippers, the apostates, their crosses, their borders, and their ballot boxes'.[56] Everyone fights for something for the sheer sake of fighting. The enemy becomes little more than a convenient tool for regaining one's lost self-worthiness and self-fulfilment.

Some tried to escape the discrimination, stigmatisation and scapegoating they experienced at home in exchange for a life as the hero in their favourite movie. For many, lack of direction was replaced by a new sense of meaning, loneliness by a new sense of belonging. Maybe even an alternative career path: many European fighters were quick to move into prominent positions within ISIS. The salary? Four hundred to 1,200 dollars per month (before ISIS had to cut the salaries due to exceptional circumstances in early 2016). 'Why not?' the 17-year-old Brit Aseel Muthana may have concluded before starting to pack his suitcase in early 2014. All he had to do was get on the next flight to Turkey; everything else was arranged for him. Shortly afterwards, he would advise other teens on his Ask.fm page: 'Don't tweet about *dawlah* [the Islamic nation state] or jihad; don't tell all your friends; don't tell your family.'

ISIS offered a simple, ready-made alternative to complex problems: a new utopian world – the caliphate – which promised to bring fighters sense, sex and salvation. Their unique selling proposition was their vast territory: by June 2015, ISIS controlled an area of some 82,940 square kilometres.[57] As our research at Quilliam showed, over 50 per cent of their propaganda output was depicting civilian life in the utopian state in 2015.[58] British jihadist Abu Rumaysah even published a Lonely Planet-style travel guide for the Islamic State. The 46-page document promised Twix and Bounty chocolate bars, 'fruity cocktails' and 'an exquisite Mediterranean climate that has all the makings of a plush holiday resort'.[59]

Most departing fighters knew that they would not embark on a tourist trip. Many knew they would be there to stay, and, most likely, to die. But they were convinced that something more fulfilling awaited them, either in this life or afterwards. So they went all in.

'It is like a drowning man catching at a straw. You yourself will agree that, unless he were drowning he would not mistake a straw for the trunk of a tree.'[60] Once the bets are placed there is no going back. *Rien ne va plus*. Living in the Islamic State was a utopia that may be entirely destroyed by now. But glorified martyrdom for the *ummah* and glamorised revolution against its perceived enemy can give rise to new forms of utopian thinking that may drive future generations into the arms of jihadists. As long as they have a clear antagonist they have a reason to exist, to fight and to chase after a utopian world, in which all perceived evil is absent. One of their most obvious antagonists today is the rising far right, which makes life for Muslims in the West a constant struggle.

3

The Far-Right Renaissance

ON 7 MAY 2002 THE LIFE OF KENZA ISNASNI CHANGED DRASTICALLY. 'I WAS 18 years old when my parents were murdered,' Kenza tells me as we meet in Tunis. A Belgian of Moroccan decent, Kenza grew up with a loving family who taught her that the values of Islam are compatible with those that shape Belgian society. 'I was always proud to be Belgian and Muslim,' she says. 'But I could feel the rising anti-Muslim hatred in the wake of 9/11.' It was 4 a.m. and her parents were in the middle of the dawn prayer when far-right sympathiser Hendrik Vylt entered Kenza's family house in Brussels. He started shooting at her parents before setting the entire building on fire. Kenza and her two younger brothers, who both suffered serious injuries, managed to escape.

Vylt was a supporter of former French ultra-far-right presidential candidate Jean-Marie Le Pen, who is even said to be too radical for his daughter Marine. 'He will win. That's good,' Vylt said after seeing Le Pen's high scores in the first round of the 2002 elections. 'The only thing we'll have to do now is take a Kalashnikov and kill them [foreigners] all!' In the second round of the elections on 5 May 2002, however, Le Pen lost the run-off against Jacques Chirac. Two days later Hendrik stormed Kenza's house.

'It was the climate of hatred and the fear of the other that killed my parents,' Kenza tells me. Since the death of her parents, she organises a campaign to raise awareness about far-right hate crimes on 7 May of every year. In her *Letter to the World: How Islamophobia Killed My Parents*, Kenza writes:

> I wanted to let the world know that my parents had once existed among us and that they had also contributed to a righteous and tolerant society. I fought for the memory of my parents so that a tragedy like this would never happen again. I fought with all my strength for this tragedy to become a lesson.

Since the collapse of the World Trade Center towers on 9/11, the far right has expanded on all levels: from far-right populism to far-right terrorism, from German neo-Nazism to American alt-right movements – membership numbers of both non-violent and violent far-right groups have risen at rapid speed. Hate crimes and terrorist attacks related to anti-Muslim and anti-immigrant sentiments have surged dramatically.[1]

Today's far-right landscape consists of an eclectic mix of traditional and novel ideological elements. As with Islamist extremist movements, far-right groups draw on a wide range of concepts and strategies. But they also increasingly communicate and cooperate across borders and show signs of collective learning.[2] In much the same way as it is necessary to consider rising Islamist extremist attacks as part of a larger Islamist extremist insurgency, it is important to see anti-Muslim violence in the context of a wider renaissance of the far right. What are the ideas that shape today's far-right movements and where do they come from?

A Brief History of Far-Right Ideas

Nationalism and Fascism

'Make America Great Again' is Trump's ambitious motto, while Marine Le Pen chose 'In the Name of the People' for her campaign slogan. Both the nation state and its people are 'an imagined community'. Nationalism is the ideology that wants to preserve this imagined singular community of the nation. As British-Czech philosopher Ernest Gellner put it, 'nationalism is not the awakening of self-consciousness; it invents nations where they do not exist'.[3] The idea of the nation became central throughout Europe after the Enlightenment, with the reduction in the importance of religion and an increase in rational secularism.

Fascism has its roots in nationalism. Although the origins of fascist ideology are contested, most scholars agree that it emerged in the nineteenth century as an attempt by the middle classes and petty bourgeoisie to counter democratic participation of the lower classes, who they feared would overthrow them. In 1919, Benito Mussolini founded the first 'fascist' movement, the Blackshirts, who sought to destroy Italy's socialist and communist structures.

Both nationalism and fascism stress national unity, preservation of the nation and the importance of cultural or ethnic traditions. But fascism goes well beyond nationalism or patriotism, says Professor Matthew Feldman, a leading expert in fascist ideology at Teesside University's Centre for Fascist, Anti-Fascist and Post-Fascist Studies. We sit in a corridor in Westminster's Portcullis House in front of Margaret Thatcher's portrait, waiting to give evidence on far-right violence and extremism in the UK. 'Trump is a nationalist, not a fascist. But he may inspire fascists.' Fascism is a revolutionary form of ultra-nationalism that builds on the conception of a nation in crisis.[4] 'Fascists perceive the nation as a living, breathing organic entity that must be cleansed from a disease,' Matthew explains to me.

Anti-Semitism and Nazism

In *Mein Kampf*, Hitler writes about 'diseases of national bodies' and an 'ethical and moral poisoning' of the German nation. German National Socialism, or Nazism, developed as an offshoot of fascism that used scientific racism and anti-Semitism to carry out 'racial cleansing'.

'I am not a Nazi,' insisted Nick Griffin. The Cambridge graduate used to lead the most successful far-right party in Britain's history, the British National Party (BNP). 'Fascism was Italian. Nazism was German. We are British. We will do things our own way; we will not copy foreigners', the BNP's 1992 manifesto argued. Although Griffin stated that 'Adolf went a bit too far',[5] his party shared fundamental characteristics with National Socialism, such as the use of scientific racism and the call for racial separatism.

Nazism gained traction between 1928 and 1932 and quickly became Germany's most powerful political force. But anti-Semitism – the hatred of Jews – dates back to the time of the Romans. In the Middle Ages, Jews had few legal rights: they were forced to marry Christians and were denied the ability to buy land or hold positions in government. In the fourteenth century, the bubonic plague was widely blamed on the Jews. It is estimated that 100,000 Jews were burnt alive in Austria and Germany during that time.[6] In 1873, the German political agitator Wilhelm Marr first coined the term 'anti-Semitism' in his work *Victory of Judaism over Germanism*. According to him, Jews were conspiring to run the state and should be excluded from citizenship. As the stereotypes of money-hungry and greedy Jews spread, the expression 'the Jewish question' became more commonplace in the late nineteenth century. Hitler later built on myths from the Middle Ages to justify his 'Final Solution to the Jewish Question', opening the darkest chapter in European history that saw the death of 6 million Jews.

'Holocaust denial and anti-Semitic hate crimes remain a serious concern,' Dr André Oboler, the CEO of the Australia-based Online Hate Prevention Institute, tells me over Skype. More than half of the social media hate crime reports he received in 2016 were anti-Semitic. Holocaust denial and anti-Semitism are also making a strong comeback in Western Europe, including in Germany. For example, books with titles such as *The Six Million: Fact or Fiction?* by Peter Winter were illegally sold through Amazon Germany.[7]

Jewish conspiracy theories remain an element in far-right rhetoric with a historic legacy. But today's far right is divided in its attitude towards Judaism: while neo-Nazis and white supremacist hardliners are openly anti-Semitic, counter-jihadists and identitarians often call themselves Judeophile or Zionist. Biological racism is increasingly replaced by cultural nativism. The new far right has found a new common enemy: Muslims.[8]

Anti-Islamisation and Anti-Immigration

Like anti-Semitism, anti-immigrant sentiment has been around for centuries and is bound up in the ideology of nationalism. Often characterised by genuine fears of being 'invaded', anti-immigrant attitudes go hand in hand with worries that mass migration will undermine the grandeur of the homeland nation. Even in the US, which is traditionally characterised as a 'nation of immigrants', there has also been a historic trend of anti-immigrant sentiment. Nativism emerged as a form of ethnocentrism, which descended from England and anti-Catholic hostility.

Modern anti-Islamisation movements have their roots in the 1980s. But today's so-called 'counter-jihad movement' gained traction after 9/11 triggered anti-Muslim resentment across the Western world. The Jewish–Egyptian writer Bat Ye'or (aka Gisèle Littman) was the first to popularise the term 'Eurabia' in her 2005 publication of *Eurabia: The Euro-Arab Axis*. The term would later inspire some of the counter-jihad movement's main ideologues.[9] For example, the Norwegian blogger Fjordman (aka Peder Nøstvold Jensen), who believes in a global Muslim conspiracy to take over Europe, drew inspiration from Bat Ye'or. His book *Defeating Eurabia* was originally published on Robert Spencer's webpage Jihad Watch. In the UK, the now disbanded BNP's Islam out of Britain campaign in the early 2000s helped make the perceived threat of Muslims part of the political discourse.[10]

'Anti-Muslim prejudice or Islamo-prejudice is the lowest common denominator that we have seen in the last 10 or 15 years', according to Matthew Feldman.[11] Hatred against Islam was further propelled by the rise of ISIS and the refugee crisis. Many right-wing groups have capitalised on these sentiments, masking their generic anti-immigrant hatred, and often racist attitudes, with the more culturally accepted anti-Muslim bigotry. Increasingly, the rhetoric of invasion and Islamification is where neo-Nazis, identitarians and counter-jihadists find common ground.

The New Far-Right Wave

'When I'm in power, all illegal immigrants shall be burnt alive', a member of the German Freitaler Gruppe wrote in the Korean encrypted messaging application KakaoTalk. The neo-Nazi group led by 30-year-old Philipp W. was disbanded and is currently facing legal prosecution in Germany. They planned their attacks in a KakaoTalk channel called 'black chat', using pseudonyms and code words to avoid detection, according to investigators. 'Extremely cool, when I have to walk home from work at night, I can combine this with smaller attacks.'[12] Smaller attacks usually meant arson, whereas bigger attacks would involve explosive devices and butyric acid. In 2016, the German Home Office counted 113 arson attacks, 10 explosive attacks and 1,313 physical assaults motivated by right-wing extremism.[13]

The twenty-first century has witnessed a global revival of far-right militant groups and terrorist incidents. In the decade after 9/11 the US saw on average 337 right-wing extremist attacks per year, resulting in 254 fatalities.[14] Since 2007, racially motivated attacks and violent plots from individuals who identify with American far-right groups have surged at exceptional speed.[15] Today, security forces and academics consider these groups a larger threat to the safety of US citizens, above the possibility of foreign terrorist attacks or those from an opposing group.[16] A clear trend in the far-right extremist movement is the focus on Islam: security forces intercepted many plots to assassinate or harm those who appear to be Muslim.[17]

In the autumn of 2016, Britain's Security Minister Ben Wallace warned that neo-Nazi radicalisation cases in England and Wales have surged since 2015. The national anti-radicalisation programme 'Channel' received more far-right referrals than ever before: its far-right cases went up from 323 in 2014–15 to 561 in 2015–16. In some parts of the country, right-wing extremist cases now exceed those linked to Islamist extremism. The Metropolitan Police now consider the terrorist threat from far-right groups to be as severe as the jihadist threat.[18] The proportion of 'white' people arrested for terrorism-related offences rose sharply over 2016, as the Home Office's terror statistics reveal. One-third of those arrested in 2016 were of white ethnicity.[19]

Today's far-right threat cannot be contained in one category. Classical fascism was a more or less ideologically coherent movement. But the modern-day far-right landscape is increasingly splintered: the wide range of country-specifics and subcultures make it difficult to draw a coherent picture.[20] Some movements emphasise a nationalist agenda, others focus on anti-Muslim rhetoric. Some groups explicitly use anti-Semitic or anti-black symbolism, others hide behind narratives of the victimhood of the white race. Ideological elements within the far right are not mutually exclusive, and often cross-fertilisation happens despite inherent contradictions. Most of them combine different elements from various traditional nativist ideologies and symbolism, linking them to twenty-first-century challenges such as globalisation, the migration crisis and Islamist terrorism.

The motivations of these groups are as varied as their narratives: many nationalist and anti-immigrant groups were formed for identity reasons, others for socio-economic reasons. Economic woes and frustration over politicians' reluctance to reform have been catalysts for the success of the far right. But the migration crisis and waves of terrorist attacks have further heightened support for far-right groups, whose mission statements promise to prevent 'the erosion of Western culture'. Although far-right groups differ hugely throughout time, region and social group, they all believe they belong to a superior or master race or culture and feel this is threatened by intercultural integration.[201]

The Far-Right Threat Landscape

'Death to traitors, freedom for Britain,' Jo Cox murderer Thomas Mair uttered in court when asked for his name. These words became the slogan of National Action, Britain's first white supremacist terrorist group. National Action was banned by the Home Office in December 2016 but an ITV undercover report found they continued to organise training camps in the Peak District in 2017. The group glorified Mair, saying that Cox '[had] it coming'.[22] Twenty-three-year-old Garron Helm, one of National Action's members, even said in front of the hidden camera: 'I do think if you're committing an act of treason against, you know, your own ethnic group then by right you should be put to death.'

National Action is an ultra-violent manifestation of a larger trend. British counter-jihad movements, American alt-right groups and continental European identitarian networks may come under different brands but their camouflage is the same: they use terrorist incidents, gang violence and immigration problems to legitimise an unwarranted intolerance towards Muslims under the guise of 'counter-Jihadism'.[23] In the Anglosphere, counter-jihad rhetoric has been forcing itself into the mainstream: in 2016, the anti-racist group Hope Not Hate counted 24 counter-jihad movements in the UK, 42 such groups in the US and 12 in Australia.[24]

Today's far right is fractured, volatile and leaderless in most countries. Prior to 2014, the British far right counted several successful mass movements. But leadership changes reduced their influence and reach: after Nick Griffin was expelled from the BNP and Tommy Robinson left the EDL, the membership numbers of both movements dropped dramatically. Their waning influence gave rise to smaller, more agile and often more militant movements. Ultra-violent and paramilitary groups such as National Action and Combat 18 – the name being a reference to the alphabetical position of Adolf Hitler's initials (A=1 + H=8) – have successfully tapped into the BNP's and EDL's former support base. In Germany, PEGIDA's sharp decline in 2016 had a similar effect.

Although fractured, today's far right is highly potent. Social media has facilitated cooperation across borders between like-minded groups, creating a powerful multiplier effect. This is the paradox of modern-day nationalists: they capitalise on the opportunities of globalisation to spread their anti-globalist views globally. British counter-jihad, American alt-right and continental European identitarian movements are strongly intertwined and their support bases often overlap. Tommy Robinson's successful EDL model influenced Lutz Bachmann's PEGIDA mass street protests; German PEGIDA then back-inspired Robinson's PEGIDA UK offshoot. One of their meeting points is Ned May's Gates of Vienna platform, which has promoted the mission statements of both the EDL and PEGIDA.[25]

Likewise, American self-described 'counter-jihadists' Robert Spencer and Pamela Geller, who co-founded the anti-Muslim organisation Stop Islamization of America and were banned from entering the UK, have openly endorsed the EDL and PEGIDA. Tommy Robinson maintains a close trans-Atlantic friendship with both of them.[26] One of their nexus points is the Los Angeles-based David Horowitz Freedom Center, which was founded in 1988 by political activist David Horowitz. It financially supports initiatives to combat 'the efforts of the radical left and its Islamist allies to destroy American values' and runs the FrontPage Mag and Jihad Watch.

British counter-jihadists like Robinson also exchange ideas with French identitarians such as Yann Valerie. Meanwhile, the 28-year-old Viennese Martin Sellner, founder of Austria's identitarian branch, receives remarkably good coverage by alt-right Breitbart News: the webpage runs headlines, features video and shares tweets of what they call Austria's 'hipster right identitarians'.[27] These international alliances between extremists give them an edge over moderates – most importantly, they help them to stretch their echo chambers and expand their influence across the globe.

'Counter-jihad' activists also mingle with the political far right, which is equally well connected: Dutch far-right leader Geert Wilders is regularly seen at American conferences hosted by alt-right figures like Pamela Geller and Milo Yiannopoulos. Wilders and his French and Austrian counterparts never miss out on congratulating each other for an election success. They express their solidarity when one is under attack by the media. On Saturday 21 January 2017, the hashtag #WeWillMakeOurCountriesGreatAgain was trending in the ancient German city of Koblenz. French Front National leader Marine Le Pen led a 'counter-summit' that brought together Europe's most prominent nationalist leaders. UKIP's Nigel

Farage and Trump, the undisputed winners of 2016, took this mutual solidarity principle a step further. Not only did Farage meet the president-elect before Prime Minister Theresa May, but Trump also told Farage, 'You'll be my friend for life', and suggested to the US over late-night drinks to celebrate their victories that he should become Britain's ambassador.[28]

This cross-border loyalty between members of different far-right factions creates a similar propaganda effect as ISIS campaigns of brotherhood and the unity of the *ummah*. It appeals to younger generations. Massive support from digital natives has enabled many far-right leaders to build a huge online followership. Between 2012 and 2016, major American white nationalist groups increased their Twitter fellowship by 600 per cent: 22,000 followers. They combine slick social media guerrilla activism with organised trolling and targeted media manipulation. Although white nationalist social media communities tend to be less cohesive than their ISIS counterparts, 'they outperform ISIS in nearly every social metric, from follower counts to tweets per day', a report by the Institute for Strategic Dialogue shows.[29]

High social media pro-activeness has resulted in organic, self-sustaining networks. This has propelled the threat from far-right self-starter attacks. The Royal United Services Institute found that far-right lone actor terrorists were likely to exhibit radicalisation signs in their online behaviour.[30] Although non-violent alt-righters, counter-jihadists and identitarians have distanced themselves from violent neo-Nazis and terrorists, they often share the belief in an inevitable clash of civilisations.

Far-Right Extremists' Inevitable War

'We enter now the age of discontent, the final battle for the soul of Europe,' white supremacist Andrew Anglin announces in a sober voice.[31] In 2013, the 31-year-old founded the number-one neo-Nazi webpage the Daily Stormer, named after the famous Nazi newspaper *Der Stürmer*. He grew up in what he describes as a 'very liberal' environment. In his youth he lived in South East Asia for several years and studied a wide range of different religious and political ideologies. 'I'm the last person you would expect to become the most extreme person in the world', Andrew Anglin says about himself.[32]

Anglin is suspicious of everyone: not just Jewish, Muslim or black people and left-wingers. He has even clashed with several self-proclaimed 'race realists' who accused him of infesting and discrediting white nationalism and suggested that Andrew is mixed-race – needless to say, this is a big insult in white supremacist circles. Most of all, Andrew despises journalists. 'I would like to assume this is honest, but journalists as a group are so dishonest that I don't ever assume that', he writes in an email to me. 'If you can guarantee this is for a book and not the *Guardian* or some other website', is the first condition he puts on our interview. He likes being quoted in books, he tells me, and the inevitability of a race war is one of his favourite topics. I offer to send him a copy of this book.

According to him, 'we are approaching a point where the lines will be clearly drawn' and each individual will have to choose between either 'the restauration of the European man' or 'his complete annihilation and replacement with non-white savages predominantly driven by Islam'. In his 2014 speech in London he announces that 'it is along these lines that the greatest war which has ever taken place is emerging'. What he calls 'traditionalism', an extreme version of conservatism, is the only way to 'save Western civilisation and the human race'. As he looks up from his notes, a smile plays on his lips. 'The white race in particular.'[33]

These words were recorded less than three years and 1,000 miles from the attack that was committed in the name of 'saving white men'. On 22 July 2011 in Norway, Anders Behring Breivik committed Europe's deadliest far-right terrorist act since the bombing of Bologna's Central Station in 1980. He first detonated a bomb in front of Oslo's government buildings, killing 8 people, and then shot dead 69 teenagers who were attending the summer camp on the island of Utøya.

Norway would seem to be an unlikely place for crime and terror. It is blessed with a GDP per capita higher than Qatar's and known for its low income inequality and high education standards. Norwegian prison models are known for their success in rehabilitation and the population has high trust in its government. Their first shock came in 2001, when the neo-Nazi group BootBoys stabbed to death a 16-year-old Norwegian-Ghanaian boy. Some may know his name from Michael Jackson's 2001 album *Invincible*, which he dedicated to Benjamin 'Benny' Hermansen. 'May we continue to remember not to judge man by the color of his skin, but the content of his character. Benjamin ... we love you ... may you rest in peace.' Yet, even though the incident mobilised almost 40,000 people who protested against racism in the streets of Oslo, there was still widespread denial of the problem. Most people thought that this had been a one-off extremist attack. 'We all thought that Oslo is a safe city,' Oslo's Vice Mayor Geir Lippestad said in his speech at The Nordic Safe Cities conference in November 2016. 'Ten years later we understood that terrorism can happen anywhere.'

Geir has asked himself many times in the last few years: 'what if he [Breivik] had been a Muslim? What kind of society would we have in Oslo today?' On the morning of 23 July 2011, the initial assumption that the attack had been committed by an Islamist terrorist led to an upsurge in anti-Muslim hate crimes and even physical attacks on Oslo's public transport. Muslims were insulted and hijabs pulled off. 'I don't think we'd have the same open, pluralistic society,' Geir concluded. 'And that scares me.'

Apart from being Oslo's deputy mayor, Geir is also a well-known lawyer. He has defended many high-profile far-right extremists, including Breivik. Before staging his attack, Breivik tweeted a single message: 'One person with a belief is equal to the force of 100,000 who have only interests.' To decipher the belief that made Breivik kill 77 innocent people, Geir read all the documents and journals Breivik had written as a child. Geir knows Breivik's childhood and youth inside out. Breivik had developed an obsession to 'win the ongoing Western European cultural war' by forming a 'Pan-European Patriotic Resistance Movement' over years before carrying out the attack. He saw himself as the soldier at the forefront in the war against 'Islamic imperialism'.

Breivik did not mind Jews or non-Muslim foreigners. Although he cared about the Christian cultural heritage, he said, 'I am not going to pretend I'm a very religious person.' But his hatred went beyond Muslims and immigrants. He also despised the establishment, especially the Norwegian Labour Party which for him represented dangerous political correctness, 'Marxism' and multi-culturalism. The Norwegian admired British right-wing movements such as the EDL and Stop the Islamification of Europe, which converged with his views about the establishment sacrificing native populations to Muslims. In his opinion, though, their approaches were not effective enough. Breivik explains his strategy in his 1,518-page manifesto called '2083', which he released online hours before the attacks.

Bjorn Ihler is probably even more familiar with Breivik's manifesto than Geir Lippestad. Being Breivik's lawyer may not be the most thankful job, but even worse was the experience of being with Breivik on that island. Bjorn was 20 and had come to Norway from Liverpool, where he was studying at the time. The summer camp he attended was organised by the Norwegian Labour Party but 'like for most teens, it was much more about flirting, drinking and spending time with friends than about politics'. When Breivik arrived on the island dressed as a member of the Norwegian Police Security Service (PST), the young people had already heard of the bombing in Oslo's governmental district. Most of their programme had been cancelled but no one thought that the island could be a potential target. Bjorn remembers hearing gunshots and thinking it was fireworks until a person was shot right in front of him. 'Even when I saw the blood my brain could still not process the information.' He managed to escape to the woods, saving himself as well as two children who were eight and nine years old, who had both lost their fathers. 'Swimming to land was not an option with the two kids,' he tells me; 'we survived by pure coincidence.'[34]

To honour his friends who had not been so lucky, Bjorn has since devoted his time to studying the minds of people like Breivik and ending violent extremism of all kinds, whether Islamist or far right. Today, he is a leading counter-extremism expert – not because he has survived a terror attack, but because of the crucial work he has done to prevent future attacks of this kind. Still, surviving terror has taught Bjorn a lot about the dynamics that produce terrorists like Breivik. The minds of criminals and the minds of violent extremists don't work in the same ways: 'Breivik killed because he thought it was for the greater good.' It was his belief that a war between Muslims and non-Muslims was inevitable; therefore his narrative was: 'either we kill or we get killed'. In his eyes, the teenagers on the island were traitors who deserved to be killed because they had different beliefs and because they challenged his worldview. According to Bjorn, 'this is the ideology that all violent extremists have in common, whether they are Muslims, Christians, atheists, fascists or communists'.[35] Breivik really believed that 'Muslims are colonialising Europe' and that 'the combination of 21st century mass media, transnational legislation, and bureaucratic feudalism helped transform Europe into Eurabia'.

Also Young, Educated and Online

When you think of far-right extremists, what is it that comes to your mind? A middle-aged, working-class, under-educated man who has a printed copy of *Mein Kampf* on his bookshelf? Maybe this description would have been accurate to describe neo-Nazis and white supremacists 20 years ago, but it certainly doesn't apply any more to today's far-right sympathisers. The new far right is increasingly young, educated and online. Whether populist or militant, the new far right are typically in their twenties, educated and internet-savvy. They call the imageboard sites and, occasionally, Reddit, their home. Anonymous discussion forums allow them to spread politically incorrect memes that mock minorities or the establishment – especially what they call 'Libtards' and 'Cuckservatives'.

Traditionally, most right-wing groups called for a return to the male-dominated nuclear family and displayed hostility to homosexuality and inter-racial relationships.[36] But many of today's far-right groups have adapted to the twenty-first century and re-invented themselves as an alternative to the mainstream conservative right. In the US, even historical neo-Nazi groups such as the Ku Klux Klan, Christian Identity and White Power Skinheads have moved beyond white, male-support bases. Many of them have compromised their male-dominated position to include female membership at around 25 per cent.[37] Richard Spencer, founder of altRight.com, was the first to use the term 'alt-right' as a euphemism for modern white supremacism. But today the alt-right is seen as a loose affiliation of different groups, ranging from counter-jihadists and nativists to neo-Nazis who reject or reassess traditional right-wing values.

Alt-right groups have increasingly managed to appeal to young people by addressing their concerns and by adapting to the volatile state of current politics. They have realigned their strategies to the problems facing today's modern world, and have gained steady support as a result of jihadist attacks and the ongoing refugee crisis. Most alt-righters, whether counter-jihadists or neo-Nazis, converge in their fear of a #whitegenocide and their opposition to multi-culturalism, calling for white nationalism as a solution. They have therefore found a nexus point in the recent US and European elections as supporters of Donald Trump, Geert Wilders and Marine Le Pen.

Many of Europe's most successful far-right groups are online movements with street wings. They organise themselves in internet forums and hold marches that often lead to racist-fuelled violence, riots and disruption. Street protest movements such as the German PEGIDA, the EDL and Les Identitaires in France have spread their anti-Muslim propaganda both online and offline. Similar to Islamist extremist groups Hizb ut-Tahrir and Sharia4UK, they have also exported their models to other countries, attracting hundreds of thousands of young, educated, internet-savvy followers.

A strong youth subculture has developed around the American alt-right movement and bled into parts of the European far right. In the depths of far-right internet forums one encounters a curious blend of different online subcultures such as the anti-feminist 'Manosphere' community, the gamer space #Gamergate and conspiracy theory forums. None of these online communities actively promotes extremism, yet they are easily hijacked by the alt-right as their topics naturally align. Like shoaling fish they all navigate in the same direction in a coordinated but leaderless way. Some fish may have bigger fins than others but most do not dare to change direction for fear of being abandoned by the collective. As a result, pick-up artists, semi-professional internet trolls and gaming geeks often meet where vulgarity, irony and trolling collide. Non-ironic Nazism hiding behind ironic Nazism 'for the lulz' is common in these meeting points. 'In an age of nihilism, absolute idealism must be couched in irony in order to be taken seriously', according to the Daily Stormer.[38]

The platform Weev is ground zero for alt-right trolling. Its main journal entry explains why hackers must become nationalists. In the wake of the US elections, the administrator wrote: 'We've had a resurgence of white identity and anger that is unprecedented for our lifetimes. We can't let it dissipate into quiet resentment. We have to capture it and use it to advance the cause of American salvation.' Alt-right trolling arguably reached its peak in 2017 when 4chan users declared war on the anti-Trump performance art project led by Shia LaBeouf. The American actor's art installation, which consisted of a webcam that livestreamed a flag saying 'he will not divide us', became subject to an elaborate sabotage game. After the flag was taken down twice, LaBeouf resorted to keeping its new location secret. But the alt-right trolls again succeeded in locating the flag, using open-source intelligence such as flight plan data, meteorological details and honk echoes. They stole the 'he will not divide us' flag and replaced it with one that featured the cartoon frog Pepe.

Pepe is one of the alt-right's favourite mascots, but pop culture references, Anime images and cult memes are diverse and commonly used in interactions. Music and video games also play an important role in far-right counter-cultures. While German neo-Nazis have co-opted hard rock and heavy metal, the Austrian far right has hijacked hip hop and rap.[39] The 1980s instrumental electronic genre of Synthwave has emerged as the music preference of the American alt-right. By defending online gamers from video game journalist reproaches and spreading misinformation, the alt-right managed to invade geek culture and sparked waves of online harassment of women and minorities in gaming. For example, a white supremacist gamer called ProgenyOfEurope created the game modification 'Make Space Great Again – Play as Europeans Only' that allows players to get rid of all non-white characters in the original game *Stellaris*. There are also more extreme games with connections to the far right: *Hatred*, which is known as 'the world's most violent game', glorifies white supremacism and 'Catholic jihad'. 'It's time for me to kill and it's time for me to die. My genocide crusade begins here,' says the sociopathic player in the video game's trailer before embarking on a shooting and stabbing spree.[40] Its creator was the Polish firm Destructive Creations, which faces neo-Nazi and anti-Muslim allegations. The ten men behind the game have not only links to far-right hate groups but also to #Gamergate, which was forced to migrate to 8chan after being banned from 4chan.

These different online subcultures have merged into a political collective united through a common problem and a shared goal. In the words of Andrew Anglin, Trump's campaign provided 'the nexus of that centerpoint' for disenfranchised, often young, white men who feel that their race is undergoing extermination.[41]

Whether through Trump, Farage or Wilders, identity politics that divide societies along ethnic or religious lines have provided an outlet for such identity crises of the angry, white man. As the following chapter will show, both jihadists and far-right extremists have benefited from the global rise of identity politics.

4

Identity Politics

ALEXANDRE BISSONNETTE WAS YOUNG, EDUCATED AND INTERNET-SAVVY. THE French-Canadian social science student had followed the tweets of Le Pen and Trump and expressed support for Generation Nationale, an interest group that campaigns against multi-culturalism. On social media, he was known for nationalist, anti-immigrant posts. 'Whites risk marginalization,' the 27-year-old told Facebook friend Martin Robin on 28 January 2017 when they discussed Trump's immigration ban.[1] Canadian Prime Minister Justin Trudeau had just reacted to the ban by tweeting: 'To those fleeing persecution, terror and war, Canadians will welcome you, regardless of your faith. Diversity is our strength. #Welcome to Canada.' Less than 24 hours later, Bissonnette went on a shooting rampage, killing six Muslims in Quebec City Mosque during their prayers.

The Quebec shooting is illustrative of how anti-Muslim rhetoric used by politicians contributes to a climate that can propel hate crimes and fuel white supremacist terrorism. It was not the first time political statements and verbal dehumanisation provided ideological inspiration for far-right militants. This is why the stories that politicians, activists and journalists tell matter: they may demonise minorities, radicalise majorities and normalise hate.

For decades, academics, politicians and practitioners have had heated debates about whether there is a natural progression from non-violent extremism to the more militant ends of extremism.[2] Where the British government stands on this question is clear: 'The extremist worldview is the gateway, and violence is the ultimate destination', former Prime Minister David Cameron said in his controversial 2015 speech in Birmingham.[3] His 'gateway of extremism' theory risks oversimplifying a complex psychological process, disregarding factors such as grievances and identity crises. Pathways into extremism are far too multidimensional to describe them through a linear model that sees extremist worldviews as the only driver. What is clear, however, is that ideologies and narratives are elements which connect non-violent and violent extremists.[4]

Multiple individuals have gone from the EDL to Combat 18 and from Hizb ut-Tahrir to ISIS. Several jihadists were formerly members of non-violent extremist organisations such as the Muslim Brotherhood, Tablighi Jamaat or Hizb ut-Tahrir.[5] The Australian terrorist Man Haron Monis, who staged the hostage-taking at the Lindt Chocolate Café in Sydney, suffered from chronic schizophrenia. But he also attended Hizb ut-Tahrir conferences and was reportedly radicalised by their members.[6] Breivik may have serious mental health issues, including personality disorders, but he was also a member of the anti-immigration Progress Party, admired the EDL and followed Gates of Vienna's hardline anti-Islam commentators.[7]

Driven by the desire to appeal to the 'ordinary people' – the forgotten, the unheard, the disenfranchised – populists and political activists often resort to identity politics. It is the *Star Wars* effect: victimisation and demonisation for the sake of simplicity. Today's global rise of identity politics has allowed stories to divide the world into clear camps based on faith or ethnicity to enter the mainstream. A perceived war between races or religions often lays the intellectual foundation for violent extremists' behaviour. It may push individuals to translate their fears into rage and their words into action. Why are identity politics increasingly successful and what does that mean for the reciprocal radicalisation effect?

From Fear to Rage

'*Indignez-vous!*' (Time for Outrage!), wrote the French diplomat and concentration camp survivor Stéphane Hessel in 2010. His book sold close to one million copies within the first ten weeks after its release, inspired the Spanish anti-corruption protests *Los Indignados* ('The Outraged') and sparked the Occupy Wall Street protests in 2011.

Today, we have passed the point where the richest 1 per cent of the world's population have accumulated more wealth than the remaining 99 per cent.[8] The gap between the rich and the poor continues to widen every day. Money grows faster in the accounts of those who depend on it the least and vanishes quickest in the hands of those who need it most. Not only do the rich become richer and the poor become poorer; the gap also becomes more visible. In an age where even people without access to clean water have access to mobile phones, the poor cannot escape Facebook and Instagram pictures that show the enviable life of the rich.[9]

Perceived socio-economic injustice is a key driver of identity politics and radicalisation. The marginalisation of the majorities – both regionally and internationally – has contributed to the rise of ISIS and the popularity of Islamist extremist organisations in the Middle East, the Persian Gulf and beyond.[10] But it has also made our Western societies more prone to radicalisation and political violence. Over the past 140 years, far-right parties have on average enhanced their vote share by 30 per cent after a financial crisis.[11] The 'outraged' who found that their street protests did not change anything had to find more radical ways to show their dissatisfaction at the status quo. By leaving their liberal, democratic home countries for what they thought would be a better world, in ISIS's pseudo-caliphate, for example. Or by voting for those on the fringes of politics who claim to represent the mainstream of society. Extremists have filled the gaps where state institutions failed.

Over the past decade, the world has experienced a series of economic, political and humanitarian crises. As the financial crisis was unfolding following the collapse of Lehman Brothers in autumn 2008, the words 'financial melt-down', 'global recession', 'liquidity crisis' and 'economic collapse' appeared on the covers of newspapers. Although most of us didn't know what exactly these words meant, they sounded quite apocalyptic. It was a bit like children who see their parents fighting – they can sense that something is seriously wrong without really knowing what exactly the dispute is actually about. The images of bankers shaking their heads were quite self-explanatory.

Then we read about bailout programmes being signed for those banks that were declared too big to fail, to save a system that we found too complex to understand. We were told that this system was just two steps away from complete breakdown, yet most people still didn't really understand what was going on. We were left with no option but to trust the establishment to sort things out. Everyone hoped it would not affect their own lives too much. And actually, for many of us, it did not pose an existential threat, at least not instantly. Yet the societal aftermath and creeping human toll of the economic crisis has only just started to take shape.

Until screens turned red in trading rooms all across the world, the negative effects of increasingly unrestricted financial markets and deregulated trade systems had remained widely hidden. Only those suffering from hunger, environmental degradation and diseases in the Global South had experienced the negative side of the international *laissez-faire* attitude shown towards multinational giants, food-commodity speculation and spiralling debt dynamics. Yet after the crash, high unemployment rates, rising national debt levels and tough austerity measures quickly spread to southern European states such as Greece, Spain and Portugal, contributing to public instability.

In other parts of Europe, a growing number of people were forced to question their bank's trustworthiness to keep their money safe and their state's ability to protect them as they grow older.[12] Low economic growth rates, a quickly morphing age pyramid and growing rifts between the rich and the poor have increased Europeans' concerns about their future. What most of us thought would be a temporary emergency situation that politicians would soon resolve, today looks more like a permanent state of uncertainty. The Western middle class might not have been the first victim of globalisation and neo-liberalism. Yet to those who see the security and prosperity they had taken for granted vanish and their living standards shrink, and who increasingly struggle to earn a living, the repercussions of the crisis were all the more agonising.[13]

Fear has increasingly turned into rage – against the left as much as against Muslims, against Theresa May as much as against the BBC. As a YouTube user called Pure Heroine writes:

FUCK YOU!!!! You must think we are just the worthless working classes, we are all fucking racist and our countries would be better off without us! Well guess what, when we are gone there is NO FUCKING barrier between the Islamist's and YOU! The limited control our governments have implemented to appease us are the ONLY things keeping your fucking LIBERAL country from becoming a fucking theocracy in 50 years!

I had always wondered why anyone would endorse such an unlikable comment with a 'like', so I scheduled a phone call with one of the 'likers'. 'What do you know about all this?', the woman is soon shouting on the other end of the line. 'You don't get it, right?' I turn down the volume. 'You are fucking part of the establishment.' I hang up, overwhelmed by her rage, and the fact that she may be right.

The financial crisis of 2008 exposed the downsides of global-isation and the interconnectedness of economies around the world. Yet many Europeans and Americans blamed the consequences of economic globalisation on cultural globalisation. Logically, the solution to them is a return to nationalism rather than a change in the economic system. Immigrants somehow make for better scapegoats than bankers.

We could have anticipated that economic failure would contribute to undermining political solidarity, according to Nobel Prize-winning economist Joseph Stiglitz. For him, today's political and societal rifts that have prevented us from effectively responding to new challenges such as the migration crisis have their origins in this first crisis.[14] The G20 were aware of the long-term dangers too. At their summit in April 2009 in London, they recognised the political and human dimension of the global financial crisis and pledged to allocate funds to mitigate its effects on the weakest parts of society.[15] In retrospect, the 2008 financial crisis was just a pre-cursor to all the other crises that were to follow: the Greek debt crisis turning into the Eurozone crisis, the Ukraine crisis, the migrant and refugee crisis. Today, we are facing a new crisis: the global identity crisis.

The Global Identity Crisis

Political and societal instability have long plagued the Middle East and North Africa (MENA). Yet the fall that followed the Arab Spring was a turning point. As pro-democracy uprisings transitioned into sectarian conflicts and civil wars, hope turned into despair. Extremists were quick to fill the vacuums of power and voids of hope. The Middle Eastern microcosm 'prefigured the battle that is now raging across the world [...] where people who claim to want the nation state are actually trying to have a pan-national movement to institutionalise separatism and division within national borders all over the world', former US President Bill Clinton noted in March 2017.[16] 'It's like we're all having an identity crisis at once', he warned.

The notion of a 'collective identity crisis' has been increasingly used recently by the media, politicians and the general public, describing all sorts of things. Indeed, a quick Google search reveals some quite surprising applications of the concept: from architects who feel unsure about whether designing or building is at the core of their profession, to peculiar flavouring trends in the food industry. In sociology, collective identity is seen as the shared sense of belonging to a group. On the basis of shared beliefs a collective identity can be an important driver of collective action. Karl Marx advocated that class consciousness, and the values, interests and solidarity that come with it, are at the root of collective identity. Max Weber criticised Marx for overemphasising production and suggested that class, status and party form the basis of collective identity.[17]

To understand how communities develop collective identity crises, it may be helpful to look at identity crises on an individual level. The German psychologist Hilarion Gottfried Petzhold describes a person's identity as a house that stands on five pillars: (1) body and health; (2) social network and social interaction; (3) work and performance; (4) material security; and (5) values. If one or several of these pillars collapse or undergo drastic changes and the remaining pillars are not strong enough to keep the house standing, an identity crisis can be provoked.[18] In many ways the pillars are linked to each other – the collapse of one can therefore also destabilise others. On a collective level, these pillars keep the Jenga tower, the collective identity, stable.

Globalisation, technology and migration have led to dynamics that are affecting all five identity pillars at varying extents:

1. New consumption and living habits in an increasingly fast-paced world have impacted on our body and health. As obligation was transformed into choice and restriction into freedom, this has opened up an ocean of new opportunities: we can be whoever we want to be and do whatever we want to do. But the fact that we can freely shape our

identities has also brought about a major burden: self-definition can be a difficult process that not everyone is prepared for.[19]

2. The internet, modern communication devices and social media have altered our social network and social interaction. Especially the development of young people's identities has been heavily impacted by the changing nature of social organisation. Global communication technologies have facilitated cultural interaction and idea exchange, which often creates multiple, conflicting identities.

3. Technological innovation, artificial intelligence developments and globalisation have changed our modes of work and our understanding of performance.

4. Economic decline, rising unemployment and the accompanying feeling of uncertainty have increased material insecurity for hundreds of millions of people across Europe, the US and beyond.

5. Most importantly, accelerated societal transformation, waves of mass migration and increased exposure to other cultures have destabilised existing value systems and culturally embedded ideologies.

In 2015, the number of asylum applicants in the EU more than doubled, reaching a record 1.3 million.[20] Yet this number accounted for only 0.2 per cent of the EU's population. And, in fact, Europe had dealt with similarly large immigration waves in the past.[21] When Merkel claimed that 'we can do this', she had reason to believe in her words. Germany absorbed roughly 800,000 immigrants in 2015 – many more than any other country – but it had given refuge to the same number of people in 1992, following the collapse of the Soviet Union and the outbreak of the Balkan Wars.

This latest crisis, however, was different. Europeans perceived the migration waves as more threatening to their traditional values, lives and habits than they did in the 1990s. Was Europe already in a profound identity crisis before the first refugees arrived? Former head editor of *Le Monde*, Natalie Nougayède, commented in the *Guardian* that 'in fact, Europe isn't confronted with a refugee and migrant crisis. It's the refugees and migrants who are confronted with a crisis of Europe.' What is clear, however, is that the migrant crisis forced Europeans into asking themselves 'who they are, how they define themselves and their actions'.[22] It also forced the migrants themselves to ask how their previously held values would stand up in a liberal democratic land.

European citizens' fears over uncontrolled migration generally boil down to three levels: (a) material insecurity caused by the perception that 'they take away our jobs and housing'; (b) concerns that 'they "Islamise" our Western societies'; and (c) anxiety concerning terrorist attacks. Election campaigns have increasingly evolved around the topic of migration, while public scepticism towards the elected politicians' ability to manage migration has surged. This has left the public more susceptible to far-right rhetoric, which thrives in this environment of fear and victimhood. For example, Le Pen's Front National capitalised on the fears of both France's traditionally communist north and its conservative south. Her national-socialist agenda addressed the socio-economic grievances of the working-class north, while her cultural conservatism responded to the wealthy south's worry that their culture was threatened by migrants. The population's universal fear of terrorism is used as a hook for the party's anti-immigration agenda: it took Le Pen less than five minutes to link the Champs-Élysées attack of April 2017 to her Twitter campaign.

The destabilisation of all five pillars is at the source of today's global identity crisis. Most of us cannot escape the deep structural changes that are underway all across the world and have therefore experienced a sense of powerlessness – often accompanied by the desire to go back to old, better times or to move forward to new, better times. When people are stuck in a game with terrible cards without any hope of getting new ones, their only chance to win is to start cheating. If they additionally notice that even those with the best cards are not playing by the rules, it is understandable that they stop believing in the game. Voting for game changers, such as Trump or Brexit, or leaving the game altogether by joining ISIS, for example, may then appear like the best solution.

The falling pillars that have uprooted our collective identities have resulted in a desire for 'radical' change and thus higher vulnerability to 'radicalisation'. The word 'radicalisation' stems from the Latin word 'radix', which means root. Caught within these dilemmas of conflicting identities, many people fall prey to groups with ideologies that offer them a return to their alleged roots. It is no coincidence that the alt-right blog of Richard Spencer is called 'Radix Journal'. One blogger tells me he identifies with the 'new, young and creative movement' because it 'provides clarity about right and wrong behaviours and attitudes in an era of relativism'. Identity crises are thus important drivers of radicalisation.[23] The shakier an individual's identity, the higher the temptation to resort to radical solutions.

In an increasingly unstable world order, everyone seeks to benefit from the growing chaos as the cards are being reshuffled. ISIS's and Russia's expansionist agendas concentrate as much on exploiting and fuelling societal divisions as emerging British and American isolationist-nationalist movements do. It is against this background that an explicit synergy between Russia and the far right, as well as an inadvertent interplay between Islamist extremists and the far right, have emerged. Hungarian party Jobbik was among the first European populist parties to foster close ties with Putin's Russia. Austria's far-right leaders visited the Kremlin in December 2016 to sign a cooperation pact. Frauke Petry, leader of Alternative für Deutschland (AfD), followed in February, and Marine Le Pen met with Putin in March. The former sought to secure financial assistance for the 2017 German elections, while the latter had accepted a €9 million loan from a Kremlin-linked bank in 2014.[24] A destabilised and polarised Europe would suit both Moscow and ISIS, suggested NATO's Supreme Allied Commander for Europe, General Phil Breedlove. He accused Putin of deliberately bombing civilians in Syria to exacerbate the refugee crisis, 'weaponise migration' and drive divisions within Europe.[25]

The rise of identity politics and the deterioration of societal rifts are therefore consequences of the global identity crisis, which manifests itself in a new wave of victimhood cultures.

Victims and Demons

On 16 November 2016, Rashad Ali and I are running through the transit area at the Paris Charles de Gaulle Airport. We don't have much time to catch our connecting flight to London, as our flight from Tunis was delayed. When I get to the security controls a uniformed guy looks at me for half a second and lets me through without asking me a single question. As Rashad approaches the checks the guard's micro-expressions change. 'What were you doing in Tunisia?' I hear him ask with a strong French accent. We had been on the same flight, are going to the same destination and ironically both worked in counter-terrorism. But I am Caucasian. A clear case of racial profiling, I think to myself. 'He was with me at a conference. And we'll both miss our plane, if you don't let him go now,' I tell the security officer in French, trying to keep my voice calm. He gives me a polite nod, ignores my request and asks Rashad to step aside.

As they finally let us go, I am outraged but Rashad seems calm. Not only is he used to getting his share of ethnic profiling, but as a senior fellow at the Institute for Strategic Dialogue he also advises governments against policies that disproportionally target religious or ethnic minority groups, including profiling. 'I don't think there is a typical profile [...] It actually could be anybody,' he had told the British Home Affairs Committee in an evidence session back in 2012. In some areas of the UK people of colour are 17 times more likely to be stopped and searched by the police than white people, a 2015 study by the *Independent* revealed.[26] Such policies are highly counter-productive; they increase the risk of radicalisation and feed into the identity politics used by extremists. Extremists have successfully channelled the outrage, fear and humiliation of sidelined communities into support for their expansionist agenda on the basis of common victimhood.

'Extremist groups' advantage is that they can build on narratives of grievance, which lament and challenge the injustices of the status quo,' Rashad tells me as we finally sit on our plane to London.[27] He used to be within the national leadership ranks of the Islamist extremist organisation Hizb ut-Tahrir, so he knows about the success factors behind extremists' recruiting strategies. For Rashad it is clear that the centre ground inherently cannot appeal to identity groups that feel persecuted or discriminated, as it is representing the status quo. 'Why is it that the Lib Dems are not successful?' he asks. 'Because their values equal those of our current society – they are not radical, so they don't promise change.'

Politicians who are in power just can't get it right: some are blamed for their action, others for their inaction. Additionally, all of them remain prisoners of their predecessors' crimes. While minority communities often feel that they are disadvantaged and treated unfairly by the majority, the majority tend to believe that the minorities are gaining economic advantage from the welfare state and putting increasing pressure on the state's infrastructure and resources at a time of economic hardship.[28] The majority's grievances might thus push them to join extremist groups that stress their superiority and call for further restrictions on migration and religious freedom, for example. Minority communities on the other hand are more prone to be recruited into extremist groups that offer solutions to overcome perceived oppression. Both majority and minority communities thus resort to victimhood narratives and insulation within their identity group.

According to a 2015 poll,[29] 55 per cent of Brits thought Islam and British values were irreconcilable, while 46 per cent of British Muslims found that societal prejudice against Islam made it difficult to be Muslim and British at the same time. The Casey Review of 2016 revealed that increasingly Muslim communities identify with the *ummah*, the global Muslim community, rather than with their home country as a result of these grievances.[30] This observation also holds true for other countries, such as France, where Muslims additionally enjoy less freedom to practise their religion in public places. Even social media platforms, which were created with the aim of 'connecting people', are increasingly contributing to online segregation according to class or political attitude through the formation of echo chambers.

Identity politics become especially dangerous at times of crises, because hardships offer extremists a precious chance to win public support. The theory of outbidding may explain such situations. Outbidding occurs in divided societies when parties try to get political support through showing themselves as the sole defenders of a societal group.[31] As parties start to use identity – based on ethnicity, religion or class, for example – to appeal to voters, they need to stick to their agenda and push their rivals to the extreme in order to win. Such movement towards the extremes is harmful for both intra- and inter-ethnic relations, because groups grow more distrustful of the behaviour of each other.[32] It is highly likely that one side's identity-group mobilisation provokes a backlash from the other side.

Islamist Identity Politics

Around 1.6 billion Muslims inhabit planet Earth. Islam is one of the most diverse and multi-faceted faiths, with a wealth of different beliefs, traditions and subcultures. One-third of the worldwide Muslim population is under 15 years old, two-thirds are under 30. Most young Muslims are tech-savvy, modern and cool – for British Muslim writer and blogger Shelina Janmohamed this is 'Generation M'.[33] But this young generation of Muslims has also grown up in the shadow of 9/11, meaning that they do not know a world without the War on Terror. New technology has enabled them to communicate with other Muslims across the world and to share their stories of oppression and discrimination. This can result in a stronger sense of collective victimhood and a desire for concerted resistance. Islamist identity groups have built on youngsters' over-identification with the *ummah* and translated it into mass mobilisation against perceived oppressors, 'the West'.

Teenage jihadi vocabulary like 'Jihobbyist' and 'YODO' (You Only Die Once) have become part of an emerging youth subculture; so have dark jihadi raps – some 'disturbingly good'[34] as Foreign Policy's Dana Stuster put it, others disturbingly bad. Everything is out there – from professionally produced rhymes with their own labels to self-styled rappers who turn their bedrooms into music studios and their phones into cameras. Before joining ISIS, the German Denis Cuspert – aka Desdo Dogg – produced raps that were viewed tens of thousands of times on YouTube. The former Al Qaeda-linked Omar Hammami had a somewhat less successful rap career. With a $5 million bounty on his head, he features high on the FBI's list of most-wanted terrorists, as former ISIS spokesperson Al Adnani used to. His poorly produced (and sung) rap 'Make Jihad with Me'[35] cannot be the sole reason for this. But its lyrics speak for themselves:

Attack America now, martyrdom or victory.
We're taking Nairobi to Addis,
Paradise inside,
come on, Muslim brother, bring your money or your life.

This Jihadi counter-culture is rooted in the feeling of marginalisation and rebellion against stigmatisation, according to counter-terrorism expert Peter Neumann at the International Centre for the Study of Radicalisation and Political Violence. 'Jihadi rap existed before the Syria conflict, but the influx of the westerners into jihadist groups means that it's getting a lot more prominent now and involves a lot more people,' he says.[36]

Immigration and cultural diversity in the age of globalisation have proven to be great drivers of progress, innovation and prosperity in Western countries. But they have also contributed a vanishing sense of belonging and a rise of identity conflicts. Citizens of increasingly diverse twenty-first-century states often have few common traits and overarching ideals with the people they share public space and resources with. This has resulted in a widespread desire to join movements with well-defined identity groups that draw a clear line between Muslims and non-Muslims, dividing both sides into monolithic blocs. These in-groups are marked by homogeneity and exclusivity: only those who are considered 'Muslim enough' can be part of it. 'This is haram, bro' started as a common joke among Muslim kids in Viennese schools. Today, teachers report rising peer pressure in their classrooms where some Muslim children lecture others on how to dress or behave.[37] This is where 'Generation haram' enters conflict with 'Generation M': those in between may experience an identity conflict.

Hatred of non-Muslims and 'otherisation' is deeply enshrined in Salafi thought – both quietist Salafism and Salafi-jihadism. Traditionally, Islamist extremist groups have formed as a direct challenge to what they perceive as the potential 'Westernisation' of *Dar al-Islam* (The Islamic World) and thus a threat to their cultural heritage. The nineteenth century saw increasing European pressure for the Ottoman Empire to replace Sharia with Western commercial and penal codes and culminated in 1923 with the complete separation of religion and politics in the new secular Turkish Republic. Such 'Westoxification' inspired the creation of many religious movements that opposed Western imperialism and the perceived destruction of Islamic values.

The Muslim Brotherhood was one such movement. Hassan Al Banna founded it in late 1920s Egypt to repel foreign influence by proselytising Islamic values in everyday life. The group's popularity quickly grew through the implementation of charitable, educational and welfare projects. As its popularity increased, the Brotherhood began to prepare for election to government and, when threatened, would instigate pre-emptive assassinations on enemies. In the 1960s and 1970s, the group suffered many constraints in Egypt under President Gamal Nasser, who saw the group as a threat to his legitimacy and so had many of its members imprisoned, executed (most famously Sayyid Qutb) or exiled. The recurring repression that the Brotherhood endured helped gain sympathy and support for their cause throughout the Muslim world, as it reinforced the notion that Islam was being suppressed by increasingly Westernised leaders.

The latter half of the twentieth century saw 'globalisation' accelerate and the perceived threat of 'Westernisation' grow in Muslim-majority countries. Many Muslims feared the forced implementation of materialism, consumption, hedonism and irreverence. This new threat has thus encouraged many Muslims to support Islamist movements as a demonstration of religious self-assertion against Western hegemony. The creation of the state of Israel as well as the military expeditions into Iraq and Afghanistan have added to the pile of grievances. As a result, many Islamist groups that go to fight in Chechnya, Kashmir, Bosnia, Iraq, Afghanistan and Palestine are praised for their defence of Islam against Western tyranny.[38]

Non-Violent Calls for Violence

Hizb ut-Tahrir is a global Islamist extremist organisation that today has branches in almost every country. It was the first organisation to popularise the idea that Muslims must establish a global caliphate. Its founder, the Islamic scholar Taqi Al Din Al Nabhani, formed it in 1953 in Jerusalem as a direct reaction to the 1948 Arab–Israeli war. Al Nabhani believed that the depressed political condition of the modern Muslim world stemmed from the abolition of the Ottoman caliphate in 1924. He thus called for the establishment of a new caliphate to restore the glory of Islam but only by peaceful politics and ideological subversion. However, as of 2015 the group has been banned in China, Germany, Turkey, Russia and all but three Arab states. It has been accused repeatedly of disseminating radical ideas through leaflets, religious sermons and online posts. Furthermore, in 2006 the Hizb ut-Tahrir leader Ata Abu-Rishta called for the death of all Russians in Chechnya, all Jews in Israel and all Hindus in Kashmir, claiming that violence is justified when spreading the word of Islam or when working to establish the new caliphate. Its strategy is based on making 'oppressed Muslims' rise up against their regimes to replace the existing order with theocratic regimes. So, while the group is not directly responsible for any extremist attacks, Hizb ut-Tahrir's strategy to capitalise on chaos, fear and disorder overlaps with that of more violent extremist groups.[39]

Inciting and channelling resentment and outrage among Muslim-majority communities is an official goal of the Islamist extremist organisation Hizb ut-Tahrir. A look at their internal teaching materials reveals their non-violent call for violence:

> The success of the movement would be measured by its ability to incite the sense of resentment among people, and to exhort them to express their resentment each time the ruling authorities or the current regime undermined its ideology, or each time the regime manipulated it according to its own interests and desires.[40]

International Exporters of Terror
Al Muhajiroun is a radical Salafist organisation now banned in the UK. Meaning 'The Emigrants' in Arabic, Al Muhajiroun was established in Mecca in 1983 by Omar Bakri Muhammad, who had been one of Hizb ut-Tahrir's leaders. The group's founding date marked the fifty-ninth anniversary of the destruction of the Ottoman caliphate. Al Muhajiroun originally began as a front for Hizb ut-Tahrir in Saudi Arabia but has since become independent. With a strong presence in the UK, Al Muhajiroun has stated that its main goals are to spread awareness of Islam, influence public opinion towards Sharia and to implement an Islamic caliphate. Despite its claims of exclusively non-violent methods, the group has repeatedly provoked controversy over the years for its statements and its alleged affiliations.

On 9 September 2002, the group celebrated the 9/11 anniversary during a conference entitled 'The Magnificent Nineteen', praising bin Laden for opposing imperialist intrusion into Muslim countries. Adam Deen, a former Al Muhajiroun member, who participated at the event, remembers not feeling anything when watching people jumping out of the Twin Tower windows to escape the fire. 'We were filled with hatred to the extent that we were immune to feeling empathy. Not for one moment did I think these people have families,' he told me.

Al Muhajiroun is known for its connections to notorious British terrorists such as Michael Adebolajo, who murdered Lee Rigby, and the five Muslims arrested in 2007 for attempting to detonate a fertiliser bomb at a shopping centre. To evade surveillance by the British government, Al Muhajiroun adopted several aliases. In June 2009 it changed its name to Islam4UK and was banned in January 2010 under the Terrorism Act 2000. It has since used several aliases to avoid detection, including Saved Sect, Al Ghurabaa, Need4khalifah, Sharia Project and Islamic Dawah Association.[41]

One of Al Muhajiroun's leaders was the notorious hate preacher Anjem Choudary, who was jailed in the summer of 2016 for inviting support for ISIS. As a trained lawyer, his legal knowledge had enabled him to escape terrorism charges since the 1990s, when he was first accused of spreading extremist propaganda. But an undercover police officer who went by the name 'Kamal' infiltrated Choudary's extremist circles in Luton over a period of 20 months and helped to collect enough evidence to eventually convict the hate preacher.

Choudary was such a charismatic orator that wherever he went in Europe, offshoots of Sharia4 were founded. The most well-known branch was Sharia4Belgium, which rose to public attention after the Paris terror attacks. Although the Belgian secret services had long suspected that the Sharia4Belgium group was linked to terrorism-related activities, these were not confirmed until November 2015, when it became clear that two of their members, Abdelhamid Abaaoud and Bilal Hadfi, had been actively involved in the Paris attacks. Many of their militant members also fought with the francophone armed rebel brigade 'Les faucons du Sham', led by Belgian jihadist Abdel Rahman Ayachi.[42] Others had connections to the French radical Islamist group Forsane Alissa (Les cavaliers de la fierté), which was formed in 2011 and banned in 2012.

From Extremist to Jihadist
The question is: what distinction, if any, really exists ideologically between violent Islamist extremist groups and self-proclaimed non-violent groups? Virtually all forms of Islamist extremism agree that

Islam must be the principal or only source of morality and identity in life. Thus they usually perceive the world as divided into two spheres: the abode of Islam (*Dar al-Islam*) and the abode of heathens (*Dar al-Kufr*). Furthermore, both non-violent and violent Islamist extremist groups believe that Muslims belong to a de-territorialised, global community that is under constant attack, a perpetual danger that drives the Islamist narrative of victimhood and grievance. Both groups also believe that Sharia must be implemented, either in their respective countries or as part of a greater caliphate. The main (and perhaps only) difference, then, between the two groups is how this goal should be achieved. Islamist extremist organisations all share the same tendency to criticise the secular, democratic model of government common in the West. They try to draw a picture of a West that is a symbol of imperialism and thus presents a threat to Muslims' culture and religious identity. Islam is presented as incompatible with modern Western values, such as democracy, in order to create a distinguished identity that can serve their political agenda. Consequently, they encourage the view that Islamic values are at odds with Western norms and morality, and create a dividing narrative of 'us vs. them' among Muslims.[43]

Although most extremist groups do not openly advocate violence, they often express some sympathy towards jihadist movements and have even legitimated certain circumstances in which violence would be justified. It is perhaps unsurprising, then, that in some instances non-violent extremist groups have actually set individuals on an indirect path towards terrorism, as shown by the fact that many terrorists previously belonged to non-violent extremist groups such as the Muslim Brotherhood, the Muslim World League, Hizb ut-Tahrir and Tablighi Jamaat. Most groups, both violent and non-violent, generally reject Western values such as democracy, freedom of speech and individual rights. It is therefore unclear whether those groups that choose to take part in elections are doing so out of some ideological moderation or whether it is merely a superficial strategy to exploit their host society. Despite having no direct affiliation to extremism, President Erdoğan of Turkey (head of the Islamist AKP party) famously made a somewhat incriminating comment regarding his true motives by comparing democracy to a train: 'you get off once you have reached your destination'.

Charles Kimball in *When Religion Becomes Evil* identifies five indicators of religious extremism:[44]

1. Blind obedience.
2. Claims of absolute truth.
3. The aim to establish an 'ideal' time.
4. Claims that any means justify the end.
5. The declaration of holy war.

Based on the list above, it appears that the values and goals of violent and non-violent extremist groups are virtually identical except perhaps for number 5, but even then the non-violent groups have repeatedly shown some form of sympathy towards holy war to the point almost of legitimising it. In short, the main (and perhaps only) difference between non-violent and violent extremist groups is their choice of strategy, and even then the disagreement is based not on a disagreement over morality but rather on context.[45]

Far-Right Identity Politics

Andreas joined PEGIDA's Monday street protests in 2016 along with around 20,000 other marchers. The weekly marches in Dresden have attracted a curious blend of disaffected middle-class citizens, from Christian conservatives to neo-Nazis. They are united in their fear of an 'Islamised West' in which they would lose their social status. 'But you don't really have a strong percentage of foreigners or immigrants here in Dresden,' I say to Andreas.

'Look, the people here in Saxony have a stronger sense of patriotism.' The middle-aged man's voice goes up. He was born in Dresden, a former Nazi stronghold and the birthplace of PEGIDA. 'But we are also tired of being messed around with by those in power. Over the past 100 years, we had World War I, the Weimar Republic, World War II, the communist German Democratic Republic, then the reunification, and now once again people here are being fucked over. We are tired of it.' He believes that politics and democracy have reached their limits.

Andreas gets a decent salary from Deutsche Post. 'They pay well and on time,' he says. Today, he owns a house in a village just outside Dresden, where 'it's calm and you won't find any foreigners'.

'That doesn't sound like you would have to worry too much,' I remark.

'No one here in Dresden would have to, really,' he replies. 'It's about the principle. The gigantic lobbying machinery behind politics have been trying to make fools out of us. They keep increasing the taxes while the gap between the rich and the poor is widening. They invest the money in foreign people and foreign infrastructure, while our own people and our own infrastructure bite the dust. Then I see the smiling faces as the stock markets are up 2.5 per cent again. The real war criminals are the adventurers; they got us into this situation.'

'But the people suffering on the other side of the Mediterranean, they are real people after all,' I say. 'How do you feel when you see pictures of drowning refugees?'

He hesitates and, as he replies, I can sense that the question is upsetting him. 'You know, this is something I've been struggling with. But all these terrible pictures from the German Press Agency come in combination with clearly articulated opinions; it's all so dishonest,' he argues. 'You see, the only reports that I trust nowadays are those put out by the DFB (the German Football Association). All other news is merely an interpretation of events. I don't know what to believe any more. This is what drove people to the streets in the first place.'

Lutz Bachmann founded the PEGIDA movement in 2014 after a diverse professional journey from cooking, graphic design and professional soccer to running a nightclub. On the side, he was dealing cocaine and involved in 16 burglaries, which got him a hefty prison sentence. In 2016, he was found guilty of 'inciting racial hatred' and fined €9,600 for a Facebook post that called refugees 'cattle', 'scumbags' and 'filth'. His anti-immigration attitude did not prevent him from emigrating twice to escape prison.

When Bachmann says that PEGIDA is 'a peaceful movement', he is technically right: nowhere does the group's 19-point manifesto call for violence. Nonetheless, it has attracted violent militants, mobilised neo-Nazis and inspired countless attacks against immigrants. Three months after PEGIDA's first demonstration on 20 October 2014, hate crimes against migrants and refugees had more than doubled in Dresden, according to a study by the German political magazine *Report Mainz*.[46]

Margins Turning Mainstream

'The big coalition in Austria is in an artificial coma.' A vendor of the street paper *Uhudla* stands in front of my table in a Viennese café. He points at the headlines of the newspaper that I am reading. Tony has been homeless in Vienna for over 15 years. One day he just found himself without a place, he tells me. He must have been in his early thirties when an alcohol problem cost him his job, his friends and eventually his apartment. 'It happened a lot faster than you'd think,' he says. Now Tony has replaced his alcohol addiction with a passion for writing. Had he not worn torn trousers and a dirty jacket, I would have guessed that he was a professor. 'I also want to write a book,' he tells me, staring at the cappuccino next to my laptop for a few seconds before adding, 'but it's a bit harder for me.'

'I'll buy one of your newspapers,' I say and invite him to take a seat. I like the *Uhudla*; it's fair and transparent: I pay him two euros, knowing that one euro goes to him, the other to the organisation. He now makes enough money to buy himself two hot meals a day, he says.

Tony tells me about his life on the streets. He has seen what remains invisible to those of us who enjoy the luxury of having a roof over our heads. He has seen the refugees arrive in 2015, watched people freeze to death, steal food for their hungry children, and he has increasingly witnessed racist and anti-Muslim hate crimes in the streets.[47] 'Things were different when I first arrived on the streets,' he recalls. 'Life and people have changed quite a lot in recent years. People are afraid now, I can see it in their eyes; the way they look at the homeless, refugees and migrants reveals more than how they treat us.'

It is within this context that over recent years Austria's mainstream parties have lost ground at an unparalleled speed. They have desperately been trying to reanimate their support base, yet without success. But Austria is not the only country where the mainstream is clinically dead. All across the Western world, the disproportionate fear of uncontrolled migration, terrorism and the changes that globalisation bring to life today has led to a growing hostility towards liberalism and democracy.[48] Entire strata of society have lost trust in the democratic institutions and belief in the fundamental values that shaped the post-war order. Strong anti-establishment attitudes that used to be exclusive to the lower-revenue and less educated classes in society can now be found across all social classes.

Trust in mainstream political parties and transnational organisations has been collapsing throughout Europe and the US. Recent figures from the Eurobarometer show that even though trust in the EU and national political institutions has slightly improved since the economic crisis in 2008, it remains very low at 40 per cent and 31 per cent respectively. Trust in national parliaments is also at a very low level, with 62 per cent of EU nationals not trusting their national parliaments.[49]

A 2014 survey by YouGov showed that while distrust in British politicians is not new, it is increasing, with only 10 per cent of voters believing that politicians are doing the best they can to serve their country. In the UK, less than 1 per cent of the British people are members of a political party.[50] The US population's declining faith in 'the establishment' may have begun as early as the 1960s, when the government started burdening the country's constitution with regulations that protect '*certain* special interests' and champion agriculture and labour cartels instead of emphasising public interests.[51]

Polling conducted in the US revealed vanishing trust in democracy and the rule of law. Voter turnout, party identification and trust in political institutions has dropped dramatically over the last three decades. A poll in the *Journal of Democracy* reveals a rapid drop in the number of people who believe that democratic values are 'essential'. While 72 per cent of the generation born before World War II give maximal priority 'to live in a democracy', only one in three Millennials (those born after 1980) attribute the same importance to democracy. 'Even in some of the richest and most politically stable regions of the world, it seems as though democracy is in a state of serious disrepair', concludes the study.[52]

Populist politicians have exploited this crisis of confidence and rising anti-system mood to change the direction of contemporary politics. This has led to a breakdown of mainstream political parties that have dominated across Europe ever since World War II. Traditional large parties are losing their supporters to small, often far-right, ones. Had you asked someone five years ago what the chances were of having Brexit, Trump as US president and far-right leaders across Europe, most people would have answered 'Zero'. Peace and security may have been the costliest treasures to the post-war children; their parents had passed on the fear of conflict and division to them. But this has changed – today's generations are no longer risk adverse. Their appetite for change is too big to contain, their frustration too high to sustain.

Voters increasingly feel that the elected establishment is incapable of tackling mainstream social, economic, political and cultural problems such as migration and extremism, leading to a widespread sense of disillusionment with the traditional political parties and governments.[53] When political elites additionally decide to campaign against public opinion, as was the case in the Brexit vote, this contributes to the widening divide between people and their governments. Populist and fringe parties – whether on the right or on the left, focused on immigration or on social reform – have used this window of opportunity to engage with the electorate and gain public support from the disillusioned. YouGov calls the new trend that is emerging 'Authoritarian populism', which 'could be the defining political phenomenon of the next decade'. Trump, Brexit, the National Front and AfD are, according to its study, 'branches of the same tree'.[54]

Populism is not new but it is has been gaining momentum, thus pushing leaders of traditional parties to adopt different policies to cope with the new situation. Populist and anti-establishment parties such as the far-right National Front in France, the anti-EU Five Star Movement in Italy, the left-wing Podemos movement in Spain or the nationalist Finns Party in Finland have been gaining ground rapidly.[55] In Austria, the neo-fascist Freedom Party has nearly doubled its share of the vote since 2006. The leaders of all these parties have exploited rapid economic changes and the sense of insecurity and fear associated with them.[56] Immigration, Islam and austerity are among the most controversial and inflammatory issues that such parties are using to appeal to voters. Thus, the growing support for populism might be the result of 'cultural alienation and the persistent erosion of the social fabric'.[57]

Calls for change appear loud and pressing. The sheer speed at which new fringe movements are catching up with mainstream parties demonstrates this. For example, Podemos was established only in 2014 in Spain but was gaining votes and competing with long-established Spanish parties within a few months. The same can be said about the UK, where the rapid rise of UKIP signalled strong competition for the country's three major parties.

When the centre ground shrinks, people on all sides tend to be pushed towards extremes, making it more difficult for parties to reach agreement and make decisions. Increasingly, outsiders benefit from shrinking trust in the establishment and widening divisions within our societies. The Icelandic Pirate Party, which was founded by activists and hackers, has moved from fringe to front-runner. Its parliamentary seats increased threefold in the 2016 elections. But not all of the outsiders are as benign as Iceland's Pirates. In Austria, the political landscape has recently seen successes of a far-right gun enthusiast, a rapping dental technician with Nazi links and an 82-year-old billionaire who featured himself on his campaigning posters as a clown holding his 25-year-old *Playboy*-model wife.

A decade ago no one would have taken these figures seriously as political candidates – until 2016, commentators laughed at Brexit and thought of Trump as a joke. A year prior to the US presidential election, the audience of HBO's *Real Time with Bill Maher* burst out in laughter when American conservative commentator Anne Coulter predicted Trump's victory.[58] Yet voters decided that the establishment was more of a joke than the outsiders who were deemed ridiculous. In today's world, which is increasingly dominated by the fringes, we have no option but to take them seriously. 'What began with a stunt, lampooned as a joke and dismissed as a fantasy', has become a 'historical truth', as the *Guardian*'s Washington correspondent David Ian Smith noted.[59] From Vienna to Reykjavik, from Icelandic hackers to Austrian rapping clowns, the margins are turning mainstream.

As mainstream politicians are facing pressure from the fringes, their reactions to crises sometimes become irrational. In their struggle to maintain power and control, they tend to opt for the politically most favourable rather than strategically best answer. Visibility of action becomes more important than its effectiveness. For example, the series of terrorist attacks across Europe in 2016 led many governments, in particular the French and the German, to adopt counter-terrorism policies that cut down on civil liberties purely for the sake of shutting down the far right. Not only have these sacrificed the very values they are trying to defend in the face of extremism; they have also tended to exacerbate existing intra-community tensions.

Major events that spark fear and insecurity – such as the global financial crisis, the refugee crisis and terrorist attacks – accelerate polarisation dynamics. Their negative impacts on community cohesion are palpable, both within the wider society and within religious, ethnic and political communities.[60] On the macro-level, the result of this has been binary-choice elections with diametrically opposed camps: Remain versus Leave in Britain, Trump versus Clinton in the US, a green party-supported professor against a right-wing gun enthusiast in Austria. Regardless of the outcomes of these elections, the aggressive campaigns that preceded them left international institutions, political parties and the general public permanently fractured. For example, intra-party divisions have widened within the British Labour Party, the French Socialist Party and the US Republican Party. On a societal level, minorities within minorities are often the first ones to suffer from intra-community conflict. For instance, Muslim communities within Europe are increasingly split, as their members accuse each other of not being Muslim enough.

A loss of faith in the establishment, widening rifts within society and its communities, increased polarisation, scapegoating and finger pointing: this all sounds alarmingly familiar. The ascendance of the National Socialists in the 1930s started with the German public's loss of faith in their government. Hitler managed to convince the population that the country's mainstream parties were corrupt and that he could significantly improve the workers' welfare.[61] The Nazis presented themselves as the true defenders of lower-class workers' interests, in contrast to other elite politicians. As a result, mainstream parties were destroyed and the public were attracted to the Nazis' convincing propaganda.

Recent changes can be seen as a movement of far-right political parties and social groups from 'the margins to the mainstream'. Increasingly our societies are drifting towards the extremes, or rather: the extremes are becoming the new normal.

Normalisation of Hate

In December 2011, Thomas F. raised his hand in an auditorium full of philosophy students at Vienna University. The professor had asked the students about the most pressing problems facing the world. 'The Islamisation of the Occident,' Thomas said in reply. Everyone looked at him. The professor raised his eyebrows and Thomas's seatmate even moved a few centimetres to the left, as if to distance himself. But today, more than five years later, something has changed. Making anti-Muslim and anti-immigrant statements may still cause raised eyebrows but expressing support for far-right parties has increasingly become socially acceptable. Controversial discussions about the compatibility of Islam and Western values have become commonplace; even universities have been forced to address the issue.

'This is because politicians have exploited the public's fears and exacerbated their paranoia,' a Hungarian activist whose organisation defends minority rights tells me. 'Everyone who doesn't speak Hungarian is labelled a potential terrorist, that's how far they've gone now. People have called the police just because they heard a person in the street speak in a foreign language.'

It's hard to say when Pandora's box was opened. In the first round of the Austrian presidential elections on 24 April 2016, far-right politician Norbert Hofer, of the Freedom Party, received more votes than any other candidate. A few days later in the UK, Nigel Farage warned that the newly proposed EU policy to prevent illegal migrants from drowning in the Mediterranean Sea would cause ISIS terrorists to flood into Britain. A few weeks and several terrorist attacks later, the Brexit referendum had turned almost entirely into a vote on immigration. In the last month before the vote, immigration surpassed the economy as the top issue for voters.[62] The fringes had successfully moved into the public arena and what used to be a taboo had now become a legitimate dinner-table conversation.

'If Britain votes to leave the EU it will be because of hostility to immigration', wrote deputy director of the London-based Centre for European Reform Simon Tilford prior to the referendum.[63] On 23 June 2016, 52 per cent of Britain's population voted Leave. An Ipsos MORI poll shows that immigration was the main driver behind Brexit votes: more than half (52 per cent) of Leave voters cited immigration as an issue of concern.[64] Although many Leave voters were not convinced by Farage's xenophobic rhetoric, UKIP supporters and far-right sympathisers felt confirmed and empowered by the outcome of the referendum.

In the aftermath of the Brexit vote, the public's confidence in expressing anti-immigrant views publicly surged and hate crimes spiked both online and offline. Between 24 June and 1 July, Demos identified 2,413 unique online reports of hate speech incidents and xenophobic abuse in British streets. Within the same period, it registered 13,236 tweets sent from the UK that contained xenophobic or anti-immigrant contents.[65] A similar pattern could be observed in Austria, where the effects of the Freedom Party's aggressive campaigning were palpable both on social media and in the streets. In 2016, the country witnessed a major spike of hate crimes against ethnic and religious minorities, which both rose at unprecedented speed.[66]

The populist far right has gained ground at rapid speed all across Europe and the US. Countries with no far-right party seats in parliament have become the exception rather than rule. The French Front National, Alternative für Deutschland in Germany, the Freedom Party in both Austria and the Netherlands, Italy's Lega Nord, the Danish People's Party, the Sweden Democrats, Belgium's Vlaams Belang, Golden Dawn in Greece, Hungarian Fidesz, Law and Justice in Poland have all managed to appeal to voters who believe that liberalisation, globalisation and cosmopolitanism have gone too far and who fear the extinction of their culture. Despite the many positive effects of immigration on innovation, competitiveness and cultural diversity – even Austrian far-right leader H. C. Strache admits to eating ten kebabs a year[67] – far-right voters do not see themselves as beneficiaries of multi-culturalism.

The 2017 Dutch general elections saw the surprise victory of the liberal People's Party for Freedom and Democracy. But it's not game over for Geert Wilders's Party of Freedom, whose programme includes prohibiting the sale of the Qur'an, shutting down mosques and Islamic schools, closing the Dutch borders and introducing a ban on Muslim immigrants. 'We were the 3rd largest party of the Netherlands. Now we are the 2nd largest party. Next time we'll be nr. 1!', Wilders tweeted after the election results were released.[68]

Prior to Trump's election victory the rise of far-right populism was widely perceived as a pan-European phenomenon. However, during the US election campaign, more and more taboos were broken, without severe consequences. Trump's statements about banning Muslims from coming to the US, and his offending the family of a Muslim war hero, led to short-lived condemnation and temporary drops in polls but did not prevent him from being elected president. Between June and October 2016, Trump's popularity increased drastically among white women without college degrees, suburban voters, conservatives and white Catholics.[69] Even though Trump supporters were steadily getting louder over the campaigning months, Trump's victory took almost everyone – whether social scientist, journalist or activist – by surprise. It shook the world as a political earthquake because it made something that had long been undeniable official: far-right populism had become a worldwide trend.

Trump's cabinet picks confirmed that his anti-Muslim campaign rhetoric had not been purely for the sake of election point-scoring. Trump's chief strategist Stephen Bannon, who ran the alt-right Breitbart News, is known for his racist and anti-Muslim views. He believes that 'Islam is not a religion of peace'. Under his leadership, Breitbart featured articles with headlines such as 'political correctness protects Muslim rape culture', blaming the 'epidemic of rape cases across Europe' on Muslim migrants. US Army lieutenant General Michael Flynn held his post of national security advisor for less than a month, setting a new record. His claim that 'fear of Muslims is RATIONAL'[70] reminded one of Breivik, whose manifesto's declared aim was to show that 'the fear of Islamisation is all but irrational'.[71] At an event of the anti-Muslim group ACT for America in Dallas, Flynn declared that Islam was 'a political ideology' that 'hides behind this notion of it being a religion', adding that it was comparable to 'a cancer'. Again, this sounds alarmingly similar to Breivik's words. In his manifesto, the terrorist emphasised multiple times that 'Islam is less a personal faith than a political ideology that exists in a fundamental and permanent state of war with non-Islamic civilisations, cultures, and individuals.'[72]

From Populist to Militant

Belgian Hendrik Vyt, Norwegian Anders Breivik, British Thomas Mair and French-Canadian Alexandre Bissonnette have something in common: they all admired and actively followed far-right politicians. Their examples show that terrorists may be influenced and motivated by far-right propaganda and identity politics.

Populist and militant extremists agree on both narrative and ideology: while the former is used to describe the world, the latter is used to rule the world. Narrative provides the link between vulnerability and ideology. Both far-right and Islamist extremists explain grievances with black-and-white narratives that link evil to ethnic or religious identity. As identity for them is unmoveable, evil becomes impermeable. Their exclusivist ideology then offers a framework to judge and treat evil.

Embracing violent, total solutions is only taking it one step further: from the *Star Wars* effect to the Final Battle effect. 'She was idealistic with an inborn loathing of compromise. She longed for the absolute, the total solution', the famous German writer Günter Grass said about the German Red Army Faction terrorist Gudrun Ensslin. According to Austrian psychologist Paul Watzlawick, it is the claim to absolute truth, perfection and infinity that makes ideologies dangerous. Their all-embracing – and therefore universally binding – nature can turn the most honourable utopia into the most disgraceful 'total solution'.[73]

Neither Trump nor Wilders, Le Pen or Farage endorse far-right hate crimes. UKIP has actively attempted to distance itself from far-right extremism. Anne Marie Waters' name disappeared from UKIP's London Assembly list shortly after she joined PEGIDA UK in 2016. While 69 per cent of UKIP members identify themselves as being 'right-wing', only 10 per cent label themselves as being 'very right-wing'.[74]

Nigel Farage's 'Breaking Point' poster, which showed a queue of refugees, was released just hours before Thomas Mair killed Jo Cox. The timing of the incident at the height of UKIP's aggressive anti-immigrant Vote Leave campaign speaks for itself. Common connections of UKIP members and Thomas Mair are equally suggestive: for example, both Mair and UKIP's leader in Wales, Neil Hamilton, were found to be linked to the Springbok Club, a London-based white supremacist pressure group.

Spikes in online hate crimes in the wake of Brexit, Austria's far-right successes and Trump's election were mirrored in real-life incidents. Multiple studies found that online and offline far-right activities are closely related[75] – self-starter terrorists tend to be inspired by or involved in online hate speech.[76] For example, Dylann Roof, the white nationalist who murdered nine people at the Emanuel African Methodist Episcopal Church in South Carolina in June 2015, was a regular commenter on the Daily Stormer and other white supremacist platforms, according to the FBI.

It is hardly surprising that Trump's cabinet choices were celebrated by alt-right and neo-Nazi movements. People like Richard Spencer, the white nationalist who is banned from 27 European countries for his extremist views, and David Duke, the former Imperial Wizard of the Ku Klux Klan and Holocaust denier, immediately endorsed the cabinet. Duke praised Trump on Twitter for his 'great' cabinet choices and Daily Stormer founder Andrew Anglin wrote: 'It's like we're going to get absolutely everything we wanted [...] Basically, we are looking at a Daily Stormer Dream Team in the Trump administration.'

Trump was called 'a kind of alt-right hero'. Although he distanced himself from the alt-right movement after being elected, claiming that he did not want to 'energise the group', he has effectively created an environment in which white nationalists can thrive. As Richard Spencer said: 'Trump was the first step towards identity politics in the United States [...] The alt-right is fundamentally about identity, the Trump campaign was fundamentally about identity, we're connected to him.' In reaction to Trump's victory, Spencer shocked many with cries of 'Hail Trump, hail our people, hail victory!' that prompted his audience to imitate Nazi-style salutes. Although Spencer later argued that this was 'done in exuberance and fun', his supporters took it more seriously. 'Hitler definitely made Germany great again', one of them told the *Guardian*.[77]

Far-right groups have strategically blended their violent views into everyday discourse to normalise their views and minimise disapproval.[78] Inflammatory rhetoric against ethnic and religious minorities might not always translate directly into criminal activity from smaller right-wing groups. Yet their statements are conducive to the formation and empowerment of small violent groups grounded in similar ideologies.[79]

In short, nativist populism and far-right terrorism interact as much as online and offline hate crimes: all of them are part of an emerging new far right. Their common element, the story, is also the connecting element to Islamist extremists: they all tell the same binary stories. Their stories of victims and demons are then transmitted and amplified through the media.

5

The Media

WHILE HISTORY BOOKS SHAPE THE STORIES OF THE PAST, THE MEDIA FRAMES the stories of the present – both can feed into extremists' narratives. Far-right and Islamist extremists have successfully capitalised on opportunities offered by the rapid changes that the media has undergone since the internet has rendered information abundant and transformed attention into a scarce commodity. While politicians and activists often deliver the ideological inspiration for far-right and Islamist extremists, the media has a strong record of amplifying and spreading their stories. Mass media sensationalism, biased reporting and fake news have all made their own contribution to extremists' success in spreading their binary worldviews. Hijacking stories has become easier in a new media landscape that is marked by rising interconnectedness, increasing competition for clicks and views, soaring speed of news circles and vanishing trust in 'mainstream' media. Entirely new modes of storytelling have formed and shaped our virtual space as much as our real lives.

i-Propaganda and #Mobilisation

The progress we have made in the transmission of stories since ancient times is one of our biggest achievements: first, stories were passed on through word-of-mouth and painted on cave walls, then documented manually on papyrus, later printed in books. Now we can choose from a wide array of visual, auditory and even multi-sensual channels, ranging from glossy, photo-shopped pictures to sophisticated motion pictures with integrated special effects. This has revolutionised the art of storytelling. In an increasingly interconnected world, the transmission of existing and new stories become easier, faster and more inclusive. With the invention of the internet and social media, literally everyone with a mobile device and internet connection can disseminate new stories or even new narratives. While centuries ago the creation of narratives was reserved for the most privileged in society, today anyone can spread their stories on a global level at incredible speed.

Narratives are traditionally the most powerful tools of control but, paradoxically, they are now also the most uncontrollable determinants of power. Since the first edition of Johann Carolus's weekly newspaper *Relation* was published in the Holy Roman Empire in 1605,[1] traditional print and broadcasting media have played a decisive role in spreading and shaping collective stories. Over the past four centuries, we have seen that the media can play a decisive role in both the escalation and resolution of conflicts. New media has multiplied the potential reach and speed of storytelling a thousandfold: live news streams, blogs and social media can cross borders and even languages to reach millions of people within less than a minute. For example, the fast food chain Chipotle Mexican Grill's video campaign 'Food with Integrity' went viral instantly,[2] while a random British couple managed to get worldwide views on their wedding invitation within 18 seconds.[3] The Arab Spring has demonstrated all too well the crucial role that social media plays in mobilising people under a common narrative that creates a shared goal and calls for collective action. Large-scale demonstrations that previously took months or even years of preparation and coordination, the delivery of thousands of pamphlets, letters and speeches, can now be achieved within a matter of days if not hours.

Today's leaders are well aware of the omnipresent threat this poses to their regime's stability. In post-coup Turkey, Erdoğan used a combination of positive and negative counter-insurgency measures: while censoring, blocking and shutting down any dissident media to suppress critical voices, he also used social media as a vehicle for his propaganda and mass communication.[4] The Chinese state employs an army of at least 100,000 bureaucrats[5] – almost the size of the French Armed Forces – to maintain its 'Great Firewall', control its 700 million internet users and keep the internet clean of any threats to the imagined order. Any suspicious item is removed, any open opposition or allegation prosecuted.

Extremists have embraced the new opportunities offered by social media more than anyone else. Social media enables them to bypass traditional channels. Even those groups and individuals that are denied a platform by mainstream media can now easily spread their ideas and narratives on a global level using the internet. As Jamie Bartlett, author of *The Dark Net*, noted, 'terrorists and far-right extremists will always be early adopters' of new communication tools.[6] Their campaigns sometimes go viral faster than those of multinational communication firms and their social media accounts often attract more followers than mainstream political parties. While Islamist extremists have in the past hijacked major Twitter hashtags such as those of the World Cup and of the i-Phone 6 release,[7] far-right groups have used the hashtags #StarWars and #Taylor Swift to leverage their respective hate messages.[8] A handful of people are often enough to make a lot of noise.

The #Mosul Effect

In June 2014, the world's eyes were on ISIS. No one could believe the breaking news of the conquest of Mosul, a northern Iraqi city of 1.5 million residents, by a militia of 2,000 ISIS fighters. Politicians, military strategists and news commentators all asked: why did a 30,000-strong Iraqi army, an army trained and equipped by the American military for more than a decade, an army that outnumbered its attackers by over fifteen to one, abandon the city without even fighting?[9] 'What happened?' one of the infantry soldiers who fled the Al Ghazlany base after checking their mobile phones asked. 'There is a mystery here.'[10]

The answer was equally surprising: tweets and a movie. Some months before the offensive, ISIS's propaganda wing designed an Arabic-language app called the Dawn of Glad Tidings, which allowed users to hand over their social media accounts to ISIS operatives.[11] On the day they approached Mosul, tens of thousands of messages were posted simultaneously, swamping the social media feed of users worldwide.[12] The sheer number of retweets conveyed the impression of a gigantic, invincible army marching towards Mosul, creating shockwaves across the ranks of the Iraqi army. It was enough to make the ISIS fighters appear so invincible that even the bravest Iraqi soldiers stripped off their uniforms and fled.

The content of the Twitter campaign played a crucial role too. One of the items they shared was the ISIS-produced video *The*

Clanging of the Swords IV. Visually in the style of Hollywood, the film starts with the words 'Allah is great', followed by 'My lord, (grant us) the victory that you promised'.[13] This is a reference to the so-called End Times prophecy, which predicts a bloody war between Muslims and non-Muslims following the reappearance of the final Mahdi (the twelfth imam). This war, so the prophecy says, will eventually end in the victory of the 'true believers' over all infidels and apostates in an epic final battle in the Syrian city of Dabiq.[14] The assumption is that justice will be restored and the world will be purified of all un-Islamic influence on the Day of Judgement.[15]

The prophecy is deeply embedded in Islamic culture, spanning its various systems of belief and scriptural interpretations. According to a study conducted by the Pew Research Center in 2011,[16] 92 per cent of American Muslims believe in the End Times prophecy. Another Pew Research study[17] found that in nine of the 23 surveyed nations, half or more of Muslim adults thought that the return of the Mahdi was imminent and would occur during their lifetime.

The Clanging of the Swords IV presents ISIS fighters as the vanguard of the Muslim community, the *ulema*, whose jihad is supported by Allah and will eventually be rewarded with the fulfilment of the prophecy. The movie also emphasises the signs that supposedly indicate the approach of the end of time and the successes of ISIS in leading the way towards the Day of Judgement: 'Indeed, openly speaking the truth and revealing the path of Ibraheem leads to a real conflict between truth and falsehood. [...] And after patience, combat, strife, and tribulation, we now see The Islamic State is controlling a vast area in Iraq and Syria.' It succeeds in conveying the idea that the eventual victory of 'truth' over 'falsehood', of Islam over the West (or what ISIS refers to as the Crusaders) is inevitable and that everyone who is fighting on the 'wrong' side will be punished.

Mission completed – #AllEyesonISIS worked. It was a storybook psychological operation that even the strategic communications and information warfare experts of the British Army's 77th Brigade were impressed with. ISIS soldiers essentially told their story before it happened, turning it into a self-fulfilling prophecy. According to Zaid Al Ali, author of *The Struggle for Iraq's Future*, 'the image that they convey of themselves has convinced people in many parts of the country, and that [was] clearly a factor in encouraging people to leave their posts as ISIS was advancing'.[18]

The idea of an army that enjoys the support of God and is on its way to fulfilling a millenniums-old prophecy sounds indeed a bit intimidating. No wonder the Iraqi soldiers panicked – anyone who believes that story would. Anyone who believes that enough people believe the story would do too. This example demonstrates the power that stories can have. They can hold together groups, communities and armies, inspire action (or inaction) and make people change their behaviour in anticipation of a certain outcome, thereby rendering the expected outcome more likely. There is no weapon more powerful and no driver of change more effective than a good story.

It was at that moment, when tens of thousands of well-trained Iraqi soldiers were too afraid to defend Mosul, that the West started taking ISIS seriously. The event was the first portent of what would follow in the succeeding months. It was also a first indication of the nature of the threat that ISIS would pose to Western governments. Policy makers should have realised back then that the biggest challenge in fighting ISIS would not be their military capacity but their ability to communicate and to convey stories to a wide audience. Yet, even three years later, the discussion on defeating jihadism still revolves primarily around sharpening national security measures and increasing troops in warzones. Although governments worldwide have stepped up their efforts to monitor, block and counter ISIS's propaganda, they are always lagging one step behind. A Brookings study[19] counted at least 46,000 Twitter accounts used by ISIS supporters in the period between September and December 2014. By the time Twitter started taking down accounts associated with extremist activities, in mid-2015,[20] ISIS recruiters had already moved on to encrypted messaging applications such as WhatsApp, Telegram, Signal and Surespot.

The one with the better army may win the battle, but the one with the better story wins the war. This is because the ultimate battle that decides the war does not take place on a physical level but in our minds. All that we are fighting for and against are abstract ideas and products of our imagination. The two opponents in the conflict (the West and the *ulema*) and their respectively desired outcomes (democracy and theocracy) are entities and concepts that exist nowhere but in our heads. The war is therefore not primarily fought with fists, guns or drones but with our imagination. More than anything else it is a fight for the hearts and minds of the young generations. This fight is in many ways shaped by those who set the agenda for the stories that reach the masses: journalists.

Sensationalism

'I was incidentally on Twitter when the news broke that a four-year-old child had been beheaded by ISIS back in the summer of 2016,' Jonathan Russell, who co-chairs the EU's Radicalisation Awareness Network's working group on communications and counter-narratives, recalls. 'So I decided to do an experiment and stay on Twitter until I'd see the first account sharing a picture of the dead child. I was interested in seeing who would first be tweeting it.'

An elderly woman on the table next to us looks up, slightly confused about our conversation.

'Guess who it was?' he says.

'A far-right politician?' I start guessing. 'A terrorism expert, a jihadist organisation?'

He shakes his head, taking a sip from his coffee. 'Mainstream media.'

A few hours later I awake with a start, trying to shake off the pictures of a man burning in a cage and to stop his howls from echoing in my head. I had not expected to find the video of the Jordanian pilot who was burnt alive by ISIS so quickly. One does not have to navigate through the Dark Net or even visit dodgy fringe websites to come across it; the full unedited footage is still publicly available in the archives of Fox News. 'It is disturbingly easy to access videos of terrorist atrocities,' Jonathan had warned me. One quick Google search with the key word 'ISIS propaganda' is enough to dive into a vast ocean of beheadings, shootings and crucifixions – pages from Heavy.com, Breitbart and the *Daily Mail*[21] appear at the top of the search engine results.

Journalists are storytellers too. It is their job to make sense of events by connecting them through narration that appeals to their audience. In doing so, they automatically cherry-pick information, determine tonality and add interpretation. Mass media, unsurprisingly, seeks to appeal to the masses. In that sense their strategy is driven by the same dynamics as that of populists: they tell the stories that the public wants to hear.

'Does the public really want to hear stories of violence and horror?' I ask strategic communications expert Joshua Stewart.

'Audiences love their daily dosage of macabre scenes, tragedy and, most importantly, sensationalism. It sells.' Clearly, Josh knows what sells. If you Google the words 'porn' and 'ISIS', his name is among the first ones to appear.[22] He has analysed the media's tendency to show graphic images of bodies covered in blood, perpetrators posing with guns, and real-time displays updating the numbers of terrorism victims.[23] 'If we didn't want to see it, read it or view it, the papers wouldn't gun for it. Yes, they'd inform us, but it wouldn't be such a spectacle. We demand it and the papers oblige.' Everyday media culture has sensitised and socialised the public towards expecting this kind of imagery and horror, according to Josh. 'Just think of the past few years' unending frenzy of books, films, TV series and video games that hinge on hyper-violence, the apocalypse and nihilism – *Walking Dead*, *True Blood*, *Game of Thrones*, *Twilight*. It's only natural that this should bleed into our consumption patterns regarding geopolitics and terrorism,' Josh concludes.

The 'if it bleeds, it leads' principle has become even more pivotal in the media's competition for readers' all-time-low attention span. A Microsoft study revealed that the average online user's attention span is estimated to have fallen from 12 seconds in 2000 to just 8 seconds in 2016. It is now shorter than that of a goldfish.[24] As a result, human attention has become a scarce and precious commodity. With 24-hour news loops and the rising scramble for clicks and views, traditional media's business models have become outdated and the pressure to maximise online readership has grown.

Reporting needs to be faster, content easier and headlines catchier. The modern-day media ecology is dominated by the constant fear that 'if we don't do it, someone else will'. Charlie Beckett, the director of the journalism think tank POLIS, confirms this. 'Media outlets will all say "we don't want to be first, we want to be right",' Charlie tells me over coffee at the London School of Economics campus, where his think tank is based. 'Nonsense.' He sighs. 'Everyone wants to be fast. Some might not be first but no one wants to be three hours later either.' Charlie has 20 years' experience of international journalism at the BBC and ITN's Channel 4 News. Having witnessed and studied the rise of online journalism and citizen journalism, he is a leading expert in media change.

Now add tabloid-style dehumanising language to sensationalism. 'Barbaric ISIS mangle 250 children in industrial dough kneader and cooks rest alive in oven', was the first thing you could read when opening the *Daily Express* on the morning of 26 October 2016.[25] The *Sun* and the *Mirror* regularly talk about 'ISIS monsters' and 'evil savages'.[26] Often articles stress the racial or religious background of the perpetrators and use words such as Muslim, Islamist and Jihadist interchangeably, thereby demonising entire communities.

In December 2016, the *Sun* ran a 'Cut Out and Keep Guide' to explain how to distinguish a terrorist from an 'innocent (white) OAP'. It showed picture of bin Laden in his turban, the White Widow in her hijab and Jihadi John in his black mask, below the words: 'Here's what terrorists look like'. The message was: terrorists wear hijabs, turbans or masks. A few months later, the *Daily Mail*'s headline was saying: 'They think they can get an AK and get forgiven by God at the same time: Channel 4's *Extremely British Muslims* revealed how young Asian men want to join ISIS because it's "the biggest most baddest gang in the world".'[27] The corresponding article is far more nuanced than its title suggests but many readers might not even get that far. 'When I was in the EDL, I never read the story in the paper. I only ever read the headline,' ex-EDL Regional Organiser Ivan Humble admits. He agrees that negative coverage of Muslim communities by media outlets such as the *Daily Mail* or the *Sun* adds to the problem. Stories of victims and demons decrease empathy and reinforce prejudices, ultimately providing the fuel for identity politics.

'How do you feel when you see these kind of stories?' I ask Mohammed, a 22-year-old Muslim history student based in London.

'Outraged and annoyed – how can they lie about me, put me in a category and define me as someone I'm not? It's also scary because the people develop this deep hatred against people like me, my friends and my family.'

This is why Richard Peppiatt drafted an open letter to *Daily Star* editor Richard Desmond in March 2011.[28] Starting with the words 'you probably don't know me, but I know you', the young journalist's letter accused his then boss of encouraging 'inciteful instead of insightful' reporting. Calling the now-imprisoned Islamist hate preacher Anjem Choudary 'to see if he fancied pulling together a few lines about whipping drunks or stoning homosexuals' was nothing unusual, he reports.[29]

When media outlets sensationalise jihadist terrorist attacks and demonise entire communities, they inadvertently work in tandem with extremists. 'Terrorists don't think like army generals; they think like theatre producers', Harari wrote in a piece for the *Guardian*.[30] Irresponsible media could be seen as the theatre that hosts and sells the tickets for the plays written by terrorists. Meanwhile, the public watching the spectacle urge politicians into going on stage to join the play, acting in accordance with the terrorists' scripts. Whenever this happens, it means a happy end for the terrorists.

The Perceptual Gap

Terrorism is 'under-reported', Trump claimed in February 2017 and released a list of 87 supposed terrorist attacks to support his statement.[31] Riddled with errors and inconsistencies, 'the list proved to be a bit of a fail', a US-based terrorism expert tells me. Trump was right about one thing though: some types of terrorism are underreported: far-right terrorism, for instance. Most attacks motivated by far-right ideologies are smaller in scale than those of their Islamist extremist counterparts. Yet, even bigger incidents such as the Munich shooting, which killed nine people in July 2016, lost the label 'terrorist' as soon as it became clear that the perpetrator had not acted in the name of Islam. Accusing the media of deliberately keeping the public in the dark about jihadist attacks is not new. Breivik kept far more comprehensive lists of what he called 'Islamic terror attacks against non-Islamic civilisations' in his manifesto. He complained about the lack of global terrorism databases for jihadist attacks and the 'multi-culturalist' media's reluctance to comprehensively report on what he called 'jihadi genocides against Christians'.[32]

If Anders Breivik has been watching the news from his high-security cell just outside Oslo, he's probably done so with much satisfaction. Although right-wing terrorist attacks are more frequent, political violence related to Islamist extremism is covered far more extensively by the media than far-right incidents. Terrorism perpetrated by Muslims receives an excessive and disproportionate amount of attention. Attacks committed by Muslims receive around 4.5 times more news coverage than other attacks in the US, a 2017 study found.[33] 'Headlines can mislead. The main terrorist threat in the United States is not from violent Muslim extremists, but from right-wing extremists. Just ask the police', American terrorism experts Charles Kurzmann and David Schanzer stressed in the *New York Times* in 2015.[34]

Intuitive public reactions to the Quebec mosque shooting in January 2017 exposed how the media's sensationalisation of jihadist attacks and inconsistent use of language have manipulated our minds into automatically linking the label 'terrorism' to 'Muslim'. Likewise, social media users instantly associated the words 'Allahu Akbar' (or 'God is great') with violent action rather than a peaceful expression of faith. The levels of inaccurate and premature reporting, which were – mildly put – astonishing, did not help. Right-wing media outlets such as Fox News and alt-right activists such as blogger Pamela Geller jumped to the rash conclusion that the attack was committed by a Moroccan Muslim, who found himself in the midst of a frenzy, subjected to vast negative media attention and online accusations. But after many twists, the Arab man arrested turned out to be a witness rather than a perpetrator and the only man charged for the shooting was white 27-year-old nationalist Alexandre Bissonnette.

Despite the extensive evidence of the increasing number of far-right attacks and the prevalence of far-right groups, terrorism of this kind is often not labelled as such and receives less attention from the media. It is true that in many cases far-right terrorists demonstrate lower levels of coordination and preparation than their jihadi counterparts. As a result, right-wing violence is often overlooked or dismissed as less menacing and less newsworthy. The unorganised and often amateurish nature of right-wing hate crimes and terrorist attacks has, however, not made them less dangerous. The Extremist Criminal Database counts 38 Islamist extremist and 177 far-right extremist homicide events between 1990 and 2014.[35] European terrorism follows a similar pattern: between 2000 and 2014, right-wing attacks were responsible for 94 deaths and 260 injuries across Europe. The Royal United Services Institute (RUSI) has declared it the number-one terrorist threat, warning that right-wing terrorist plots, often carried out by self-starters, are particularly hard to detect and pre-empt.[36]

The media, and consequentially politicians and the general public, tend to downplay right-wing attacks by framing them as isolated acts committed by mentally ill loners.[37] The risk of far-right terrorism is 'often ignored or underestimated because of the devastating impact of the 9/11 terrorist attacks', according to researchers at START.[38] Far-right perpetrators are frequently labelled as psychopaths rather than terrorists. For example, Breivik's first court-ordered forensic report diagnosed the man as having paranoid schizophrenia. When this led to widespread criticism, a second evaluation was conducted – its results were published just a few days before his trial. This latter report concluded that Breivik suffered from a narcissistic personality disorder and was in fact not in a psychotic condition before, during or after the attack.[39]

The man who attempted to mow down a crowd of worshippers in front of a mosque in the Parisian suburb of Créteil on 29 June 2017 was not declared a would-be terrorist. He was reported to have made 'confused references to the Bataclan attack' and was quickly declared schizophrenic.[40] A few days after this incident, two hooded men opened fire in front of a mosque in the French city of Avignon. injuring eight people including a seven-year-old girl.[41] Neither of the attacks received much coverage and the Community Against Islamophobia in France (Collectif contre l'Islamophobie en France) heavily criticised the 'euphemisms used to describe these kind of terrorist acts' in its press release.[42]

On the morning after Jo Cox's murder, there was a heated debate at Quilliam: endless email chains discussed the wording of a press release to condemn the incident. 'Let's call it terrorism,' some advocated. 'No, let's go for terrorist-inspired,' others argued. Half of the team had worked through the night to analyse the motives behind the attack; we knew it was technically terrorism. Although there is no universal definition of 'terrorism', most academics and policy makers agree that deliberate acts of violence aimed at provoking political change by instilling fear should be referred to as terrorism.[43] Thomas Mair's attack on Jo Cox clearly fell into this category: it was a deliberate, premeditated killing for a political cause. His bookshelves and web browsing history were filled with German military books and Nazi materials. The police even found books such as *SS Race Theory and Mate Selection Guidelines* and *The Politics of the Holocaust* as well as a *Daily Mail* news extract about Breivik's terrorist attack.[44] Yet some were petrified of labelling the attack 'terrorist' because no one had used the term yet. Had Mair shouted 'Allahu Akbar' instead of 'Britain First', the word 'terrorism' would have been in the headlines of all newspapers on the next morning.[45] When our press release was finally published, we were indeed the first voice to call the incident an 'act of nationalist far-right terrorism'. Several media outlets followed suit and the *Telegraph* wrote that Quilliam 'does not mince its words'.[46]

Far-right political violence is one of the most underestimated forms of political violence. A combination of insufficient empirical basis, limited academic interest and political neglect has led to widespread ignorance concerning the threat of far-right terrorism.[47] Coupled with the hesitancy to classify far-right political violence as terrorism, many right-wing attacks do not receive enough attention to be publicised. This reinforces the disproportionate understanding of its prevalence. The vast gap between reality and perception has resulted in wrong policies and threat assessments of far-right radicalisation.[48] Right-wing extremist groups have grown and become normalised in contemporary society. Their influence on everyday political debate has substantially increased; the tabloidisation of their discourse makes it favourable and digestible for the general public.[49] This has allowed both far-right parties and militant groups to thrive in Europe and the larger Western world.[50]

'America will kill you all Muslim cockroaches', one Twitter user wrote before his account was blocked and his tweet removed. It is not surprising that disproportionate demonisation and fearmongering provoke and reinforce binary worldviews and apocalyptic visions of far-right and Islamist extremists. The comments sections of Breitbart stories prove this all too well. In reaction to the beheading of German hostage Jürgen Kantner by Abu Sayyaf militants, one reader commented: 'Should be compulsory viewing for all Germans. They need to be desensitised. Ready for when Islamic raping moves on to the next stage – plan B – in Germany. Beheading. It's coming.' A few hours later all explicit graphic materials and videos disappeared from the Surface Web. Cyber-security officers have become much faster at removing raw footage and graphics of violence. 'This webpage is unavailable to your geographic region at the request of your government', a pop-up tells me, as I try to access the raw footage on ZeroCensorship.com.

But there is a dilemma here, Charlie Beckett warns. "If mainstream media doesn't articulate some of the public's anger, in a funny way that can actually foster it. When those who are angry feel that their views are not being represented by the media, they become more conspiratorial and seek refuge in more extremist sources.' Indeed: 'Plot twist, the U.S. funds Isis, the US did 9/11', one 4chan user claims soon after the shutdown in the discussion group on Jürgen Kantner's execution.[51] The perception that 'mainstream' politicians and 'mainstream' media are complicit in keeping 'the truth' from the public has fostered a sense of censorship and prompted societies to question everything and everyone, including facts and experts.

Alternative Facts

'This was the largest audience ever to witness an inauguration, period', Trump's former Press Secretary Sean Spicer wrongly claimed in his first White House briefing. Presidential counsellor Kellyanne Conway's comment that 'he gave alternative facts' set the internet on fire. The hashtag #alternativefacts trended for hours, if not days, following her interview on 22 January 2017. Social media users flooded the Twittersphere with memes and comments such as 'The moon is a big pizza pie. period! #alternativefacts'. Spicer's claim even prompted award-winning designers to create a card game entitled *Alternative Facts*, to be played by two or more 'legal US citizens',[52] and inspired American actress Melissa McCarthy to embody Spicer in a surprise performance on the American comedy show *Saturday Night Live*, which instantly went viral. The *New York Times* adopted the slogan 'No alternatives, just facts' to advertise its subscription offers.

The Trump administration's attitude towards facts as comparable to the weather forecast was good news for political satire and creative memes. But it was also illustrative of today's return from logos to mythos. In times of crisis, we often turn back to seeking salvation in the supra-natural, spiritual and divine rather than the earthy and scientific. Human beings are not inherently rational animals. Our ability to think rationally may distinguish us from other animals but it requires an active decision to make use of these rational thinking capacities – Aristotle never said otherwise.[53] 'A lot of people enjoy the false stuff', was the conclusion reached at a fake news event of the London-based meeting point for journalists, the Frontline Club. Simple explanations and straightforward solutions can provide comfort, even if these are based on lies. Extremists have exploited this: their narratives are often based on a mixture of real stories and invented or exaggerated details, resulting in half-truths and conspiracy theories. For American historian Darren Mulloy, the appeal of conspiracy theories is obvious: 'they offer certainty in an uncertain world'.[54]

Extremists' strategy is to devalue the entire concept of truth. Facts are presented as partisan, as part of the corrupted system and directed by the elites. Heightening mistrust and cynicism towards mainstream media is a good start for that.[55] Both far-right and Islamist extremists rub their hands at Trump's open war with the 'dishonest' and 'rigged' media. At one of Trump's campaign rallies in Pennsylvania an entire stadium full of 10,000 voters erupted in 'CNN sucks' chants.[56] Far-right leaders banned leading media outlets from reporting their 2016 Koblenz summit, accusing them of having 'failed to meet journalistic standards in past reporting'.[57] One of Al Muhajiroun's press releases speaks of a 'Western media crusade against Muslims' and accuses 'Kuffar sources' such as CNN and the BBC of spreading lies and misinformation.[58]

The public increasingly distrusts the fact-based media and turns to consulting alternative sources for information such as social media. 'The press is sitting on a trust time bomb', Jonathan Heawood, founder of the independent press regulator IMPRESS, told the *Guardian*.[59] According to an Ipsos MORI poll, only 25 per cent of the British public trusts journalists to tell the truth.[60] A similar study conducted by Gallup reveals that in the US, trust in the mass media has reached a historical low: less than a third of those polled expressed confidence in the press 'to report the news fully, accurately and fairly'. Since reaching its highest level at 72 per cent in 1976 thanks to extensive investigative journalism into the Watergate scandal and the Vietnam War, trust levels have declined gradually and steadily. The sudden drop in Republicans' trust in the media from 32 to 14 per cent over the past year is all the more remarkable.[61]

In an effort to exhibit impartiality, many big newspapers introduced fact checks. Yet, with less than 30 per cent of Americans trusting fact checks, even these find little resonance with the public.[62] Thirteen million people listen to radio talk show host Rush Limbaugh every week.[63] It is not hard to imagine the impact Limbaugh had when he told his listeners in September 2016 that fact checks were merely a vehicle 'to do opinion journalism under the guise of fairness'.[64] According to him, the *New York Times*, the *Washington Post* and *USA Today* all use the fact-checking technique to fool their readers. But he also has a loose relationship with truth. In 2015, Limbaugh gave his listeners a history lesson on migration that was based on invented facts, claiming that from 1924 to 1965 there was zero immigration in the US.[65]

Ultra-conservative news outlets have become so powerful within the widening right-wing echo chambers that people increasingly 'refuse to believe any news or opinion that wasn't vetted by the network', Bruce Bartlett, former advisor to both Presidents Ronald Reagan and George H. W. Bush, showed. When tested on general news knowledge, Fox News viewers score even lower than people who consume no news at all.[66] Bartlett called this the Fox News effect. Fox News remains the US's most watched news channel, Rush Limbaugh its most listened-to radio commentator and the *Sun* and the *Daily Mail* are Britain's most read newspapers. But as alt-right news sources like Breitbart News, which even finds Fox News too policed and moderate, are becoming more popular, the Fox News effect is accelerating further. The average age of Fox News viewers is now 68. Their younger audience is increasingly shifting to online news shows, which often have no fact checking at all. This has benefited extremists because it allows them to discredit all mainstream narratives and replace them with their own alternative facts and conspiracy theories.

What is it that leads entire strata of society to renounce mainstream news sources and instead believe in unbelievable hoax stories? Michael Fellner, who teaches 16-year-olds in the special programme *Teach for Austria*, has a theory: 'It's a mixture of ignorance and misinformation.' When Michael discussed the ongoing fighting in Mosul with his pupils, one of them told him: 'You cannot believe what they say, the media always lies.' As many of his pupils considered Austrian mainstream newspapers like *Die Presse* to be part of a global conspiracy against Muslims, they stopped consulting official news sources and resorted to information from their Facebook and WhatsApp groups instead. 'It's hard to get them to believe me because they are so disconnected from reality. Conspiracy theories are somehow the new currency.' For example, 9/11 was staged by Bush, and the Boston Marathon saw the conviction of the wrong people. As a result, 'they don't take a nuanced approach to politics any more', Michael tells me. The narrative 'H. C. Strache is a Nazi' quickly turns into a narrative of 'All Austrians are racist Islamophobics'.[67]

Ralph Keyes' book *The Post-Truth Era*[68] has gained almost prophetic value today. When he wrote in 2004 that the lines between true and false, reality and fiction, are becoming more blurred than ever, he did not know how right he would prove just a decade later. Post-factualism might indeed be one of the most defining features of our time. The campaigns in the run-up to both the Brexit referendum and the 2016 US presidential election have shown quite starkly that political rhetoric is no longer limited by a necessity to tell truth. Facts are presented as lies, untruth is presented as truth. Socrates' modes of persuasion don't apply any more. Who cares about logos and ethos? If you want to win an election today, you only have to appeal to the people's pathos. Even the UN has voiced concern over the rapid growth of alternative facts: in September 2016, their human rights chief Zeid Ra'ad Al Hussein called for action to stop 'demagogues and political fantasists' from using 'half-truths, manipulation and fear' as the basis for their campaigns.[69]

Both the Leave and the Remain camps used exaggeration, deception and bluffing. 'The UK can do nothing to stop Turkey joining the EU', Penny Mourdant, a Tory MP and then armed forces minister wrongly claimed in the run-up to the Brexit referendum.[70] Not only was Turkey far away from meeting all requirements in the EU's 35 defined policy areas; the UK would also have had the power to veto any accession claim.[71] Vote Leave repeatedly argued that EU membership cost Britain £350 million a week without taking into account the reductions before payment such as the UK rebate mechanism. Their campaign claims were deemed deceptive by independent bodies such as the UK Statistics Authority[72] and the Institute for Fiscal Studies.[73] Not only was the number based on wrong calculations – some may call this cheating – it was also used to feed another lie. While Vote Leave had decorated entire buses with the pledge that the equivalent amount would go to the NHS in the case of Brexit, Nigel Farage publicly admitted that this was 'a mistake' just hours after the vote.[74] For Trump, facts are not a priority either. Within his first few weeks in office, his administration mixed up Jean-Claude Juncker and Donald Tusk, conflated Iran with Yemen's Houthi rebels, confused the US and Saudi Arabia, misspelt Theresa May's name and referred to Malcolm Turnbull as Australian 'President' instead of 'Prime Minister'.

Political language has become more fluid and ambiguous too. Trump can claim that President Obama is 'the founder of ISIS'[75] and Boris Johnson can maintain that the EU forbids reusing teabags.[76] Objectively, these statements are false. The American journalist Nathan Heller called this *the collapse of public language*: 'to know what Trump means, despite the words that he is saying, you have to understand – or think you understand – the message before he opens his mouth'.[77] 'Trumpism', with all its 'Trumponyms', has become a dialect, but one that is widely understood. Trumpism does not require sophisticated syntax or fancy idioms. In fact, Trump might even purposefully avoid them. Simplistic language has become one of his most successful political tools. Linguistic analyses of Trump speeches show that his active vocabulary barely exceeds that of a primary-school pupil.[78] His linguistic minimalism appeals to a wide audience precisely because it is *per se* a political statement. This is playing to his advantage because it reinforces the image that he paints of himself: he is on the side of the people, using their language rather than that of the elites.[79]

The use of basic-level cognition helps Trump to create concrete images in the heads of his audience. He conveys his messages on an emotional rather than informative level; in this process facts become irrelevant. Instead of saying, 'Obama's action in the Middle East has contributed to the rise of Islamist terrorist groups', he simply claims, 'Obama was the founder of ISIS.' The effect of this rhetoric is immediate and powerful: the creation of images makes words appear real, regardless of whether they are accurate or not.[80] In

Politics and the English Language, George Orwell warned of the dangerous political implications that inaccurate public statements can have: imprecise language prevents us from thinking clearly and makes us reproduce 'foolish thoughts'.[81]

But Trump's untrue statements go beyond negligence and inaccurate language. Telling lies has become part of his standard operating procedures: Hillary Clinton, he claimed, was drugged in the second presidential debate and regularly goes to secret meetings with international banks 'to plot the destruction of US sovereignty', while climate change is a hoax created by China. Even Trump's central campaign topic of migration was drawing on a lie: the lie that migration is a problem in the US. In fact, the country's illegal immigration has been stable since 2009 and the number of illegal immigrants entering the US each year is offset by the number of illegal immigrants who are deported.[82] Once in office, he went on to deploy an arsenal of wrong numbers, half-truths and flawed logic to defend the immigration ban, and he invented attacks in Bowling Green and in Sweden that never took place.

At the dawn of the Cold War, US Senator Joseph McCarthy levelled wild accusations and groundless allegations against his political opponents before Trump could pronounce his first words. George W. Bush made misleading and exaggerated statements after 9/11. Yet today's level of conspiracism, scaremongering and lying within the ranks of high-profile politicians is unprecedented. Is Trump mimicking Putin's strategy of obfuscation? By polluting the entire space with lies and misinformation he can make up his own reality, suggested Pulitzer-prize-winning historian Anne Applebaum.[83] Everyone who wants to succeed in his world has to pretend his lies are true. The more people are playing by his rules, the more Trump's lies become a collectively imagined reality. Untrue things enter the public discourse and become true for hundreds of millions of people. Enough people believe them or want to believe them. Many only hear what they want to hear, some just don't care and others even seek the tone of conspiracy. The narrative that Clinton has a secret agenda became mainstream in the run-up to the elections and 43 per cent of Republicans still believe that Obama is a Muslim.[84]

Websites such as Infowars, the platform headed by conspiracy theory mastermind Alex Jones, provide the basis for self-sustaining news circles of alternative facts. These are then recycled in far-right echo chambers, for example by the Daily Stormer, which considers itself 'The World's Most Visited Alt-Right Website'. Citations from *Mein Kampf* are as common as discussion of whether National Socialist speeches make for a better German-language learning tool than Duolingo and Rosetta Stone. 'LEARN GERMAN THE FUN AND EASY WAY WITH DR. GOEBBELS! "Das Volk" is the NS term currently under discussion by our work group', the headline of one discussion reads.[85] In May 2016, Stormfront's founder Andrew Anglin announced that the website's traffic had doubled over the previous six months. A few months later, he successfully mobilised his followers to register for the 'IRL [In Real Life] Troll Army AKA the Stormer Book Club' to prepare for 'the coming race war'.[86] By the end of 2016 the page had reached over 120,000 daily visitors, surpassing even Stormfront, the web's first hotspot for racial hate, in page views.

Stormfront was founded by former member in 1995. In many European countries, such as France, Germany and Italy, the neo-Nazi webpage is not listed in Google Index. The page is to the militant far right what Telegram is to ISIS. As in ISIS Telegram channels, it is hard to spend more than a few hours in the platform's forums without reading apocalyptic race war prophecies and explicit calls to violence. In fact, the page even has a category called 'Race War', along with 'Jewish Problem'. Unlike with Twitter, inflammatory posts are rarely taken down. This is where neo-Nazis meet the militant alt-right; this is where anti-Semitism fuses with anti-Muslim hatred. It's where a benign Trump supporter may come across a KKK recruiter.

This is where I meet Cathy. Cathy is inexperienced, having only been active on Stormfront for a few weeks, but says she has already made some good online friends. She likes that she can say and comment on whatever she wants in the 'community of racial realists and idealists' without being judged for it. She had felt lonely and misunderstood by many people in her community. 'I like that everyone's honest here … I've really had enough of all this political correctness.' Cathy has lost all faith in traditional media outlets, which all have their own political agenda and fail to report the truth. 'We are constantly kept in the dark. Imagine how much we actually don't know. The way the German media covered up for these immigrant rapists proved that', she writes, referring to the

2015 New Year's sexual assaults in Cologne. Several German media outlets failed to report the incidents, resulting in a huge social media frenzy that reinforced the idea of 'Lügenpresse' (literally, lying press), a term first coined by the Nazis.

As social media and blog pages increasingly replace conventional information sources, 'disinformation, hateful language or horrific images […] encourage the creation of outgroups, reinforcing the categorical thinking that pushes an extremist to take action towards others', finds a case study on the effects of Geert Wilders' rhetoric.[87] It is often when facts meet fiction that narratives turn into conspiracies and meeting grounds turn into battlegrounds.

Fake News

On YourNewsWire.com it is hard to distinguish between facts and fiction. The substance of the webpage's section 'news' is similar to that of its section 'conspiracy'. Headlines like 'New 9/11 Evidence: CIA Built Remote-Controlled Passenger Jets' and 'NATO spy behind the assassination of Russian Ambassador to Turkey' feature under 'News'.[88] Under 'Conspiracies' one would find articles claiming that the CIA and Mossad were behind a Washington DC paedophile ring[89] and the 2017 best picture Oscar was given to *Moonlight* to avoid a race war. Needless to say that YourNewsWire and Infowars cooperate closely on these stories. Yet even YourNewsWire concedes that some of their claims are a little peculiar, which is why they created an entire category entitled 'Weird'. 'Queen Elizabeth Reveals She is Ready to Flee Britain' can be found there, for example.[90] The rest of it reads like a mixture of *Harry Potter*, *Alien* and *The Terminator*: 'Real Life "Dementor" Appears in Africa, Terrifying Residents' is seen next to '"Real" Alien Selfie Results In 4Chan Being Taken Offline', while apparently 'Photos "Prove" Donald Trump is Time Traveller John Titor'. Sean Adl-Tabatabia, the editor in chief of the website, claims that he has been 'speaking truth to power since he learned to talk'. His motto is 'live without fear'. For someone who believes in a world that was created by aliens and is governed by the CIA and Mossad, this seems rather appropriate.

Sean's YourNewsWire is just one out of an emerging arsenal of webpages that circulate misinformation and false stories, often universally labelled as 'fake news'. BuzzFeed's Craig Silverman defines fake news as 'completely false information that was created for financial gain', while lies and myths created for ideological or political reasons are propaganda. 'Fake news is not state-sponsored disinformation, bad reporting, a news story you don't like or ideologically-driven news that goes against your views', he writes.

Since lies and hoaxes have turned out to sell better than the truth, the wild invention of facts has increasingly become a business.[91] Entrepreneurs have made money off the generation of fake news that attracts lots of clicks, using online advertising networks such as Google AdSense. A BuzzFeed investigation found that a group of teens in Macedonia was running more than 100 pro-Trump websites that spread fake news. 'Yes, the info in the blogs is bad, false, and misleading but the rationale is that if it gets the people to click on it and engage, then use it', one of the students who had started a US politics site told BuzzFeed.[92] The emerging fake news market has given rise to a new market niche: the identification of fake news. First Draft is a leading verification agency that works with Facebook and Google to tackle everything from commercially incentivised hoax production to politically motivated conspiracy theories and trolling. But there are also 'fake' fake news checkers. For example, the webpage Fakenewschecker.com claims to expose fake news stories, using the Daily Stormer as one of its primary sources.[93]

The line between misinformation and deliberately fabricated falsities is thin. New media has enabled computer-savvy people and people-savvy computers to manipulate contents and online users at whim. We recognise, verify and make sense of information by comparing it to lists of previous experiences in our memory. We can tell that something is an apple because we have seen apples before; because we have memorised the concept 'apple'.[94] In today's increasingly fast-paced, complex and globalised world, our brains are often left with neither access to complete information nor adequate means of comparison.

In the virtual space, our ability to compare received information with reality has been particularly limited, making it hard to distinguish between facts and fiction. When ISIS releases utopian images of smiling, soccer-playing kids, vibrant markets and crowded streets on Islamic State territory,[95] it is hard to know whether these places really exist, as most people will never know what war-torn Raqqa looks like. Likewise, when the Pentagon commissions a British PR firm to produce fake 'Al Qaeda' videos for half a billion dollars, no one who doesn't coincidentally sit in an investigative journalism bureau would even have the means to uncover the lie.[96]

Anti-establishment movements – often in the form of populist and extremist groups – have exploited information gaps, filling them with lies and half-truths that suit their narrative and support their conspiracy theories. The alt-right and Nordic nationalists have been especially good at trolling, subversion and media manipulation, according to Charlie Beckett. 'They use bots to retweet their stories, which then shoot up in rankings and are more likely to get attention in search engines and on social media,' he tells me. Like terrorists, they are attention seekers and instigators of chaos. 'We should also go back to rule 1 of trolling. Like terrorism, it's all about prompting an overreaction from your adversary,' Joshua Stewart explains. 'When done properly and *en masse*, it can amount to something like a digital nuke.'

The effects of some of these efforts have gone beyond imagination. In 2015, students were forced to halt their protest against racism at the University of Missouri. The Daily Stormer's Andrew Anglin had miraculously managed to manipulate them into believing that 'KKK has been confirmed to be sighted on campus', using the hashtag #PrayForMizzou. Thousands of Twitter users, including the university's student body president Payton Head, shared the invented story.[97] In December 2016, a man opened fire in the Washington pizza restaurant Comet Ping Pong because he believed the so-called 'Pizzagate' conspiracy theory.[98] Three weeks later, Pakistan's defence minister threatened to go nuclear after reading a fake news piece about Israel.[99]

These examples show: it does not matter whether stories are real or fake. Ideas can become reality once enough people believe in them – this is the #Mosul effect. Not only ISIS masters it; the far right does too.

The explosion of new media has turned blogs, vlogs and social media into primary news sources. Google, Facebook and Twitter are struggling to keep the spread of fake news stories via their platforms under control. But this turns out to be a Sisyphean task. Clinton won the popular vote. By 15 November 2016, she had received 770,000 votes more than Trump. Yet, over the weekend after the elections, the myth that Trump was ahead of Clinton by 700,000 votes was circulated on the internet. When users typed 'final election results' on Google the first website that appeared was 70news.[100] 'Trump won both popular and electoral college votes', the website (wrongly) claimed. After readjusting its algorithm, Google apologised for the error but the damage was done – thousands of people had shared the wrong numbers.

In August 2016, Facebook fired up to 26 human editors to replace them with robots. It took only two days until stories such as 'Breaking: Fox News Exposes Traitor Megyn Kelly, Kicks Her Out for Backing Hillary' started trending.[101] In September 2016, a Facebook post that wrongly claimed that Pope Francis had expressed support for Trump was shared over a million times.[102] Two days prior to the elections, the invented headline 'FBI AGENT SUSPECTED IN HILLARY EMAIL LEAKS FOUND DEAD IN APPARENT MURDER-SUICIDE' was circulated on Facebook, purportedly reported by the *Denver Guardian*, a newspaper that doesn't even exist.[103]

Facebook now reaches almost two billion people each month. Sixty-two per cent of US adults get news from social media, 44 per cent of those use Facebook as a primary news source, according to a poll conducted by the Pew Research Center.[104] In an attempt to reassure the public, Mark Zuckerberg posted that 'of all the content on Facebook, more than 99 per cent of what people see is authentic'. To cut down on fake news, Facebook had launched a tool in early 2015 that enables users to report hoax stories and spam posts.[105] The social network is also part of a coalition with Twitter, Google and traditional news outlets that committed itself to tackling the spread of fake news.[106] Yet a BuzzFeed study[107] of six hyper-partisan political pages on Facebook found that 19 per cent of extreme left posts and 38 per cent of extreme right posts contained wrong information. Articles that were based on fake news were furthermore shared more often than others. Instead of fulfilling its mission statement of 'connecting people', Facebook's biased algorithms threaten to further exacerbate political polarisation.

Facebook accounts for 50 per cent of fake news traffic, according to Jonathan Albright, an award-nominated journalist and researcher in fake news and hashtags. But much of Facebook's fake contents is organically 'seeded' rather than promoted. This means that tackling the problem with algorithms alone will be difficult. Albright found that strategic micro-targeting and emotional manipulation were the number-one force behind the dissemination of misinformation during the 2016 US elections. When typing in 'Why Brexit Won' an Infowars article would feature on top of both Google's and Facebook's organic ('top public posts') results.[108] This has given rise to new, data-driven election PR strategies.[109]

'WE NEED TO REACH THE NORMIES', says a Google Doc called 'Make Everything Great Again (MEGA)'.[110] The document was circulated in pro-far-right chat groups in 2016. It outlined a trolling master plan for manipulating the elections in Austria, the Netherlands, France and Germany. The administrator of the chatroom, 'The Great Liberation of France', called on French and Francophone users to get involved 'so it looks authentic, not just like Americans trying to take the Trump Train to Europe'.[111] His goal was to make Le Pen appear the most credible candidate. The plan was to create chaos on social media by infiltrating Facebook pages and news comments sections and flooding them with memes, jokes and rumours. Fake accounts should ideally be 'young, cute girl, gay, Jew, basically anyone who isn't supposed to be pro-[FN]', he explained.

What are the consequences of this post-factualism? 'Post-truthfulness builds a fragile social edifice based on wariness. It erodes the foundation of trust that underlies any healthy civilization', wrote Ralph Keyes.[112] Apple CEO Tim Cook expressed concern that clicks-driven fake news might be 'killing people's minds'.[113] The executive producer of *Democracy Now*, Amy Goodman, went further, warning that it may even cost people's lives. 'When the media acts as a conveyor belt for liars it matters because liars take lives', she said in the documentary *Truth, Deception, and the Spirit of I.F. Stone*.[114]

Fake news fans the flames of extremism. Post-factualism in conjunction with rising fears has created the perfect conditions for extremists to thrive. As the OECD has warned, the brainwashing effects of fake news make young people more vulnerable to radicalisation. The inability to distinguish what's wrong from what's right is exacerbated on social media, where users increasingly live in bubbles.[115]

Inside the Bubble

Facebook uses algorithms that prioritise updates that users find pleasant.[116] This is done to maximise the time people spend on the platform. As a result, social media users remain increasingly within their own echo chambers. Users follow people with similar interests and attitudes, while social media platforms are algorithmically programmed to show tweets and posts automatically based on assumed interests. The vanishing trust in fact-based media is conducive to the expansion of extremist echo chambers, which turn their members into prisoners through 'self-brainwashing'.[117]

Echo chambers have an amplification effect on extremism. Social psychologists found in experiments that group attitudes tend to become more extreme in the course of group discussions, resulting in so-called 'group extremity shifts'.[118] This can lead more people to hop on to the bandwagon of extremists.[119] The anonymity that users enjoy in online communities exacerbates this effect by reducing social constraints and inhibitions. The American cyber psychologist John Suler explained that people tend to be nastier in remote communication than they would be in real life because of 'toxic disinhibition'.[120]

But bubbles don't just have a filter function; they also act as support networks. Extremists have successfully established international alliances – against the immigrants, against the Crusaders, against the 'Islamisation of the West', against the 'Westernisation of Islam'. For this reason, extremists tend to be better at connecting with each other than moderates. The US political establishment lives in its enclosed DC bubble, its British equivalent in the Westminster bubble and EU bureaucrats in their Brussels bubble. There is a bubble for almost everyone: the bankers bubble in the City, the entrepreneur bubble in Silicon Valley, the #Gamergate bubble on 8 Chan.

Extremist networks have become increasingly international. New media has made it easier for members of extremist groups and movements to connect through their shared perceived victimhood that is tied to a common identity – be it on the basis of race, religion, political affiliation or class. Hizb ut-Tahrir has offshoots in almost every country, its members are united through their common narrative and vision. Likewise, ISIS and Al Qaeda's communication networks reach into every corner of the world. The same is true for the far-right networks: Gates of Vienna, Atlas Shrugs, Jihad Watch, FrontPage Mag, Breitbart and Français de Souche exchange information and share each other's stories globally.[121]

When Pamela Geller shares her anti-Muslim thoughts on Facebook she doesn't have to wait long until her post is liked, commented on and shared hundreds of times. Top influencers like her can make a story circulate in their echo chambers within a matter of minutes. While mainstream politicians and moderate commentators are struggling to enhance their online fellowship, the profile pages of extremists are flourishing and their echo chambers widening.[122] The success of a tweet depends entirely on its re-tweetability. Extremists' fake news feeds and inflammatory statements just attract more young people who look for exciting content worth sharing. The diplomatic, often unemotional, statements of moderates look lame compared to this.

In December 2016, the Islamist extremist organisation Die Wahre Religion ('The True Religion'), which was banned and disbanded by the German government in November 2016, could count 165,423 likes on Facebook. This is more than the national account of the governing Christian Democratic Union of Germany reaches.[123] With over 330,000 followers, Tommy Robinson's Twitter account has attracted almost as many followers as British Prime Minister Theresa May's. With more than 1 million Facebook likes, Marine Le Pen has a bigger social media audience than former president François Hollande and his former prime minister Manuel Valls combined.[124] In the UK, the online popularity of extremist groups increased substantially following events such as the election of London's first Muslim mayor Sadiq Khan, Jo Cox's murder and the Brexit vote.[125]

But this is just the tip of the iceberg. As Twitter has shut down 235,000 accounts deemed as Islamist extremist over the course of 2016,[126] most members of the more violent extremist organisations have moved to encrypted messaging apps. 'We are now starting to shut down far-right accounts as well,' a Twitter representative tells me in the autumn of 2016.[127] As a result of the social media crackdown on extremists, it is becoming increasingly hard to get into their echo chambers.

The 4Chan's forum 'pol/ – Politically Incorrect' is what the Daily Stormer describes as the Ground Zero of the alt-right. Anonymous users here may exchange conspiracy theories and chat about the end of the world. Apocalyptic predictions are met with responses such as:

> I've got 2000 rounds of 5.56 and 2000 rounds of 9mm. I keep thinking 'Man, I should get more ammo', but then I realize how fucking long it'd take me to burn through 4000 rounds. If I was in a firefight, I could only carry maybe a few hundred rounds total. So like 200rds 5.56 and 100rds 9mm. Anything more than that would slow me down.

Those people who do spend their days infiltrating online extremist platforms tend to keep a low profile. Susan is a terror intelligence analyst and a professional hacker who works with the US military. But if you ask for her profession, she will say she is a cyber-security expert. What she actually does is track down and dismantle ISIS recruiters and monitor their sympathisers. 'IS members, supporters and affiliates use anti-Muslim sentiments to their advantage in propaganda, although it's not as prominent or useful to them as the consequences of airstrikes on civilians, for example.' By propaganda she means the propaganda that is circulated all over the web primarily produced by their unofficial media outlets and random supporters.

Extremist online communities move fast, as their members are avid aggregators of current events. They often respond to articles and headlines and other events faster than the people who work in national security or journalism. And as a result, something might be useful to their propaganda goals in a headline or a statement made by someone and they may write little blurbs on Telegram or Facebook or Twitter, 'but it's often just a blip because quickly they are onto the next thing – the lifespan of any potency is pretty short,' says Susan. Some of the people who work on unofficial ISIS channels also work for more 'official' media outlets, according to her. 'It's just much more informal and they aren't physically located in ISIS-controlled territory.' They only issue new links to channels periodically throughout the day, which are active for 30 minutes to an hour, during which time you can join before the link dies.

Extremist propagandists spend an exorbitant amount of time online. Susan watches them closely. 'On the Western-oriented ISIS side, many extremists gravitated to the online community because of the isolation they felt in real life, whether as a result of discrimination or a host of other factors depending on the individual,' she says. The people they meet online become their friends and most active supporters. 'I honestly don't know how they would find the time to have friends in real life given the amount of time they spend on social media. The sense of community is something fierce though. In my opinion, that is at the heart of the struggle we face.'

Twitter accounts and Telegram channels led by ISIS supporters have a short life cycle, of course. The more obvious accounts get shut down quickly and often. @RasslerFred, for example, joined Twitter less than 24 hours ago. When I access his account, half of the content and links he shared are already taken down. It's only a matter of time until his Twitter profile is entirely taken down. He is aware of that – within 12 hours he fired out more than 60 tweets, most of them linking to official ISIS propaganda videos and press releases.

The account called @ThatCoffeeTho seems to be an exception. It has existed since 2012, has 14,000 tweets and 7,785 followers. I'm not surprised to recognise some familiar Islamist faces among its most active followers: Mohammed Rao for example. Initially I assume that Twitter has kept the account open for monitoring purposes. Yet a few hours after I flag it to them, it is taken down. There are too many accounts popping up on a regular basis for Twitter to avoid missing some. Clearly coffee was not a bad cover. The profile picture and cover were as innocent as the name sounded: espresso cups and the coffee beans. Ironically enough, drinking coffee is considered an offensive act (*makrooh*) by many Islamic scholars. The profile only looks innocent until you scroll down to see the content. A mixture of posts about Mosul war atrocities and Islamophobia in Western countries, coupled with messages in support of ISIS, awaits the reader.

I also catch @akhi_anon before his account is shut down. He knows that he doesn't have much time. Within less than one hour of opening the account he fires out 645 tweets but they are all taken down instantly. Like many other extremists, he is good at hijacking trending hashtags such as #Florida, #myvote2016, #ThankObamaIn4Words, #NotMyPresident, #WhatsNext. Posts from both @ThatCoffeeTho and @akhi_anon often combine right-wing hashtags or news of anti-Muslim crimes with a link to official ISIS propaganda, such as their Khilafah News #DailyReport. For example, @akhi_anon shared the picture of a fallen ISIS fighter adding the hashtags #NotMyPresident #FoxNewsUS.

According to Carl Miller, two trends can be observed in extremist echo chambers: on the one hand, social media algorithms drive their members further apart on a daily basis, effectively limiting their exposure to cross-cutting content.[128] On the other hand, there are irregular spikes in their interaction when something happens that penetrates both echo chambers. After extremism-related events, both far-right and Islamist extremists tend to quote the same sources, use similar hashtags, and even reference each other in their posts. For example, in the aftermath of terrorist attacks or hate crimes, Twitter often becomes a place of direct confrontation between members of different echo chambers.[129] Often extremists' echo chambers do not engage directly with each other but talk about the other extreme to a third party, the potential support base.[130]

In short, one extreme's echo chambers echoes the other side's echo chamber. That's a lot of echoing. In the end, all of them are prisoners caught within the boundaries of their increasingly segregated online and offline space. Our increasingly interconnected and globalised world has not necessarily widened our cultural horizon. It has also given rise to global echo chambers that are reserved for people of a specific race, religion or sex. Over time, the victimhood narratives spread by extremists within such echo chambers have been carved deeper and deeper into stone, changing our global political landscape. Increasingly, widespread confusion about the reliability of information helps extremists spread their conspiracy theories that are designed to denounce 'the other' as well as the ruling elites.

6

Escalating Extremes

SASCHA L. IS A FORMER NEO-NAZI TURNED SUSPECTED WOULD-BE ISLAMIST terrorist.[1] In 2013, he warned that native German people were 'dying a creeping death', uploaded an anti-migrant video entitled 'tips for fighting cockroaches' and urged German non-Muslims not to make friends with Muslims: 'Even a dog knows where it belongs to – and where do you belong to? Don't be sillier than a dog and save the German race from going extinct!'[2] But in 2014 he converted to Islam himself and went from drawing forbidden swastikas to spreading the forbidden Islamic State flag on the internet. His story, of course, calls to mind that of Joshua Goldberg, the artist who posed as a neo-Nazi, a violent jihadist and a radical feminist all at once because he liked the thought that his ideas would give him power.[3]

The consequences of Joshua's tweets as ISIS-supporting 'Australi Witness' were bad enough: he was accused of having encouraged the attack on a Muhammad caricature contest in Texas in May 2015.[4] But unlike Joshua, Sascha L. was not trolling at any point. In February 2017, he was arrested for planning to bomb German security forces, and chemicals used to create explosives were found in his flat in Lower Saxony. To him, being a Muslim meant being a radical Salafist who hates the West, both before and after his converting to Islam. Even when going from one extreme to the other, Sascha L.'s worldview didn't change. 'Neo-Nazism and Salafism are comparable in their attractiveness to individuals in search for orientation and guidance: the overly simplistic dichotomous worldview of both reduces the societal complexity that the person may have experienced as overstraining,' Chief of Detectives at the Criminal Police Bureau in Bremen, Daniel Heinke, tells me. Both far-right and Islamist extremists believe in a monolithic, literalist and political Islam that is opposed to a culturally homogeneous West.

'Just as little is seen in pure light as in pure darkness', Hegel wrote in 1812.[5] In Hegelian dialectic,[6] contrast is the source of identity; yet the two polar opposites are identical. The perfect complementarity of the far right's view that 'Islam is at war with the West' and the Islamist extremists' narrative that 'the West is at war with Islam' reflects this unity of opposites. One allows the other to thrive. As they are telling the same stories, they reinforce and escalate each other.

Two Sides of the Same Coin

'Dirty kuffar', a jihadi rap video by Sheikh Terra (featuring Soul Salah Crew), has been downloaded to millions of computers since its release in 2004. The 'Dighad' logo that introduces the jihadi clip is identical to Combat 18's website logo – except that the swastika was removed.[7] While extremists' collective identity draws on the opposing side's rhetoric, the end product is strikingly similar. They are two sides of the same coin.

There are two Tommy Robinsons on Twitter. The first with the User ID @TRobinsonNewEra[8] is the founder of the EDL and PEGIDA UK. But the second Tommy Robinson with the User ID @Tommy_Robinsons[9] has created his parody profile entirely in reference to the real Tommy. Both profiles indicate Luton as their place of residence and use the cover of Tommy Robinson's book *Enemy of the State* as their background picture – the only difference is that the wrong Tommy wears a full beard and a green prayer cap.[10] The second Tommy also replaced the poppy seed in the corner with a Pakistan flag. 'We must unite to fight Christianism. Fight against Christian Paedo's like Jimmy Savile & Rolf Harris & against Democratic Terrorists bombing the Middle East', reads his Twitter bio, mirroring Tommy's anti-Muslim rhetoric. His Twitter feed is filled with posts about 'white American terrorists', 'secular liberal paedophiles' and 'gay terrorists'.

'Hi @TRobinsonNewEra; did you know that you have a doppelgänger on Twitter?' I ask, without expecting an answer since Tommy devoted an entire chapter in his autobiography to criticising Quilliam's 'belief in moderate Muslims' and insulting some of my former colleagues as 'squealing morons' and 'cheeky bastards'. But he replies, nicely. He wasn't aware of his doppelgänger account, he admits later over the phone.[11] 'I wonder why someone would do that.' So I ask the other Tommy, who is just as forthcoming and friendly. His primary goal was 'to make a point about racist rhetoric', he says, although he also found it funny to troll Tommy. He decided to open up the account to see how racism, hiding behind the socially more acceptable anti-Muslim bigotry and xenophobia, works. 'I watched what Tommy was doing and imitated him.' For Robinson, any crime committed by a brown-skinned person or with a Muslim name becomes a Muslim crime. 'I thought this was interesting, as why would you refer to criminals using their Muslim identity? Why would he stress the white identity of "Muslim gang" rape victims?' So the wrong Tommy Robinson replicated this with a gang of white paedophiles who were convicted of raping babies and titled it 'Christian paedophiles'.

Tommy's doppelgänger gives me a crash course on how he operates. 'It is not hard,' he tells me. 'You pick an identity based on race, religion or sexual orientation, and associate every social ill and crime to that label. The label can be anything: "Black", "Jew", "Gay", "Asians", "Polish", "Irish".'

Demonisation on the basis of such labels is, of course, not a new phenomenon. 'GIANT NEGRO DISABLES 4 POLICEMEN IN FIGHT',[12] a *New York Times* headline from 1927 announced. 'The murderers of Germany' was the title of an article that warned of a Jewish conspiracy against Europe in a 1934 edition of the anti-Semitic newspaper *Der Stürmer*.[13] This is not the only parallel to today's extremist rhetoric. *Der Stürmer* labelled itself as the German weekly that is at the forefront 'in the fight for truth'. This notion of fighting for truth is something that modern-day far-right and Islamist extremists have in common. 'Tell the truth and fear no one', says the slogan of the neo-Nazi website Stormfront. Whether Hizb ut-Tahrir, ISIS, PEGIDA or neo-Nazis, 'truth' and 'falsehood' play a crucial role in both violent and non-violent extremists' rhetoric. The post-truth era where nobody trusts anyone increasingly inspires young people to turn to those who claim a monopoly over absolute truth, which in other words means extremists. 'You can continue to pretend that all is well, I will continue to tell the truth,' PEGIDA UK leader Anne Marie Waters tells me. Anne Marie's truth is that the word 'moderate Muslim' is an oxymoron. Her 15,000 Twitter followers all agree that Islam is an evil political ideology rather than an individual faith. 'NO SUCH THING AS MODERATE

MUSLIM', one of her followers rages as I question his conviction. Others would go as far as to view it as a disease that needs a cure. 'It's SAD and a shame they only understand VIOLENCE to cure.'

Waters and Tommy Robinson founded the UK offshoot of Germany's PEGIDA movement together. They make a good duo: while he tries to be the voice of the neglected white middle class, Anne Marie claims to champion women's rights and freedom of speech. Tony Davies, former professor at the University of Birmingham,[14] calls this phenomenon anti-humanist humanism. 'It is almost impossible to think of a crime that has not been committed in the name of human reason', Davies wrote in his book *Humanism*. For example, the German philosopher Martin Heidegger, who considered himself a humanist, inspired Nazi propaganda by applying the concept of humanism to the German race only.

Islamist extremists have also used the pretext of defending human rights to push their political agenda. CAGE is a self-declared human rights charity. But it is also known for glorifying Jihadi John as a 'beautiful young man'.[15] The members of the advocacy group, many of them former Guantanamo Bay prisoners, claim to protect Muslims from the crimes of the West and the global War on Terror. Like PEGIDA, the group may attract some constructive-minded individuals but it also appeals to a considerable number of militant extremists and conspiracy theorists. According to one of their more militant followers, Rehan, the West masterminded the bloodshed in Aleppo and used its allies to execute genocide against Muslims. In the same way that far-right extremists have twisted humanist values for their purposes, Islamist extremists have distorted Islam to fit their political agenda.

Ultimately, Rehan, Robinson and Waters all agree that the establishment has failed, badly, at protecting their identity group. 'People have had enough, they look for other options,' Robinson tells me. As a result, he opts for anti-Muslim hate groups, Rehan for a caliphate. After an hour over the phone Robinson's voice sounds impatient and exhausted. 'You know, I would be a Labour voter otherwise,' Tommy admits. And Waters might be a Lib Dem. The *ummah* must rely on a #Khilafah instead, Rehan says. 'Islam is not up for reform or negotiation – so we have no other choice than to fight it,' Tommy claims. Despite all these similarities, there is no room for dialogue; all of them prefer to talk at cross-purposes.

Extremism is not linear. The French philosopher Jean-Pierre Faye described the relationship between different forms of extremism as a horseshoe, where the far right and the far left sit on its ends, therefore being closer to each other than each are to the political centre. The theory also applies to far-right and Islamist extremists, who resemble each other more than they resemble the moderate middle. The two Tommy Robinsons provide a perfect metaphor for this connection between far-right and Islamist extremists. They demonstrate just how close is the rhetoric of their perfectly inverse narratives. Both Tommys portray themselves as enemies of the establishment and defenders of their respective identity group. They tell the same stories, just from different perspectives.

The same is true on the other side of the Channel. Pierre Conesa, former senior official at the French Ministry of Defence, wrote in 2015:

> The similarity between the National Front and Salafism is reflected in their founding myth that plots the French Nation against the Ummah. The parallels regarding their goal of excluding the other through fragmentation, their life philosophy and their set of convictions is striking. It is therefore surprising to see that the rise of the European far right is analysed in political debates, while the Salafist jihadist insurgency is only seen through a security lens, as if the two phenomena were not part of the same political process.[16]

Indeed, Islamist extremist and far-right thought even draws on common sources of inspiration. For example, the French doctor and biologist Alexis Carrel inspired two of modern history's most destructive forces: the Nazis and Al Qaeda. In his pseudo-scientific bestseller *L'homme, cet inconnu*,[17] which was published in 1935, the doctor argues that there is a form of 'hereditary biological aristocracy'. He suggests that suppressing 'deviant' human beings through voluntary eugenics can provide a solution to society's problems. It is widely known that this claim formed the intellectual basis for the pro-fascist Vichy Regime in France. What is much less widely known is that Carrel's biological-Christian study of human nature also fed into the doctrines of Al Qaeda's favourite Islamist ideologue Sayyid Qutb. In fact, there is no man that Qutb cites more often than the Vichy supporter Alexis Carrel.[18]

A look at the social media contents of today's far-right and Islamist extremist groups in Germany illustrates the similarities in their propaganda. In Berlin, I meet Götz Nordbruch, one of Germany's leading experts on Islamic youth cultures. He monitors Islamist extremist online contents as part of his work and knows their communication strategies inside out. 'Much of their rhetoric overlaps,' he tells me. Right-wing discourses often show clear parallels to Salafi ideology, as both are taking up issues such as globalisation, social and cultural diversity and international crises. In right-wing discourses, a return to the nation or the 'Volk' is presented as a solution for existing problems and concerns; in Salafi discourses, it is Islam and the global *ummah*.[19] Their topics, occasions and lines of argumentation are similar, if not identical. Hashtags such as #Kilafah, #jihad, #Islamophobia and #Trump are used on both sides. Islamist extremists prefer to combine it with #UmmahsDarkAges, #NoKilafahNoHonour, #MuslimsSalvageYourselves or #WarOnIslam, while the far right combines it with #BanIslam and #IslamIsTheProblem. There is a growing #Sharia4 and #NoSharia interaction and #kufr is used more often by the far right than by Islamist extremists nowadays.

Experiences of racism and discrimination are exploited in Islamist extremist propaganda and used to foster the narrative of 'Muslims are victims of a Western war against Islam'.[20] Germany's most famous Islamist extremist preachers have used attacks on refugee camps and anti-Muslim rhetoric of the right-wing party Alternative für Deutschland to justify their anti-West rhetoric. Germany's most prominent Salafi celebrities often use far-right crimes to push their own agendas. For example, Pierre Vogel (aka Abu Hamza) released a video in reaction to the murder of Egyptian Marwa Ali El-Sherbini that went viral.[21] In another of his videos, Pierre Vogel suggests that it is only a matter of time before there will be a genocide against Muslims. 'On the internet you find hundreds of posts that call on Germans to massacre Muslims and weirdly politicians are just watching.'[22]

Sven Lau, the German Muslim convert and former firefighter who went on to preach Islamist extremist doctrines, wrote an entire book about anti-Muslim hatred and discrimination that he encountered in Germany. 'Everyone speaks of the progress of tolerance that we achieved but where is the tolerance towards Islam?' he asks in *Fremd im Eigenen Land* ('Alien in My Own Country'). 'Camel jockeys, Stone Age men, hate preachers, terrorists, illiterates, and similar words are established terms of the 21st century.'[23] Repeatedly reading threats and hate posts like 'Only a dead Salafist is a good Salafist', 'Get out of Germany' and 'Traitor to the Fatherland! What shall we do with those? Imprison them for life and torture them until the bile comes out' made a lasting impression on him. 'Until today I ask myself why I cannot – or rather mustn't – be German in their eyes.'[24] Today, Sven is being tried for allegedly supporting and funding Jaish Al Mujahireen wal-Ansar (JAMWA), an Islamist group with direct links to ISIS.

Many far-right supporters reach the conclusion that 'Kuffarphobia' has to be fought and the #WhiteGenocide prevented by staging a #WhiteJihad. The banned British neo-Nazi group National Action even released a one-minute clip called 'The White Jihadi', which borrows communication elements from ISIS propaganda videos. It shows National Action members during a training session, practising their fighting skills in ISIS style. 'A war is brewing. It is inevitable. We are not the ones responsible for instigating it, but we will be the ones fighting it. And we fight,' one member says before the group performs a Nazi salute. 'The irony is that we actually need a jihad', one of their most prominent leaders, Kai Murras, claimed.[25]

Far-right and Islamist extremists have a long history of reciting and referring to each other. Breivik quoted Islamist extremist ideologues in his manifesto's extensive section 'Islam 101' in an attempt to show that all Muslims are evil and prove 'Muslim apologists' wrong. Over the past few years, references to xenophobia and anti-Muslim bigotry in Islamist extremist propaganda have increased sharply. In Germany, for example, Islamisches Erwachen has repeatedly referred to US police violence against Afro-Americans in their propaganda as an example of hate crimes committed by the West against minority communities. A turning point was the *Charlie Hebdo* attacks in Paris in January 2015, according to Götz. The attacks provoked a surge in far-right support and overt anti-Muslim hate speech on social media, including the widespread use of the Muhammad caricatures as a mean of provocation. Subsequently, anti-Muslim hate crimes committed by far-right sympathisers have become a major discussion topic on social media. Islamist extremists have hijacked these discussions and skilfully exploited newly arising grievances for their purposes.[26]

In January 2016, Al Shabāb Al Mujāhidīn released a propaganda video that featured Trump and framed the US as a society founded upon racial bigotry: 'Yesterday America was a land of slavery, segregation, lynching, and Ku Klux Klan. And tomorrow it will be a land of religious discrimination and concentration camps. The West will eventually turn against its Muslim citizens.'[27] A few months later, after the Brussels attacks, ISIS also published a video that showed Trump.[28] Even Tommy Robinson's anti-Muslim tweets are well known enough to ISIS that his name appears in multiple ISIS Telegram channels.[29] For example, the Telegram channel Contestants of Jihad tweeted '#Palestine – Former #EDL leader Tommy Robinson pictured holding gun on Israeli tank near Syrian border', quoting the *Evening Standard*.

Meanwhile, far-right commentators are often the first ones to share ISIS's newest propaganda. In 2015, Marine Le Pen was probed by the police for sharing graphic ISIS materials on Twitter, including pictures of the beheaded body of American hostage James Foley and dead, blood-soaked bodies of the Bataclan attack victims.[30] It is worth noting that this was in response to a discussion between French counter-terrorism expert Gilles Kepel and radio commentator Jean-Jacques Bourdin about the parallels between ISIS and the Front National. 'These two phenomena take part in the same congruency, they resemble one another,' Kepel told Bourdin. When Le Pen responded angrily by retweeting ISIS propaganda, she ironically proved exactly the point that Kepel was making.

There is a paradoxical mixture of competition and cooperation between far-right and Islamist extremists. As much as they despise each other, they also need each other. Both build on the two basic principles of victimisation and demonisation. Both spread the conspiracy theory that the other is seeking to conquer their lands. They all thrive in today's environment, where rage has replaced reason and is reinforced within echo chambers.

Self-Fulfilling Prophecy

In early 1991, a 13-year-old boy called Adam Deen was outside in the playground of Southgate School in North London. When the bell announced the end of break, a group of pupils passed by him. 'Shouldn't you be supporting Saddam?' one of them asked. Some were giving him odd looks, others were laughing. Adam was too confused to reply. First, he did not know what they were talking about. He had barely heard about the ongoing Gulf War; it was not something they had covered in school. When he learnt about British involvement in the US-led Operation Desert Shield in response to Iraq's invasion and annexation of Kuwait he figured that his fellow pupils' comments must have had something to do with the fact that he was Muslim.[31] Although the Coalition forces had come to the defence of the Muslim-majority country of Kuwait and were supported by Saudi Arabia, Saddam claimed he was fighting for the unity of Arabs and Muslims. As French political scientist Gilles Kepel argued, he 'sought to make the rape of Kuwait a kind of moral and social jihad', accusing Saudi Arabia of being an unworthy vanguard of the holy cities of Medina and Mecca.[32]

Adam had grown up in London. His parents were from Turkey but he felt 100 per cent British – that is, Muslim and British. He liked playing computer games and spent his breaks playing football, just like all the other kids in his school. But his classmates saw him as an outsider. He was the only Muslim in an all-white class. Adam had felt excluded before but this was the first time they sidelined him so overtly for his religion. They started bullying him on a regular basis. He later found out that some of the troublemakers' families were affiliated with the far-right National Front.

Four years later Adam was introduced to London's Islamist extremism networks and recruited to the now-proscribed Islamist extremist group Al Muhajiroun. Of course, his traumatising experience as a secondary-school pupil was not the only thing that led Adam to seek refuge in Islamist extremism. Yet, more than 25 years later, he still remembers that day vividly. The West-versus-Islam rhetoric used by Syrian-born Salafi Islamist and then leader of Al Muhajiroun Omar Bakri Muhammad found instant resonance with the teenager, who recalled being sidelined and bullied by the other kids. 'We often played the anti-Muslim bigotry card.

Muslims were perceived as evil and labelled as terrorists, the far right's generalised accusations against Muslims enabled us to make generalised accusations against the West.'[33]

By this time, he no longer consulted official neutral news sources. His information came exclusively from his friends within Al Muhajiroun. There was no way forward, yet there was no going back either; he was suffocating in his own bubble. 'It was quite a long journey to get out of the extremist network – it all appeared so normal. It was when a few members started leaving that I began to question.' Extremists don't perceive themselves as extreme. In a sense, everything and nothing is extreme in their binary world: there are no grey zones between the black and white, the good and bad, the guilty and the innocent. Compromise doesn't exist. 'We did not distinguish between moderates and extremists on the other side. You were either with them or with us,' Adam tells me. Al Muhajiroun members knew little about the far right but their anti-Muslim bigotry suited their victimhood narrative. They saw them as representative of all *kufr*, all non-Muslims, the West. 'The West was perceived as everything contrary to Islam and the cause of all ailments in society,' Adam says. For some this was sexual perversion, paedophilia and rape; for others it was capitalism, social injustice and inequality. For many it was discrimination, racism and anti-Muslim bigotry. However evil manifested itself, to Islamist extremists it is clear that its roots lie in the West.

The conflation of Islam and Islamism is just as endemic as the conflation of the far right and the West. When CNN's Anderson Cooper asked Trump if he thought that Islam is at war with the West, Trump replied: 'I think Islam hates us.'[34] This attitude suits ISIS well: by explaining 'Why We Hate You and Why We Fight You', they want to reinforce this 'Islam versus the West' narrative.[35] Its propaganda wing even wrote that Trump 'has yet to learn that what he refers to as "radical Islamic terrorism" is nothing but the teachings of Islam, plain and simple'.[36]

In one of their *Dabiq* issues entitled 'Break the Cross'[37] ISIS explain:

There are exceptions among the disbelievers, no doubt, people who will unabashedly declare that jihad and the laws of the Shari'ah – as well as everything else deemed taboo by the Islam-is-a-peaceful-religion crowd – are in fact completely Islamic, but they tend to be people with far less credibility who are painted as a social fringe, so their voices are dismissed and a large segment of the ignorant masses continues believing the false narrative.

Fox News published an article about the *Dabiq* issue, claiming that the author's goal was finally to prove that ISIS is Islamic and to mock those who claim Islam is a religion of peace.[38]

'Confusing Islam with Islamist extremism is extremely dangerous,' the Cambridge graduate-first-turned-extremist-then-counter-extremist, Usama, tells me. As an intervention provider for the British government's radicalisation referral programme, Channel, he sees young people radicalise – and deradicalise – on a daily basis. He has accompanied dozens of them on their way out of extremist networks and mindsets. However, over the past few years he has noticed several changes: radicalised individuals are younger, more often inspired by ISIS, and reciprocal radicalisation effects have accelerated. One of his mentees was a 17-year-old boy who had vandalised a local mosque and was convinced that all Muslims were ISIS sympathisers. He had closely followed the stories about Islamist hate preacher Anjem Choudary and seemed obsessed with the idea of fighting him. 'If I had a chance to meet Anjem Choudary, I would kill him,' he told Usama. His resentment of Islamist extremism had turned into anti-Muslim hatred and he could no longer distinguish between Islamist extremism and Islam.[39]

'It's a vicious circle! That's why extremists are strengthening!' exclaims Fiyaz Mughal. His words reverberate so loudly that the tourists sitting around us in the lobby of the Churchill Hyatt Residence Hotel turn around to look at us. Fiyaz Mughal is the founder and director of Faith Matters and Tell Mama and has over 15 years of experience in community work. The London-based organisation monitors anti-Muslim incidents across England and Wales and offers help to victims through an emergency line. As all reporting happens on a real-time basis, Fiyaz often receives intelligence on anti-Muslim hatred faster than the police.

Tell Mama's observations confirm that the circulation of far-right tweets that caricaturise Muslims as groomers, rapists and terrorists has become much more widespread over the past few years. 'The claim that all Muslims are paedophiles five years ago you would have laughed at,' Fiyaz tells me. 'Today, we can find you tons of people who say "Muslims are groomers, paedophiles".' Increasingly, people from within the political centre have started to reproduce the same narratives that previously came from the margins of society. These narratives have gone from the extreme fringes to the political mainstream, thereby gaining massive credibility: xenophobic statements have moved from the BNP to UKIP, calls to ban Muslims from Pastor Terry Jones of Stand Up America Now to *President* Donald Trump.[40]

Jihadist attacks tend to increase the support base of far-right movements. For example, in the days after Lee Rigby was murdered, the EDL's Facebook likes jumped by 100,000.[41] Likewise, the Front National achieved its highest score of 30 per cent in the national elections that were held one month after the Paris attacks of 13 November 2015.

In turn, far-right actions have been important 'recruiting sergeants' for Islamist extremists.[42] Most importantly, they have strengthened the hard-core Islamist extremists who do not believe in the possibility of reconciling modernity and Islam, giving credibility to their claims that there will be a 'Muslims versus non-Muslims' confrontation in the long-run. Moreover, it has fed into the victimhood narratives perpetuated and instrumentalised by what Fiyaz calls 'softer Islamists'. By systematically conveying the impression that Muslims are under direct threat and blaming the establishment for doing nothing to prevent them from becoming the new Jews of the 1930s, these 'softer Islamists' act as amplifiers on the Islamist extremist end. They contribute to growing fears and alienation, rendering Muslims more vulnerable to violent extremist alternatives.[43]

In short, far-right and Islamist extremists feed into and amplify each other's radicalisation strategies, leading to a bizarre interdependency between the two. This is the paradox of competition and mutual reinforcement between different forms of extremism. One depends on the other, for the 'us against them' only works if 'they' also play the game. As Al Muhajiroun's founder Omar Bakri Muhammad put it: 'People, when they suffer in the West, it makes them think. If there is no discrimination or racism, I think it would be very different for us.' Both need a credible counterpart for their process of 'othering', ideally one that is perceived as an imminent and existential threat. Islamist extremists use outrage provoked by anti-Muslim rhetoric and biased news articles to recruit alienated Muslims for their violent causes. All the far right then has to do is translate the fear generated from Islamist extremist action back into outrage – it is a perfectly coordinated vicious cycle that turns the predictions of extremists into a self-fulfilling prophecy. 'They want to make examples out of us so that we fear them but they have forgotten that hatred breeds hatred', warns the French hip hop group Expression Direkt in one of their raps.[44]

Forsane Alizza (Knights of Pride), a French Islamist extremist group, was accused of planning terrorist attacks in 2015, resulting in a major crackdown and the imprisonment of many of its members.[45] According to its founder, Mohammed Achamlane, the group was created in 2011 with the goal to 'end Islamophobia' and to counter French identity movements by adopting a 'tit-for-tat' strategy. This meant, for example, burning the French penal code in retaliation for the nationwide ban on wearing the veil in public. Indeed, Forsane Alizza managed to attract many youngsters who had been victims of far-right extremism and anti-Muslim rhetoric both online and offline. It has offered refuge to people like Maajid, who fell prey to Hizb ut-Tahrir recruiters after being repeatedly exposed to neo-Nazi violence,[46] or like Adam who was mobbed for being Muslim by his Front National-affiliated classmates before joining Al Muhajiroun.

Mohammed Merah, the self-styled French Al Qaeda jihadist who killed seven innocent people in March 2012, had reported links to Forsane Alizza. 'Abdelghani Merah, allô?' His brother, who today challenges extremism, picks up the phone. He tells me that Mohammed's experiences of anti-Muslim hatred and racism played a crucial role in his radicalisation. 'He went through a lot of troubles with discrimination when applying to car repair shops outside of our neighbourhood.' Their sister was regularly insulted in the street when she was wearing her veil. He recalls a moment in 2010 when he sat next to her, as people called her a monster, a clown and a ghost. 'I admit, for a short moment even I fell into the trap that could have led me down the same path as my brother.' It was at the time of the burqa controversy in France and, intuitively, he felt the need to be on the defensive. 'I felt more Muslim than French Republican at that moment.'

In many cases, the family reinforces these grievances that result from daily hostilities, according to Abdelghani. For example, many parents would console their kid after a bad performance in school by saying, 'Don't worry, it's because you're Arab that they gave you a bad grade.'[47]

The current dynamics in France are worrying Abdelghani. Before 1998 it was almost normal to be racist, he remembers. But France's victory in the 1998 soccer World Cup changed this: it was not just a victory for *Les Bleus* but a victory for diversity and tolerance. 'When Jacques Chirac stressed that France owed its success to its multi-ethnicity, he brought together whites, blacks and Arabs. It became a disgrace to be racist.' Yet, since the recent series of attacks on French territory, people are no longer ashamed of being openly racist. This new wave of outspoken hatred is likely to cause a backlash, because 'the one thing that unites National Front and Al Qaeda is their hatred'.[48]

Houria Bouteldja, founder of Mouvement des indigènes de la République, gave a speech soon after the 2012 Toulouse attack by Mohammed Merah:

> Mohamed Merah is me. The worst part is that it's true. Like me, he is of Algerian background, like me he grew up in a poor district, and like me he is Muslim. Mohamed Merah is me. How old was he on 9/11? 12 years old. A child in the process of constructing himself. Since then, like me, he has been subjected to the incredible islamophobic political and media campaign that followed the attacks against the twin towers.[49]

Her activism against racial and anti-Muslim hatred has effectively turned her rhetoric into one that reflects strong anti-white hatred. Labelling her anti-white propaganda as racism is inappropriate, as sociologist Christine Delphy has pointed out, because racism is inherently committed by those in the dominant position. Whether we call Houria a racist or simply angry and oppressed, her tit-for-tat racial accusations reassured French identity movements.

The French usually love word games but not when they go against them. On the TV show *Ce Soir*, Houria turned 'Français de souche', an expression used by the far right to describe White French natives, into its neologism 'sous-chiens', which also means underdog. The General Alliance Against Racism and for the Respect of the French and Christian Identity (AGRIF), which is closely linked to the French far right, accused her of Francophobia and even wanted to initiate a legal process against her at the Toulouse court for racial insult. The circle of hate was complete.

Trump's Gift to ISIS

On Tuesday 8 November 2016, Twitter and Facebook were busy places. The usual #TuesdayMotivation is not trending. Instead, everyone gives their #ElectionFinalThoughts. They reach from 'Justin Bieber should be next president' to 'the end is near!' Even Facebook becomes much more of a political discussion space than normal. Few kitten and puppy pics are posted, even fewer holiday pictures shared.

As the evening progresses, I monitor over 100 Islamist extremist Twitter and Facebook accounts and multiple ISIS Telegram channels to watch their reaction to the election results.[50] When the quintessential swing states Ohio and less than 40 minutes later Florida swing for Trump, two seemingly paradoxical trends quickly crystallise in Islamist extremists' online echo chambers: victimhood and enthusiasm. Several radical groups use Trump's victory as a piece of evidence that confirms their victimhood narrative. Others go as far as to welcome and even celebrate the election results as another milestone in their strategy to destabilise the *kufr* countries. Regardless of their emotional spin, they all share a certain 'we told you so' attitude.

'We told you so; they are all against us.' The fact that a major Western country voted for an overtly Islamophobic president is used as the ultimate proof that 'the West is at war with Islam'. Abu Muhammad Al Maqdisi, an Al Qaeda member and mentor to former Al Qaeda affiliate Abu Musab Al Zarqawi, tweets that Trump's victory exposes 'the true mentality of the Americans, and their racism toward Muslims and Arabs and everything'. Trump merely reveals what his predecessors have kept hidden – so runs the argument. Meanwhile, on Telegram, ISIS-affiliated groups are actively sharing content related to Trump's victory – in English, French, German, Arabic and Russian. In between the many posts about Mosul fighting scenes there are references to Trump's hateful rhetoric.

In the days after the election, the administrator of the ISIS-supporting Telegram group Contestants of Jihad, which reaches over 500 members, reports racist and anti-Muslim incidents. One of his posts said: '#America – Muslim student brutally assaulted by two #DonaldTrump supporters in #Louisiana. #Hijab ripped off.' The KKK's David Duke's enthusiastic tweet that 'this is one of the most exciting nights of my life, our people have played a huge role in electing Trump' was also shared in several ISIS Telegram groups.

On the morning after the election, Omar tells me, 'I know that when I go back to prison they will say: "Omar, what did I tell you? They hate us."' Omar, who de-radicalises British prison inmates convicted for terrorism, knows his mentees' problems well: in his teenage years, he joined and then left Islamist extremist organisations more often than some people change membership of sport clubs. To him it is clear that Trump's election poses a big obstacle to the reintegration of radicalised individuals. 'It will be difficult to convince them that there is a place for them in our increasingly anti-Muslim societies,' he tells me.[51]

'We told you so; democracy and capitalism don't work.' At the Khilafah Conference held in Chicago in May 2016, Hizb ut-Tahrir's American spokesperson Haitham Ibn Thbait warned Muslims not to fall into the 'electoral trap'. His narrative was that they had been tricked into voting for Clinton, Bush and Obama in the past. In the wake of the election, ISIS Telegram channels shared the YouTube link to Ibn Thbait's speech and adopted similar lines. Many branches of Hizb ut-Tahrir commented that either candidate was a poor option for president, highlighting Hillary Clinton's history of support for Israel and for US intervention in Iraq.[52]

They hit the nail on the head – the overwhelming majority of American Muslims and non-Muslims alike felt that they had to choose 'the lesser of two evils'. The *New York Times* and CBS News' final pre-election poll revealed that eight out of ten voters were disenchanted by the election campaign. The majority of Americans wanted neither Clinton nor Trump to win the election.[53] Naturally, the question that was on everyone's minds was: how did we end up here? Islamist extremists across the entire spectrum had the same tailor-made reply: the fundamentally flawed system and its underlying values are to blame. The system ensured that voters ended up with the choice between two 'unelectable' candidates.

A few hours after the election results were released, the Chairman of the British branch of Hizb ut-Tahrir, Abdul Wahid, posted on Facebook that: 'This election is more proof that capitalism is a "sick man" in decline – but which still has the capability to harm others.'[54] Likewise, Hamza Al Karibi, spokesperson of Jabhat Fateh Al Sham, a former Syrian affiliate to Al Qaeda, writes: 'Trump's victory is a powerful slap to those promoting the benefits of democratic mechanisms. [...] From this day forward we will no longer need videos explaining the West's plots, we will only need to retweet what Trump says.'

'We told you so; the only solution is to overthrow Western regimes and establish a caliphate.' The perceived failure of Western democratic systems aided Islamist extremists in their calls for action. After Trump's victory was announced, many extremists reiterated the need for Muslims to renounce democracy and establish a worldwide Islamic State. For example, one of Hizb ut-Tahrir's followers wrote: 'Trump victory. Whatevr claims US had as exampl of "leadership" is again eroded. Time 4 Muslim world 2 reestablish own lrdshp. [sic]' Abdullah Al Muhaisny, a key affiliate of Al Qaeda in Syria, states that Trump's victory was an important step towards the victory of Sunnis, since the new president will sow greater division in the US: 'The American strategy will not change much, what has changed is that the war is open and not secret, and that is a good thing.'

ISIS's official propaganda outlets remained surprisingly silent in the run-up to the US elections. But its supporters shared their attitudes towards the two candidates on the encrypted messenger app Telegram. Months before the election, the administrator of the ISIS-affiliated Telegram Channel Nashir wrote: 'I ask Allah to deliver America to Trump.' Another one posted: 'The "facilitation" of Trump's arrival in the White House must be a priority for jihadists at any cost!!!'

Seventy-two hours before the polling stations opened, the Al Hayat Media Center – one of ISIS's official media outlets – broke the apparent silence. They published a seven-page document on 'The Murtadd Vote' (the apostate vote).[55] A few things were special about this release, as my former colleague Charlie Winter highlighted in *The Atlantic*.[56] Not only was this their first media product on the US elections, it was also one of very few publications that explicitly targeted American Muslims. The essay claimed that both Trump and Clinton represented the 'Crusader enemy', and advised American Muslims to abstain from voting and instead stage an attack against US voters. The group said that 'the blood of Crusader voters is even more deserving of being spilled than the blood of Crusader combatants'. For Charlie, ISIS's call on Muslims to abstain from voting had a clear strategic background: given the high levels of Muslim support Clinton enjoyed in the race, it was indirectly designed to aid Trump to victory.[57]

After the elections, ISIS no longer hid its enthusiasm. The ISIS-affiliated network Al Minbar Jihadi Media encouraged Muslims to 'rejoice with support from Allah, and find glad tidings in the imminent demise of America at the hands of Trump'. This was echoed by their sympathisers and followers: many of them understood the strategy and supported Trump for dividing the US population. 'I voted for Trump', one Islamist extremist admitted, taking the concept of strategic voting to a new level. Another one wrote: 'We love supporters for hating us! hahahaha.' He quoted anti-Muslim lines chanted at a Trump rally with the comment: 'I wish the British were as vocal in their hate for Muslims as the Americans are ... Maybe then the Muslims here would unite against falsehood.' Likewise, one of ISIS's most prominent accounts, which got shut down a few days after the election, tweeted: 'I prefer a straightforward Donald Trump telling Muslims what half of America thinks of them than a wicked, hypocrite Clinton snake.' The tweet received 23 likes and 33 retweets.

ISIS Telegram channels also talked about the anti-Trump demonstrations across the country, celebrating the election as a sign of America descending into chaos and bringing ISIS one step further in its ultimate goal: the final confrontation between the *Dar al-Islam* ('Land of Islam') and the non-Muslim *Dar al-harb* ('Land of war'). The ISIS-supporting Telegram group Contestants of Jihad shared a picture of Trump holding a sign that quotes Hadith number 56 in the Book of Knowledge: 'The Prophet said when the power of authority comes in the hands of unfit persons, then wait for the hour (Doomsday).' The same group wrote:

You fear Trump more than Allah. Trump being president is a sort of poetic justice. I say this because how long have we been warned about being engaged deeply within this government which is nothing but kufr? […] How many times were you told either give dawah or make hijrah and you refused with nothing but scorn and anger?

The group's administrator went on to call upon Muslims to join the jihad against the *kufr*, against people like Trump, against the Americans. In one of his shared videos, a certain Zahid Akhtar explains in broken English with a mixture of amusement, confusion and anger: 'I have to say something about the Muslims. The Muslims are so upset that Hillary didn't win, as if Hillary is the Mahdi that we are waiting for. I don't know what's going on with brothers and sister. […] It sounded like Donald Trump got into office beyond Allah's will, as if God did not want it.' The Al Qaeda-affiliated Ansar Al Sharia in the Arabian Peninsula even noted in its official newspaper that 'Americans will remember 11/9 the way they remember 9/11'.

Islamist extremists' apocalyptic vision might indeed become a self-fulfilling prophecy. Clinton was not exaggerating when she told Israel's Channel 2 that 'ISIS were terrorists praying to Allah to make Trump president' in September 2016. Trump might turn out to be the biggest gift American voters could have offered Islamist extremists. The radicalisation experts who gathered at the EU's Radicalisation Awareness Network Conference on the morning after the election agreed. Internal Security Director in the EU Directorate-General Home Affairs Luigi Soreca opened his speech with the words: 'Both right-wing violent extremist groups and Daesh are benefiting from growing polarisation.'

The aftermath of Trump's victory showed that hate speech can fuel political violence and proved the connection between populist far-right politics and militant extremism. But the far right does not only exacerbate itself; it also reinforces the threat from Islamist extremism. Trump gave ISIS and Al Qaeda an opportunity to prove that the elected establishment is racist and anti-Muslim. His victory normalised the extremist narrative as being resonant with reality.

Tit-for-Tat

'If you don't want to live the way we live, don't come,' the Front National mayor of the French Riviera town Cogolin said in the midst of the burkini controversy of August 2016. Marc Etienne Lansade was among the mayors who not only advocated the burkini ban but also vowed to ignore the court ruling that declared it illegal. In February 2017, French police arrested three women for planning to blow up Mayor Lansade. The female trio had connections to jihadist recruiter Larossi Abballa and were believed to be following the directives of ISIS executioner Rashid Kassim (aka Abu Kassim). This was not the first time that ISIS explicitly reacted to Front National's anti-Muslim politics. In February 2016, ISIS had declared Le Pen's Front National and its members as its 'target of first choice'. In the French editorial of its propaganda magazine *Dar-al-Islam*, it threatened to launch an attack on the far-right party's protests.

Revenge is a recurring factor in terrorists' radicalisation profiles. Salman Abedi, who killed 22 people, including children and teenagers, at the Ariana Grande concert in Manchester in June 2017, is a case in point. In May 2016, Abedi lost his 18-year-old British Libyan friend, who was run down by a car and then stabbed in Manchester. As he believed this to be a religious hate crime, he vowed for revenge at the funeral and shortly afterwards opened a bank account, which he later used to buy items related to the suicide bombing.[58]

Likewise, the Finsbury Park attacker Darren Osborne reportedly showed changes in attitude and behaviour following the London Bridge attack. 'I want to kill Muslims [...] you deserve it [...] I did my bit,'[59] he shouted when he drove into a crowd of Muslim worshippers. While white supremacists celebrated the incident as the 'beginning of a race war', Islamist extremist channels exploited the incident to inflame anger among Muslims.

As the process of radicalisation on the side of both far-right and Islamist extremism has accelerated in recent years, we have entered a spiralling violence effect. One side's action increasingly leads to a retaliatory reaction from the other side. But if this is so, then we should be able to see a correlation between far-right extremist and Islamist extremist incidents. Looking at the statistics, the Global

Database on Terrorism (GDT) records domestic, transnational and international acts of terrorism that occur anywhere across the world. It contains data on over 150,000 terrorist attacks, making it the world's most comprehensive unclassified database on terrorism incidents. An analysis of this data suggests that far-right extremist violence correlates with Islamist extremist attacks. Indeed, a closer look at the incidents that occurred in the period between January 2012 and September 2016 across the US, Australia, the UK, France and Germany, reveals that far-right and Islamist terrorist attacks tend to spike at the same time.[60]

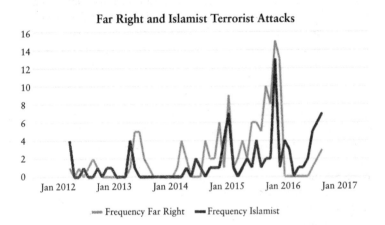

Far Right and Islamist Terrorist Attacks

▬▬ Frequency Far Right ▬▬ Frequency Islamist

A look at other global terrorism bases reveals similar trends. In the first decade of the twenty-first century, the Combating Terrorism Center recorded three peaks in far-right violence in the US in 2001, 2004 and 2008, with each wave surpassing the previous one.[61] All three waves came in years that also saw major jihadist attacks: 9/11 in 2001, the Madrid bombings in 2004, closely followed by the London tube bombings in 2005, and the Mumbai bombings in 2008. In the aftermath of 9/11, far-right attacks and hate crimes against Muslims committed on US ground increased by 1,600 per cent.[62] Following the 7/7 bombings on the London tube, anti-Muslim violence in Britain rose sixfold, and after *Charlie Hebdo*, by 281 per cent in France.[63]

The date 5 July 2016 marked the end of one of the bloodiest Ramadans in history. Terrorist attacks had been carried out all across the world from Orlando to Madinah, hitting both Muslims and non-Muslims. Earlier in the year, Carl Miller and his colleagues at the London-based think tank Demos had noticed irregular spikes of Islamophobic posts on Twitter. Carl and I were having tea in their modern open-plan office when he told me that major Islamist-related incidents such as terrorist attacks have a remarkable digital aftermath: they provoke a real-time reaction from far-right sympathisers. 'We observed an event-specific prevalence of Islamophobic hashtags,' Carl says.[64] Over the month of July alone, Demos identified a total of 215,247 Islamophobic tweets, which were sent in English from around the world. Demos found significant spikes within the 24 hours that followed major terrorist incidents in the West. For example, in July anti-Muslim hate tweets spiked in the immediate aftermath of incidents such as the Dallas shooting on 7 July, the Nice attack on 14 July and the Normandy church attack on 26 July.[65] Carl's findings are in line with Tell Mama's observations. The real-world impact, however, shows slightly later than that of the online space. 'The hate crimes usually start mounting within the 24 to 120 hours that follow an extremist-related event,' says Fiyaz.[66] The murder of soldier Lee Rigby in southeast London by two British Muslim converts in May 2013 was a classic example of reciprocal radicalisation. In its aftermath, Tell Mama registered a fourfold increase in anti-Muslim hate crimes. The organisation counted 114 cases in just five days, while the usual average was 25–35 a week at the time. In the three months following the incident, there were 34 mosques attacks across the country. Their scope ranged from the lowest level, such as graffiti, to arson and even bombing plots, such as that of Ukrainian neo-Nazi Pavlo Lapshyn. 'Within those three months the Islamist narrative kicked in virtually at the same time,' Fiyaz tells me. The number of Islamist accounts online increased substantially – Tell Mama counted around 120 newly opened Islamist accounts in that period. Many of those were reflecting on retaliation attacks against the far right. Fiyaz remembers that some people posted things like: 'Let's attack the EDL' and 'Let's have a go at Tommy Robinson's address.'[67] This period coincided with the conviction of six men who had planned to bomb an anti-

Muslim EDL rally in Dewsbury.[68] Apart from shotguns, explosive devices and knives, the police had also found a long printed message which explained the would-be attackers' motivations:

> To the EDL (English Drunkards League). O enemies of Allah! We have heard and seen you openly insulting the final Messenger of Allah [...] you should know that for every action there is a reaction [...] Today is a day of retaliation (especially) for your blasphemy of Allah and his Messenger Muhammad. We love death more than you love life. The penalty for blasphemy of Allah and his Messenger Muhammad is death.

Year on year Tell Mama sees the basic level of anti-Muslim hate crimes rise.[69]

The organisation tends to observe stronger reactions after national incidents than international incidents. Yet the 2015 attack on the *Charlie Hebdo* office in Paris provoked the same level of anti-Muslim hate crimes across the UK as Lee Rigby's murder. The spike that followed the Paris attack of November 2015 was, significantly, even higher than after Lee Rigby's murder, and the post-Brexit increase further gained in amplitude. Each of these events is having a cumulative effect in terms of hate crimes. 'This is the result of widening echo chambers of both far-right and Islamist extremists,' Fiyaz explains. Every time there is an extremist attack, the fabric that holds together our societies changes because of the spike of hate crimes. Fiyaz is genuinely worried about this cumulative building effect. 'How long can our society keep taking hits?' he asks, shaking his head. 'And in an environment where there are fewer resources.'[70]

To conclude, a symbiotic relationship between far-right and Islamist extremists occurs on at least two levels: (1) as their stories are two sides of the same coin, they reinforce each other; and (2) as their actions provoke each other into more radical retaliation, they turn each other's predictions into self-fulfilling prophecies. As a result, reciprocal radicalisation leads to an unwitting cooperation of ever-escalating extremes.

While the online interaction of extremist narratives is empirically observable, the offline symbiosis is harder to determine. Both anecdotal evidence and statistical data suggest a spiralling violence effect between far-right and Islamist extremism. But how do we know whether this is coincidence, correlation or causality? It is important to avoid rash conclusions about the nature of the relationship between far-right and Islamist extremist attacks. So, let's dive deeper into the dynamics on a local level.

7

Geography of Hate

THERE ARE MANY DANGEROUS PLACES IN THIS WORLD: THE DURAND LINE along the border of Pakistan and Afghanistan, the Mexican Ciudad Juarez, the favelas around Rio de Janeiro, the Pakistani side of Balochistan, the townships of the Cape Flats southeast of Cape Town – to name just a few. Citizens of Western democracies are lucky not to be plagued by drug cartels, gang crimes and border conflicts to the same extent as people born into such areas, where death and crime are an integral part of their daily lives. Yet our home countries host some of the world's most underestimated danger zones: mutual breeding grounds for far-right and Islamist extremists. While these may not pose imminent threats to their residents, they have produced globally some of the most troubling extremist groups, terrorist ringleaders and self-starters – from both the Islamist and far-right viewpoints.

In Europe, the most notorious breeding ground for Islamist extremism is Molenbeek, the Brussels borough that was all over the news after the Paris attacks of November 2015. Albeit less well known, there are also several far-right extremist hotbeds, such as the north-eastern German town of Jamel, which was dubbed 'the neo-Nazi village'. In a remarkably large number of cases these breeding grounds of far-right and Islamist extremists overlap geographically, forming what I call reciprocal radicalisation hotbeds.

A 2016 report of the Combating Terrorism Center at West Point found that foreign fighter recruits tend to cluster geographically in areas where they can capitalise on existing grievances. Of the 854 foreign fighters they analysed, almost 70 per cent of them came from the same city as at least one other fighter.[1] In France, suburban Paris and cities along the French Riviera such as Lunel and Nice are considered primary hotspots for foreign fighter recruitment. In the UK, Luton, Birmingham and Portsmouth are among the places with the highest foreign fighter numbers. In Germany the town of Dinslaken ranked among the top cluster areas. Many of these geographic hubs for jihadists are also primary hotspots of far-right extremism.

Many reciprocal radicalisation hotbeds have formed in areas that have undergone rapid transformations at the expense of their populations' living standards. The east London area of Barking is one example. Two of the three perpetrators behind the London Bridge and Borough Market attack of June 2017 were from there. The borough has been a stronghold for both the BNP and Al Muhajiroun. In June 2010, Barking saw clashes between far-right and Islamist extremists at a homecoming parade for British soldiers from the 1st Battalion Royal Anglian Regiment, which had just returned from Afghanistan. Forty members of Muslims Against the Crusades held up 'butchers return' banners, while a hundred EDL supporters shouted 'Muslim bombers off our streets'. Between 2014 and 2015, Barking's anti-Muslim hate crimes almost tripled, and in 2016, EDL and NF logos were found on numerous Muslim-owned shops and restaurants.[2]

Reciprocal radicalisation hotbeds are unique in many ways. They often display a bizarre mixture of cooperation, competition and overt fighting between different groups. Extremists on opposite sides of the equation have unwittingly cooperated in driving anti-establishment resentments, while competing for the same potential support base: disenfranchised youth. It is no coincidence that they have established their strongholds in similar geographic areas, often those that have undergone deep structural changes. What all reciprocal radicalisation hotbeds have in common is that their communities are desperate for change – either back to an idealised past or forward to a utopian future. A lack of perspective and disenchantment with establishment politics are typical features of these breeding grounds. Whether in the UK, France, Germany or the US, extremists tend to thrive in areas where grievances exceed morale.

As a result of growing fear and anger, competition for resources in these places becomes fiercer and divisions between communities grow deeper. This leads to a downward spiral that accelerates the radicalisation process and feeds into recruiting successes on both sides. For this reason, far-right organisations often pop up in areas with a high Islamist extremist presence and activity. Likewise, Islamist extremist groups are frequently formed in reaction to far-

Yet the 26-year-old Robinson was outraged by the protest. After organising a small, rather unsuccessful counter-protest that received limited media coverage, he teamed up with his second cousin Kevin Carroll to stage something bigger. They mobilised all their contacts within the BNP, their local football clubs, and smaller groups such as the United British Alliance, to form what they called the 'United People of Luton'. Soon, people from all across Britain joined their quickly growing network. This was the beginning of the UK's biggest far-right street movement, the EDL.

Robinson knew that he had hit a nerve with his movement. 'Britain's establishment and liberal middle class looks down its noses at angry people who march and protest, who shout and swear and chant and say enough's enough. But at least it's real, it's the voice of men and women who are patriots, who believe in their country.'[17] Indeed, there were plenty of angry, white people who thought that Islam and British values were incompatible. By 2010, membership numbers were growing exponentially and Robinson had organised dozens of demonstrations all across the country.

The EDL is formed of several groups, each with a different role. For example, members of the intellectual elite, such as computer expert Alan Lake, blog about the dangers of radical Islam and help coordinate events and demonstrations. Lake states that he and fellow bloggers tried to arrange demonstrations so that they coincided with football matches, thereby hoping to entice participation from football firms such as the Luton-based Men in Gear along with more miscellaneous far-right groups who look for opportunities to stir up racial tension. Lake cited the 7/7 bombings as justification for the EDL's activities.[18] 'The EDL hopes [...] that cumulative radicalisation on the streets will force the Government into illiberal action against Britain's resident Muslims', according to British far-right expert Nigel Copsey.[19]

Luton is where the London bombers convened before executing their plot in July 2005. In April 2007 a Luton resident, Salahuddin Amin, was jailed for conspiring to unleash a fertiliser bomb at Blue-water shopping centre in Kent.[20] No doubt as a direct result of these cases, the EDL decided to attack the Luton Islamic Centre on Bury Park Road in May 2009, just a few months after the group's inception.

The apparent willingness of the Luton authorities to allow EDL demonstrations (compared to Leicester and Bradford, where numerous restrictions have been implemented) has caused some Muslim residents in Luton to feel marginalised and unprotected. In turn, this supposed freedom gives the EDL the confidence to continue demonstrations in the area. For example, they protested against a local shopping centre's decision to construct a multi-faith prayer room. There is thus a legitimate fear among local authorities in Luton that the EDL is actually pushing young Muslims into extremist hands.[21]

In April 2013 four individuals were arrested in Luton for attempting to plant a bomb in the local Territorial Army headquarters. One month later, Anjem Choudary announced the creation of 'an EDL-type, vigilante street group called Islamic Emergency Defence (with the highly provocative acronym, IED), which aims to prevent – and, it appears, retaliate against – anti-Muslim attacks'.[22] According to the group's Facebook page, the IED's mission is 'to defend the Muslim community from anti-Muslim hate crimes'.

After ISIS declared its caliphate, Luton became one of Britain's foremost recruiting hotbeds for foreign fighters. In July 2015, the Mannan family left Bury Park for Syria, while in the same month Junead Khan from Luton was arrested for conspiring to murder a US soldier. In September of that year, a 33-year-old woman was arrested at Luton airport as she attempted to fly to Syria with her four children.[23]

These multiple Luton-based Islamist incidents provoked a clear reaction in January 2016 when Britain First organised an anti-Muslim parade through Bury Park led by Paul Golding and Jayda Fransen. A video of the parade recorded by Britain First, which now has over 3 million views on YouTube,[24] shows many Muslim residents becoming visibly angry and threatening to fight back.[25] Alt-right news outlets such as the *Daily Mail*[26] and Breitbart[27] published extensive reports on this.

The highly repetitive series of incidents around Luton from both Islamist extremist groups and anti-Muslim groups demonstrates the close links between one party's actions and the effect it has on the other party. The vulnerability that many Muslims feel in Luton has encouraged them to seek solace in authoritative Islamist groups, while the EDL has deliberately targeted the town as a direct result of the many Islamist extremist-related incidents in that part of the country.

Portsmouth

Portsmouth is a city in the county of Hampshire on the south coast. It is known for its historic affiliation with the Royal Navy and is also the home of football club Portsmouth FC. Outside of London, Portsmouth is the most densely populated part of the UK, with 210,000 people squashed into 15 square miles. Portsmouth is home to around 7,100 Muslims, most of them of Bangladeshi origin, constituting a bit more than 3 per cent of the town's total population.[28] However, unlike many parts of the United Kingdom, the Portsmouth Muslim community has no segregated cultural ghetto and its families live interspersed throughout the city, attending mixed schools with children of other ethnicities and faiths.[29]

In October 2013 a group of six Muslims from Portsmouth, known as 'The Pompey Lads', travelled to Syria to join ISIS. These jihadists had previously volunteered at the Portsmouth Dawah, an Islamist proselytising group that distributes leaflets on the Portsmouth high street along with other religious groups. They also called themselves the 'Britani Brigade Bangladeshi Bad Boys'. One volunteer, Bilal Jaff, stated that no one in the group was aware of the jihadists' intentions and that the group simply aims to educate the public on Islamic values.[30] However, a study in November 2014 showed that the Portsmouth Dawah had strong links with the Islamic Education and Research Academy (IERA), whose Salafist founder Abdhur Raheem Green has sparked repeated controversies through his sermons on anti-Semitism, homophobia and misogyny.[31]

While more than half of the Portsmouth South Asian community experience poverty,[32] there does not appear to be any direct link between poverty and the radicalisation of these six individuals. Many of the jihadists had jobs, albeit mundane ones that possibly led them to feel bored with their lives and to look for a more meaningful career path.

However, the head of the Hampshire branch of the government Prevent strategy, Sergeant John Knowles, states that many Muslims in the area suffer from low-level hate crimes, which harden extremist beliefs and reinforce the idea that a Muslim and British identity are incompatible.[33] One of the first notable altercations occurred around midday on Saturday 13 November 2010 when a group of about 40 EDL members – many of whom had travelled from London – convened outside the Jami mosque. This demonstration was a direct retaliation to an incident on Armistice Day (Thursday) in London in which a small Islamist group had publicly burnt poppies during the two-minute silence. The EDL decided to respond by painting a six-foot poppy on the Jami mosque wall the day afterwards (Friday). The Saturday protests were paused temporarily for the Portsmouth FC match but restarted in the afternoon, this time with around 100 protestors.[34]

As a response to the recent 'Pompey Lads' incident, 4 December 2013 saw another EDL protest outside the mosque, claiming that the mosque was responsible for radicalising the youths. These 20 EDL members were met by 16 members of United Against Fascism but no arrests were made.[35] Similar cases of protest and vandalism have continued in the Portsmouth area. October 2014 saw an EDL-led protest against the upcoming construction of the new Madani Academy Primary School. These protests continued in January 2016 when a severed pig's head was left outside the school and a swastika was painted on the wall.[36]

Heightened EDL activities in Portsmouth were provoked by the 'Pompey Lads' incident. While there may be several factors driving 'Pompey Lads' recruitment, repeated actions of the EDL in that area very probably incited some local Muslims to feel isolated and marginalised, leading them to seek a more meaningful life and fulfilling identity elsewhere.

Birmingham

On Wednesday 22 March 2017 at 2.40 p.m., a Hyundai Tucson driven from Birmingham careered into pedestrians on Westminster Bridge. Within a mere 82 seconds, its driver had mowed down about 50 pedestrians, crashed into the grounds of the Houses of Parliament and ran into Palace Yard where he fatally stabbed an unarmed police officer.

Tommy Robinson was quick to respond: he went straight to the scene of the attack to rage against Islam. 'It has everything to do with Islam,' he said in a video for *The Rebel*, a far-right Canadian online media platform. 'Why are you [Muslims] feeling intimidated? No one's driving cars into you. No one's raping your daughters. No one's beheading you. That's happening to our community.' What Tommy did not know at this point was that his EDL and PEGIDA UK marches may in fact have fed into the perpetrator's radicalisation path.

As more information about the attacker emerged, it became clear that his age was atypical but his geographic links were not: most traces from the investigations led to Luton and Birmingham. Like Luton, Birmingham has been a remarkable breeding ground for both Islamist and far-right extremism.

Fifty-two-year-old Khalid Masood lived in Luton between 2010 and 2012, where he worked as an English teacher. This was during the EDL's peak time: the Luton-based group's membership numbers were high and its demonstrations frequent. Khalid Masood's former boss at the language school Elas UK, Farasat Latif, told the *Guardian* that he only saw Masood angry once, when the EDL announced a protest in Luton. 'He was absolutely livid they were allowed to march', according to Latif. 'If they were to come to my town I'd kill them', were his words.[37]

Masood was based in Birmingham in the year before committing Britain's most lethal terrorist attack since the 7/7 bombings. The city in the West Midlands is known for at least three things: (1) the accent of its native citizens, known as Brummies; (2) the invention there of the industrial steam engine; and (3) its exceptionally high number of Islamist extremists and terrorists. A tenth of the country's convicted Islamist terrorists come from council wards in Birmingham.[38]

One of them is Abu Izzadeen, who also goes by the name Trevor Brooks. On the first anniversary of the 7/7 bombings, Brooks called its attackers 'completely praiseworthy' and mocked its victims in a speech he delivered in Birmingham. Although he currently sits in prison for glorification of terrorism, early reports from multiple media outlets mistakenly named Brooks as the perpetrator of the Westminster attack.

Birmingham has also seen a high concentration of activity from far-right groups: in particular, the EDL, Combat 18 and a British branch of the Ku Klux Klan have been active in the West Midlands region. Most recently, Tommy Robinson picked what he called the 'terrorist epicentre of Birmingham' for the 2016 launch of PEGIDA UK. In February 2016, about 200 anti-Islam demonstrators marched from Birmingham International Railway Station to the city's International Business Park.

The city has also been one of the EDL's favourite demonstration places. Its earliest Birmingham protests in 2009 attracted up to 900 marchers. According to EDL's own Facebook posts, the group's first protest in the city 'was prompted by Anjem Choudary who "converted" an 11-year-old white (English/Irish) boy to Islam in Birmingham city centre'.[39] The far-right group Casuals United soon started marching with the EDL in the streets of Birmingham.[40] The movement, which calls itself 'the UK's Football tribes against the Jihadists', was formed in direct response to the Muslims who protested in Luton against British soldiers returning from Afghanistan.

It did not take long until counter-jihad protests inspired counter-counter-jihad reactions: in June 2012, six Islamist extremists were arrested for planning to attack an EDL demo in Dewsbury with guns, swords, knives and explosives; five of the six would-be terrorists were from Birmingham.

One year later, a peculiar letter with neither addressee nor signature reached the Birmingham City Council. 'Operation Trojan Horse has been very carefully thought through and is tried and tested within Birmingham', the letter said, outlining a five-stage process 'to remove headteachers and take control of schools'. The Department for Education commissioned Peter Clarke, the former head of the Metropolitan Police's Counter Terrorism Command, to look into the case. His study revealed that Islamist extremists had planned 'co-ordinated, deliberate and sustained action [...] to introduce an intolerant and aggressive Islamic ethos into some schools in the city'.[41] This became known as the Trojan horse scandal of Birmingham.

Less known was Combat 18's secret plan to recruit Birmingham teachers;[42] the story did not make it beyond local news. 'Combat 18 planned to recruit teachers to pass on their ideas to young people. It was an elaborate strategy to attract new members through targeted indoctrination,' Nigel Bromage tells me. The former Combat 18 member now runs an organisation called Small Steps Consultants, which is devoted to combating far-right extremism. According to Nigel, the role of education is key to groups like Combat 18 and the KKK. They follow similar training schedules and it takes up to three years to become a leader. 'They use 70 per cent emotions and 30 per cent facts. By pointing to the other extreme's rhetoric and action, they can emphasise identity differences and foster a sense of tribalism.'

France's Identity Wars and Militant Secularism

Mohammed Chirani is a brave man. French, of Algerian heritage, Mohammed is a former representative of the French authorities in the Parisian banlieue Seine-Saint-Denis and author of *French Reconciliation: Our Challenge of Living Together*. Following the Paris attacks of November 2015, he baffled two *iTélé* moderators and won the hearts of hundreds of thousands of watchers with his passionate message to French Muslims in both Arabic and French. After denouncing the 'satanic pseudo-caliphate' and calling for more solidarity, he kissed his French passport and cited the Qur'an in front of the running camera. The video quickly went viral; it was liked more than 140,000 times and shared close to 60,000 times.[43] In the days that followed his extraordinary performance, he received multiple death threats from ISIS supporters and was added to Islamist extremists' top target list. 'I don't fear you. I declare a spiritual jihad against you', was his public Twitter reply.

But the far right dislikes him just as much, Mohammed tells me over lunch in Tunis. 'Simply because my name is Mohammed.' The ultra-right news website Riposte Laïque wrote about his appearance on *iTélé*[44] as if he himself had declared support for the caliphate. They complained that he cited the Qur'an and that 'he imposed the Arabic language on the French public'.[45]

Mohammed's case is symptomatic of the deeply fractured society in France that the famous Islam expert Gilles Kepel describes in his book *La Fracture*. Like most academics, the Sciences Po professor's year starts in September. For him, the academic year of 2015/16 was a 'terrible year' for the world, but most of all for France.[46] It is hard to contradict him: from the attacks in Paris on 13 November all the way to the attacks in Nice, terrorists have been rubbing their hands. The same is true for the far right, which has capitalised on the growing fears resulting from these repeated attacks on French ground. There are few other Western countries where the social divisions between Muslim and non-Muslim communities are more evident than in France. Identity movements have grown rapidly across France, both on the side of the far right and on that of the increasingly alienated Muslim-majority communities.

Les Identitaires (formerly Bloc Identitaire) is a French nativist, anti-Muslim movement that presents itself as a 'rally for young

French and Europeans who are proud of their roots and of their heritage'. Its founding members have close connections to the Front National. On their webpage, they proudly announce that with 2,000 members and 113,000 Facebook followers they have become one of France's biggest youth movements.[47] Increasingly, Islamist counter-movements have emerged as a form of resistance, leading to a vicious circle of identity radicalisation. There are many parallels between the two antagonists: both movements want separation, both seek a war of identities.

In August 2016, the Islamist extremist Abou Moussa highlighted these similarities in a tweet that read: 'The identity movements are those that resemble us the most, even if it's sad to say that.'[48] The statements of French writer and journalist Éric Zemmour, who is known for his racist and anti-immigration comments, confirm this. In a 2016 interview with the monthly magazine *Causeur*[49] he expressed 'respect' for ISIS jihadists because they are prepared to die for their beliefs. At the same time, he argued in 2014 that 'ISIS represents the true Islam'.[50] With these words, he reassures ISIS, whose understanding of French society corresponds to the description that the far right provides: a society where only native-born French are welcome. Islam is declared incompatible with France's Republican values by both sides. Both attempt to eliminate the grey zones.

'One thing is clear: France finds it difficult to accept its portion of Islamity', writes French-Moroccan scholar Rachid Benzine.[51] According to Benzine, France's fear of Islam has various sources, including the population's vivid memories of the Algerian war, the international terrorism threat, the worsening socio-economic situation. Profound societal transformation as seen in the accelerated 'de-Christianisation' of France and the decline of Republican values, coupled with new waves of Islamisation across the world – have added to those fears.[52] The consequence was the rise of populist xenophobia and the ethnicisation of the political discourse. A new paradigmatic enemy has emerged: 'the Islamist' – often conflated with 'the Muslim'.[53] Nativism and nationalism have melted into a struggle to conserve what they consider 'true France'. In many ways French nativists exhibit similar puritanical tendencies to those displayed by Islamist extremists in their quest to return to what they perceive as 'true Islam'. In both cases, intolerance, stigmatisation and criminalisation of 'the other' on the basis of binary thought constructs have led to identitarian radicalisation.

In this environment increasingly defined by the identity politics of the extremes there is little space for moderate Muslims like Mohammed. 'The French far right and Islamist extremists are two sides of the same coin in France. I have seen them feed off each other,' Mohammed says. 'The far right uses the arguments of ISIS, while Islamist extremists use the arguments of the far right.'[54]

This has played into the hands of terrorists. Jihadists see the rise of the French extremes as conducive to their goal of provoking a civil war. Their strategy is to widen the fissures within French society and to divide the nation into antagonistic religious enclaves.[55] Indeed, the head of the French domestic intelligence agency DGSI, Patrick Calvar, warned that 'confrontation between the extreme Right and the Muslim world' risked placing France on the 'brink of a civil war'. According to him, 'one or two more attacks and it will happen', with far-right and Islamist extremist sympathisers turning to violent responses to each other's provocations.[56]

Sevran

'Sevran has become a caliphate 40 minutes from Paris', the website laïcart.org claimed in March 2016.[57] Sevran is a town in Seine Saint-Denis, a convenient train ride away from central Paris. When I arrive at the train station, Sevran Livry, I don't initially understand why anyone would call the town 'the French Molenbeek'. Apart from the signs in front of the town hall that warn of jihadists and call on Sevran's inhabitants to report any suspicious behaviour, it seems like a perfectly normal town.

The Parisian banlieue became known as 'the French Molenbeek'[58] after 15 local youngsters went off to Syria in spring 2016. Its inhabitants experienced extensive negative news coverage, as the town became a top destination for European journalists. Achraf Ben Brahim, who has grown up in Sevran and is known as an 'expert of French suburban youth', was quickly overwhelmed by requests to take journalists around the banlieue. His frustration climaxed when a reporter brought a full-face veil with her to pretend she was a Muslim.[59] I was careful not to make the same mistake and decided to dress as I usually would.

Most of the young people who left for Iraq and Syria went to what locals dubbed 'The Daesh Mosque'. I ask a couple who seem local how to get to the illegal praying room that was shut down in March 2016 upon the request of Sevran's mayor Stéphane Gatignon. They both stare at me. 'Oh, you mean the one they talked about on TV? I don't know, to be honest.' They never go to that area, one of them tells me.

The further I walk out of the old town centre towards Beaudotte, one of Sevran's most volatile areas, the more it becomes evident that the town has an inequality problem. The small town houses that dominate the city centre increasingly turn into sad grey blocks that radiate deprivation. Of Beaudotte's roughly 10,000 people, 70 per cent live in these subsidised houses, the Habitation à Loyer Modéré (HLM). Some people would call this a ghetto.

Most of the people I pass in Beaudotte are of African descent. But like many English towns,[60] Sevran has experienced a shift from ethnic communalism where only Arabs may represent Arabs to religious communalism where only Muslims may represent other Muslims. The allegiance to the global *ummah* replaces all sense of belonging to the home country.

On the wall next to the closed praying room I read the words: 'Reality is a nightmare for those with dreams'. The town has been plagued by violence linked to drug trafficking. Back in 2011, this even led Mayor Gatignon to call for a UN intervention. The serious social divisions, low education levels and high crime rates have caused the government to add the town to its list of France's top 12 disadvantaged areas. 'Sorry, I don't speak French,' a woman tells me in broken French, as I ask her for the way.

It is true that Sevran's inhabitants are completely segregated but their lives merge for shopping and work – well, for those young people among the lucky 60 per cent with a job. On my way back to the station, I enter an oriental import shop to buy some fruits. The friendly-looking shopkeeper greets me with 'As-salamu alaykum.'

'Wa'alaykumu as-salam,' I reply.

He smiles at me. 'It's unusual for a white person here to reply in Arabic.' He is of Turkish origin and came to Sevran five years ago. When I return to the counter to pay he tells me that he encounters 'a lot of racism and discrimination in his daily life. It's not the same as in Turkey. I don't tell people any more where I'm from. I don't tell them that I'm Muslim.' He tells me that he recently entered a shop and said 'As-salamu alaykum' and received an impolite 'We're in France here' instead of a 'Bonjour'. As I leave, he gives me a few figs for free.

It's the day of the primary elections of the right, so a few people are standing in front of a polling centre. As I pass by, I catch a few words of the ongoing conversation: 'Marine Le Pen is right in what she is saying,' one of them says. 'It's not Islam that should impose itself upon France but France that should impose itself on Muslims who don't make an effort to integrate themselves.'

When Achraf moved to France at the age of eight, he could say two things in French: 'Hello' and 'No, I don't eat pork'. He was born in Djerba, an island off the coast of Tunisia. His father had moved to France several years before him; they first lived in the 17th district of Paris but in 2004 they moved to Sevran. Before turning 18 Achaf couldn't have cared less about politics. But then, in the wake of the Arab Spring, he began to care. He joined the protests in front of the Tunisian embassy and started his studies in politics. After joining ten political parties, including the right-wing Front National, to learn more about the parties' ideologies, the political science major wrote: 'I am everything the National Front despises: immigrant, Muslim, a youngster from the banlieue.'[61]

This seems to be precisely what drives many young people into the hands of ISIS. The far right makes the game fairly easy for Islamist extremists. Abou Moussa, an Islamist extremist who had been arrested at the airport before departing to an unknown destination, confesses the identity conflict that the rhetoric of far-right movements like Les Identitaires, Français de Souche ('native French') and the Front National has provoked in him. The National Front 'doesn't consider us as French, although we are', he tells Achraf. To the question of what he would reproach France for, he replies: 'a lot of injustice [...] as well as rancour and bitterness, even hatred'.[62]

I meet Mohammed Chirani again, this time in Paris. He had seen Sevran turn into a reciprocal radicalisation hotbed long before the city gained widespread media attention. 'In 2013, I understood that the situation in Sevran would explode sooner or later,' he tells me over coffee in Saint-Germain-des-Près. He recalls the moment when Islamist extremists were demonstrating in front of the local prefect, distributing flyers that claimed 'voting is haram'.

At the same time, far-right attitudes and anti-Muslim hate crimes in Sevran have been constantly rising over the past decade. Even back in 2002 the far right was a problem in Sevran.[63] But it's become a lot worse recently. When Mohammed ran for mayor in the city of Sevran after quitting his job as representative for deprived neighbourhoods, he felt the deep rifts that had formed within the town's population. He found himself in the cross hairs of the identity politics of both local Islamist movements and the far right. While the Islamists considered him a traitor whose values and goals were too moderate, the right-wing shortlist of candidates, which had close links to the Front National, withdrew their support. 'They saw me as an Arab, a "communitarist" and even an Islamist.' He ended up creating his own shortlist.[64]

These fractures are exacerbated by the oversimplified and undifferentiated media coverage of Sevran. The explanations provided by the media are often too simple, failing to reflect the complex realities of young people living in the Parisian suburb. As someone who has grown up in the town, Achraf heavily criticised the caricaturised portrayals that journalists provided of Sevran. Too often the French media reduces its explication of the drivers that made the banlieue a fertile breeding ground for jihadists to the formula: *poverty + strong Muslim community + many blacks and Arabs.*[65] The negative media attention fuelled grievances within Muslim communities and anti-Muslim attitudes of the far right, confirming both identity groups in their claims. Today, 'French Molenbeek' is one of the favourite topics of far-right groups such as Français de Souche.[66]

Nice

Our next stop takes us to the South of France, the Côte d'Azur. One of the first modern beach resorts in Europe, it was popular with British, Russian and other European aristocrats during the nineteenth century. In the early twentieth century it also became an appreciated travel destination for famous artists and writers. It has a combined population of around two million, its largest city being Nice.

The Tunisian-born Mohammed Lahouaiej Bouhlel could not have chosen a better place strategically for a terrorist attack. When he drove his truck into the crowds on Nice's Promenade des Anglais during the firework celebrations on 14 July 2016, France's hugely symbolic Bastille Day, he not only killed 86 people and injured over 400; he also hit France's Achilles' heel. One of the darker sides that tourists don't see when coming to Nice's beaches and bars is that the city and its surroundings are deeply divided along religious, ethnic and cultural lines. It is the heart of French identity politics. If Bouhlel wanted to stir hatred and fuel political tension, this was the place to commit an atrocity.

Despite its picturesque setting, many underdeveloped properties are situated just a few miles from the coast. Influential Islamist extremist preachers such as Omar Omsen and Omar Diaby have targeted disaffected French youths, mostly of immigrant origin, exploiting their feelings of marginalisation and discrimination. Such recruiters also appealed to petty criminals by claiming that their behaviour can be justified and even praised when conducting jihad. Diaby, who spent most of his early life in prison, believes in the power of reciprocal radicalisation.[67] In June 2016, he claimed in the French television show *Complément d'Enquête* that he wanted to see Marine Le Pen win.[68]

A month later Bouhel ploughed into the Promenade des Anglais. He was not a particularly devout Muslim, regularly consumed alcohol and pork, and rarely attended mosque. Neither French nor Tunisian authorities had recorded any previous affiliations between him and extremist organisations. But he was an avid follower of ISIS videos online and appears to have been indoctrinated very quickly. Discrimination and racism were part of his daily life. Stigmatisation and scapegoating of Arabs and Muslims had long become mainstream in the city. It is no coincidence that the movement Les Identitaires has its headquarter in Nice.[69]

On a sunny Thursday in March 2017, phones suddenly start ringing at a World Bank conference in Marseille. An envelope had just exploded in the World Bank Paris headquarters, so our conference venue was evacuated and our workshop turned into a live simulation. Less than an hour later, a pupil opens fire at a high school in the Southern French home of perfume production, Grasse. The 17-year-old boy, who wounded four, including the school's headmaster, was arrested soon afterwards. An investigation into his online activities revealed that he had a fascination for American shootings and European and American ultra-far-right materials.

His profile picture featured a graphic of the neo-Nazi video game *Hatred*. The Nice attack appears to have marked him. 'It's good to see how easy it is for us fools to die for nothing', was his reaction to a Twitter user's request to take down the video that showed footage of the attack.

Mohammed Chirani knows Nice well. He spent his youth between war-torn Algeria and the volatile neighbourhood of Ariane. 'Nice has one of the country's highest radicalisation rates because it is one of the cities in France where anti-Muslim discrimination is worst,' Mohammed tells me. Both the extreme right and Éric Ciotti's reactionary right, which is very close to the far right, have driven marginalisation, segregation and ghettoisation in the city. 'We are in a zone with a strong identity crystallisation.'[70] In an *Envoyé* special show, Mohammed shows how a single bridge separates segregated Arabic and white neighbourhoods. As the majority of immigrants in the area are of Algerian, Tunisian and Moroccan descent, many young people are also reminded of French colonial activity conducted in the Maghreb throughout the previous century.[71]

It is within this context that the Côte d'Azur has become a fertile ground for jihadist recruitment in recent years. According to French authorities, over 50 people have left the French Riviera to join ISIS since 2013. This makes it France's second-largest foreign fighter exporter, after Sevran. In total, the Alpes-Maritimes department of the Provence-Alpes-Côte-D'Azur region has accounted for 10 per cent of all French nationals who left for Iraq and Syria.

The Nice truck attack was not the only Islamist extremist-inspired incident in the area. Three days before the 2014 Nice carnival, local authorities arrested a man who had recently returned from Syria and planned to blow himself up at the event. In October 2014, 11 members of the same family left Nice for Syria. Various smaller-scale events occurred too: for example, Islamist extremists attacked a baker in Nice for serving ham sandwiches, while a waitress was assaulted by two men for serving alcohol on the first day of Ramadan.

These incidents have allowed the Front National to turn the region into one of its foremost strongholds: Marine Le Pen's 27-year-old niece, Marion Maréchal-Le Pen won control of the region with over 40 per cent support in the 2015 elections. In the 2017 presidential elections, Marine Le Pen's highest proportion of votes came from the Côte d'Azur.

In response to surging support levels for the Front National, local authorities increasingly pandered to the right and adopted several anti-Muslim laws. The burkini-ban controversy of August 2016 was only the tip of the iceberg. In October 2015 Christian Estrosi, the former Mayor of Nice, forbade football players from praying near or on a pitch; they would potentially receive a two-match ban for doing so. Estrosi also objected to the building of a new mosque called the Grand Mosque En-Nour in Nice, claiming that the building's owner, Saudi Arabia Foreign Minister Sheikh Saleh Ibn Abdulaziz, planned to implement Sharia law.

The French Education Minister Najat Vallaud-Belkacem stated that such examples of 'militant secularism' could further isolate Muslims and push them towards radicalisation.[72] Indeed, more than 70 Islamist terrorism-related arrests have been made since the Bastille Day tragedy, according to Riviera authorities.[73]

Lunel

Lunel is a small, medieval town in southern France. Legend says that it was founded by Jews from the city of Jericho in the first century. Its ancient synagogue serves as a reminder of its importance as a Jewish learning centre until the Middle Ages. But after the departure for Iraq of at least 20 young Lunellois from the town since 2014, Lunel's by-line has changed from 'petit Jerusalem' to 'jihad city'. Journalists, researchers and politicians all asked the same question: why has this enclave of 25,000 people been such a fertile ground for Islamist extremism?

The town is plagued by high unemployment rates, rising poverty and, most importantly, growing rifts within society. 'Lunel is a traumatised town that still can't agree on a diagnosis', according to Patrick Vignal, a local MP of the Socialist Party. For local Front National leader Guillaume Vouzellaud, the problem was clear: 'It is very simple: this mosque should be shut down,' he said, criticising the fact that the town's grand El Baraka mosque has allowed immigrants to 'impose their own values and culture' over the native French population.[74]

Between the 1960s and 1980s, Lunel experienced migration waves from North Africa, especially from Morocco. Today, Muslims make up at least a quarter of the town's population. They typically live in subsidised housing installations in the outskirts of the town and face higher unemployment rates than any other group within Lunel's society. Many locals perceive the North African population as a threat to the city's Judeo-Christian traditions and the safety of their children. 'We cannot pretend that all is fine; our culture is being eroded and our streets are endangered by them', one resident tells me. 'Why is it that this town is a priority security zone? Who do you think is responsible for the high levels of crime here?'

For Sciences Po Professor Gilles Kepel, Lunel's jihadist problem is symptomatic of deeper trends within French society.[75] As in Sevran and Nice, failed integration policies have led to rising segregation and tensions between the white middle class and second- and third-generation immigrants. 'I never felt at home in this town,' one Muslim resident admits to me. The large statue that adorns Lunel's city centre is very telling. It represents Captain Charles Ménard, a military officer who was killed in battle in 1892 against Muslim rebels who protested against French colonialisation in what is today Ivory Coast. His pistol coincidentally points at the town's North African neighbourhood.

Tahar Akermi is familiar with these segregated neighbourhoods that house up to 26,000 inhabitants. 'Tahar? He's the one we call to resolve any conflict. He knows how to speak to youngsters', the former president of the local youth and culture centre said about him.[76] Tahar's exceptional community cohesion projects in the town won him a medal from the National Assembly in 2015. The social entrepreneur is in demand at all times and barely gets a minute to himself. 'I didn't have a Christmas break,' his calm voice tells me over the phone.

'Why do we still call people who were born and raised here "Arabs"? And why do those kids call whites the "French"? This "us and them" dynamic is at the heart of the community problems,' he told France24. Of Algerian descent, he grew up in Lunel where he encountered racism and discrimination himself from a young age. 'Why are you here Algerian species?' he was told when only ten years old. Tahar explains to me that socio-economic tensions between communities in Lunel have translated into severe cultural tensions. 'When people are afraid of losing their space in society they resort to a narrative of "my identity is superior to yours". In Lunel this is very much what happened. Racist and anti-Muslim attitudes are already exceptionally strong in the region but if the far right gains ground politically, the situation will electrify even more.'[77]

Against this background it is hardly surprising that the town has attracted Islamist extremists from the entire region. Although France's Institute for Islamic Studies and the Muslim World concluded in 2010 that the El Baraka mosque was influenced by the global extremist missionary Tablighi Jamaat movement, no one expected it to become an incubator for ISIS jihadists. Here again, the transition of youngsters from non-violent to violent extremism was seamless.

Lunel's rise of Islamist extremism coincided with mounting support levels for the far right. In the 2014 elections for the European Parliament, Lunel's population voted overwhelmingly for the Front National, which won close to 38 per cent. The election results in the departmental elections in 2015 looked similarly favourable for the far right. In the first round, more than 43 per cent of the votes went to Front National candidate Louis Aliot. The second round saw a neck-and-neck race between the Socialists and Front National, which ended up gaining 48 per cent. The majority of Lunel's Muslim population had abstained from the vote.[78]

In January 2015, the hashtag #JesuisCharlie was trending across the world. People of all faiths and countries expressed their solidarity with the murdered *Charlie Hebdo* cartoonists in one way or another. In Lunel, Muslim high school students started using the hashtag #jesuisCoulibaly, after Amedy Coulibaly, the gunman who killed four Jewish people in the hostage-taking in the Hypercacher kosher supermarket in Paris. Meanwhile the Front National reacted with the hashtag #JesuisCharlieMartel, in reference to the Frankish leader Charles Martel, who defeated the Islamic Army in the Battle of Tours in 732.[79]

Like Sevran and Nice, Lunel has suffered waves of negative media coverage, which has further exacerbated tensions. 'You can't reduce all of Lunel's political activity to four jihadists and a few FN candidates,' former mayor Claude Barral insisted. 'The grand majority aren't at either extreme.'[80]

Germany's Nazi–Salafi Heartlands

Alexander Ritzmann used to shape policies in Berlin; today he analyses them in Brussels. He is the charismatic Executive Director of the European Foundation for Democracy and uses his spare time to advise EU policy makers on how to counter terrorist propaganda. Much of his knowledge about the connectivity between extremisms stems from his work on homeland security and intelligence at the Berlin State Parliament in the early 2000s. Up until 2001, the dynamics between right- and left-wing extremism had been Berlin's biggest concern. But when Alexander joined the city's parliament one month after 9/11, Islamist extremism had just become a priority on the agenda. 'The crossover effect we saw between the far right and the far left can also be applied to far-right and Islamist extremism today,' Alexander tells me. To him, the dynamics between the various extremes are a circular rather than a dichotomous phenomenon.[81]

In recent years, Germany has seen a notable increase in Islamist activity. According to the 2013 German Annual Report, membership of German Islamist groups rose from 42,550 in 2012 to 43,185 in 2013. The numbers of German far-right supporters have also been growing exponentially in recent years. 'Something is going on in society,' Hans-Georg Maaßen, head of Germany's domestic intelligence agency, declared, saying that newly formed far-right terrorist groups are posing an increasing risk. For terrorism expert Michael Götschenberg, German right-wing movements are in a sort of self-declared state of war and their willingness to resort to violence is extremely high. The growing number of attacks and hate crimes against refugees and Muslim communities from all across the far-right spectrum are a sign that the usually diverse movements have found an 'ideological consensus' on xenophobia and anti-Muslim hatred.

As a result, far-left movements are stabilising because their enemies are getting stronger and providing them with a unifying cause. While Germany's far left used to focus exclusively in the past on confronting far-right groups and the establishment, far-left extremists who attack Salafists on the basis of their motto 'Kein Gott. Kein Staat. Kein Kalifat' ('No God. No State. No Caliphate') are becoming more commonplace today. For example, a Salafist rally organised by the famous German preacher Pierre Vogel saw everyone fighting everyone. On 8 September 2016, Bremen attracted roughly 300 Salafists as well as 150 right-wing and 200 left-wing protestors. The Salafists were propagating anti-West rhetoric, while far-right supporters were demonstrating against the Salafists and the left, and far-left sympathisers were protesting against the Salafists and the right.[82] Islamist extremists have been capitalising on the rise of both far-right and far-left sympathisers. In short, any divisions and polarisations within society are beneficial to all the extremes – whether Islamist, far left or far right. 'We effectively see a circle of radicalisation in Germany. The extremists all need and reinforce each other.'[83]

Today, German populist and militant far-right groups all attack Salafism in unison. However, it is worth taking a look at how their attitudes towards and interactions with Islamist extremists evolved from fundamentally different starting points. According to the Director of the German Institute on Radicalization and De-radicalization (GIRDS), Daniel Köhler, the populist far right has traditionally had more interaction with German Salafists than militant far-right groups. One possible explanation for this is that Germany's populist far-right movements were more visible for Salafists than militant groups. There was thus more potential for friction. While the first demonstrated openly in the streets against the 'Islamisation of the Occident', the latter tended to stay underground.[84]

Both the self-conception and the actions of right-wing parties and street protest movements such as Pro NRW and PEGIDA have made them the perfect bogeyman for Islamist extremists. PEGIDA claims to represent the Christian Occident, while Pro NRW mocked the Prophet by showing Muhammad caricatures in their anti-Islam protests. They could hardly be a better fit to Islamist extremists' enemy archetype. In fact, some populist far-right supporters even appear to seek confrontation with the other extreme. They have actively tried to provoke Islamist extremists by playing with their enemy image and using their language. For example, the hashtag #ProudToBeAKafir demonstrates that far-right sympathisers have gone as far as to adopt Salafi terminology.[85]

The militant far right, on the other hand, has not traditionally seen Muslims as their primary enemy. In fact, some neo-Nazi groups have even partnered with Islamist extremists in the past. Not only have neo-Nazis welcomed the opportunity to express their anti-Semitic views freely at pro-Palestine demonstrations; the two have also jointly planned attacks on Israelis. Only recently, militant far-right groups have started to perceive Muslim migrants as enemies. In fact, the terrorist organisations Oldschool Society and Bamberg Group have become the first cases of far-right groups actively planning large-scale attacks against Salafists. Sympathisers with populist far-right movements have tended to stage smaller attacks, often arson, on refugee camps but have not planned any major terrorist acts. Köhler argues that the media has played a substantial role in provoking and exacerbating this new dynamic of reciprocal violence between far-right and Islamist extremists.[86]

It's worth noting that Germany's most prominent far-right stronghold is Sachsen, where terrorist groups such as the Oldschool Society, the Freitaler Gruppe and non-violent political movements such as PEGIDA and AfD are thriving more than in any other region. Although Islamist extremists have sought to retaliate – for example with their planned attack on PEGIDA leader Lutz Bachmann in Dresden – their networks have limited reach in the area of Sachsen. Let's therefore look into those areas in Germany where increasing far-right activity is matched by rising support for the Islamist extremist side.

The Bergisch Tri-City Area

Our first stop in Germany is in North Rhine-Westphalia, which hosts an extraordinary blend of industrial and rural landscapes. With about 18 million residents, North Rhine-Westphalia is Germany's largest state. Its capital is Düsseldorf, its biggest city is Cologne and its cultural heart is Bonn. The region is home to the highest Muslim population in Germany and contains the country's largest concentration of Salafists, which is the fastest-growing Islamist movement in Germany.[87]

In the heart of North Rhine-Westphalia lies the Bergisch tri-city area, a culturally and geographically connected triangle that is composed of the cities Wuppertal, Remscheid and Solingen. This is where the industrialisation of Continental Europe began. During the eighteenth and nineteenth centuries, the tri-city area was one of the largest industrial regions in Europe and a traditional centre for the German textiles industry. But the introduction of the Bretton

Woods system led to rising real wages in Germany. This meant that the textile industry moved to low-wage countries like China, India and Bangladesh, leaving thousands of people in Germany jobless. Textiles remain an important part of the tri-city industrial heritage tour but only account for 4 per cent of overall industrial employment.

Today, the Bergisch tri-city area is a fertile ground for both far-right and jihadist recruiters. While Salafism and foreign fighters are new trends that have emerged within the past few years, the region's far-right problems date back to at least the 1990s. German reunification and new waves of immigration in the early 1990s led to heated political debates on asylum rights and a series of xenophobic incidents.

In many ways, today's Nazi–Salafi vicious circle in North Rhine-Westphalia has its origins in the spring of 1993. This is when the city of Solingen became synonymous with far-right violence. Four German skinheads set the house of the Turkish Genç family on fire, killing a mother and four young girls and injuring eight other family members.[88] Today, two metal sculptures tearing apart a swastika in front of Mildred-Scheel-School, which 18-year-old Hatice Genç had attended, serve as a reminder of the horrendous attack. Kamil Genç still suffers the same recurring nightmares of his only daughters dying in the flames.[89] For many Turks in Solingen, the flames did not stop burning after the firefighters arrived at the scene.

On the day after the attack, around 3,000 Turkish migrants descended on the streets of Solingen's city centre, vandalising cars and shops in their anger. The police arrested 62 protestors but less than a week later another demonstration escalated into violence. Autonomist Marxists and Kurds clashed with Turks, many of them linked to the ultra-nationalist Grey Wolves movement.[90] The Grey Wolves are a paramilitary youth organisation linked to Turkey's Nationalist Movement Party. Today, Germany has tens of thousands of Grey Wolves, who often combine their nationalist ideology with religious elements and are increasingly linked to Germany's Salafist scene. 'I was forced to pray. My parents are atheists and I never had anything to do with religion. But many members of the Grey Wolves were also members of the mosque. The imam of the mosque was the chairman', a former Grey Wolf claims.[91]

Less than an hour from Solingen lies Dinslaken, which ranks among Germany's top foreign fighter hubs. Many of the town's youngsters who joined ISIS had close ties with the Grey Wolves movement.[92] Other foreign fighters were members of Millatu Ibrahim, a Salafist group that was formed in a 'backyard mosque' in Solingen in 2011. The government outlawed Millatu Ibrahim in May 2012, leading to Islamist violence in Solingen and neighbouring Bonn that same month. When Germany's 'most radical' mosque was closed down in Solingen, around 80 Salafists affiliated with Millatu Ibrahim were arrested. Many of those eventually ended up travelling to Syria.[93]

Today, the entire region is home to over 200 Salafists, according to the estimations of local authorities. Their most prominent extremist preacher is Sven Lau, who was born in North Rhine-Westphalia. In 2011, he attempted to hold a memorial service for Osama bin Laden.[94] That same year Ibrahim Abou-Nagie, the head of Die Wahre Religion based in Cologne, began to call for violence against infidels and the imposition of Sharia in Germany.[95]

Increased Islamist extremist activity provoked retaliation from several far-right groups based in the region. The climate between far-right and Islamist extremists became increasingly tense. In April 2012, Interior Minister Hans-Peter Friedrich warned of possible confrontations between members of the far-right and Salafist groups, indicating that this could have severe consequences for public security.[96]

It did not take long until his predictions turned real. On 1 May 2012, the words 'freedom instead of Islam' echoed through Solingen. Supporters of the far-right party Pro NRW marched through the streets near a Salafist mosque, showing the infamous Danish cartoons of the Prophet Muhammad by Kurt Westergaard. Some Pro NRW supporters had close connections to neo-Nazi networks. 'Deportation' was their solution. After Pro NRW announced that it would hold a 'Muhammad Cartoon' contest and post the drawings outside 25 mosques in the North Rhine-Westphalia state, the situation escalated. A group of Salafists retaliated by throwing stones, bottles and manhole covers at police and protestors. Three police officers and a passer-by were injured, 30 Salafists arrested.[97]

Less than a week later, Pro NRW supporters organised another anti-Muslim protest in Bonn, prompting hundreds of Salafists to arrange a counter-demonstration. As police staff parked their cars between the opposing camps, Salafists stabbed two police officers and injured 27 others. The events led to more than 100 arrests.[98] Two days later in Cologne, the situation repeated itself, but this time a thousand policemen from all across Germany were present and prevented violent clashes.

Prior to the demonstrations, Salafist groups mobilised their followers and urged them to take violent action in case Pro NRW marchers showed the caricatures again. 'If they show the pictures, rip them up', the Facebook page of Dawa FFM said.[99] The ex-gangsta rapper Deso Dogg, who turned into one of Germany's most famous Islamist preachers and now goes by the name of 'Abu Talha', asked his followers to 'defend the prophet'. One Islamist extremist video emerged in May 2012 that even asked Muslims to kill Pro NRW members and critical journalists.[100] Indeed, the police foiled an attack against Pro NRW leader Markus Beisicht in March 2013. The same four Salafists who were behind the planned attack had also attempted to blow up a train station in Bonn in December 2012.

In 2013, the German government officially banned and dismantled the Salafist groups Islamische Audios, DawaFFM and Al Nusra, which had led the retaliatory riots in the previous year.[101] After the government crackdown, the previously strident Islamist extremist voices of Solingen and Wuppertal became more discreet, at least on the surface. But this did not end radicalisation in the region. To keep a low profile they have resorted to spreading their propaganda elsewhere: often underground or online where the police do not have enough visibility. This has not come at any cost to their allure; they were still as appealing to youngsters as ever. In 2013, a total of around 20 youngsters from North Rhine-Westphalia left the country to join ISIS. While some former members of the dismantled groups decided to leave for Syria, others joined newly emerging movements in the region. Today, the police still monitor at least two mosques in Solingen that are believed to have Salafi links and that have invited Islamist extremist preachers in the past.

'Drinking is haram!' residents of Wuppertal were told in September 2014, while enjoying the last warm autumn evenings outside with their friends. A group of Salafists in orange uniforms was patrolling the streets of Wuppertal to ensure that residents acted in accordance with Sharia. They called themselves the 'Sharia Police', prohibiting alcohol, music and gambling under Sven Lau's leadership.[102] Outrage about the 'Sharia Police' led directly to the formation of the right-wing group Stadtschutz Wuppertal (Wuppertal City Guard), which sought to combat this new Salafist entity.[103] The month before had also seen a series of altercations in North Rhine-Westphalia between Islamists and a group of Yazidi Kurds.[104]

Hooligans against Salafists (Hogesa), an offshoot of the EDL, also seized the opportunity to get the public's attention. They staged a series of protests in other cities in North Rhine-Westphalia, such as Dortmund, Cologne and Essen, in October 2014. Many of its followers came from hooligan football-fan bases, including those of rival football clubs, which put aside their differences to unite in anti-Muslim demonstrations. Although Hogesa has stated that it is not a racist or fascist organisation, it has inevitably attracted people with such leanings to its rallies.[105] Hogesa supporters were also present at a 2015 PEGIDA march in Wuppertal, which had an 800-member turnout and attracted around 80 Salafists.[106]

Lower Saxony East

'Police arrest wrong man, culprit remains at large'. Thousands of newspapers printed headlines to this effect on 21 December 2016, one day after a man had run a truck through a Christmas market in Berlin, killing 12 people and injuring 48. While the manhunt continued all across Europe, analysts were putting together pieces of the puzzle. The young Tunisian Anis Amri was the most wanted man in Europe. He had links to Germany's most significant ISIS recruiting network, which was partly dismantled in 2016 in the states of North Rhine-Westphalia and Lower Saxony.

Of the 850 Germans who travelled to Syria between 2013 and 2017, according to the Constitution Protection Office, 550 were from Lower Saxony. Many of these individuals were in contact with the same preachers as Anis Amri. At the centre of this transregional network was the 32-year-old Iraqi Ahmad Abdulaziz Abdullah A., better known under the name Abu Walaa. 'He is the worst', German security forces said about him; 'the preacher without a face', a man who rarely showed his 25,000 Facebook followers anything more than his back.[107]

Abu Walaa had grown up in North Rhine-Westphalia but used Hildesheim in Lower Saxony as his central operational hub. Amid all the innocent-looking timber framework houses and famous churches in Hildesheim, it was hard to believe that 'the German number 1 of ISIS' was recruiting jihadists. Apart from Hildesheim, the neighbouring cities of Wolfsburg and Braunschweig have been known as Salafi hotspots. By mid-2015, the two cities had produced around two dozen foreign fighters. According to estimations of local authorities, Wolfsburg alone is home to about 30 to 40 radicalised Salafists and there are another 100 in the area of Braunschweig, although not all of these are prepared to use violence in the name of their extremist ideas.[108]

In Wolfsburg, a group of Tunisian-Germans working for a Volkswagen subcontractor went from playing football together, to handing out Qur'ans at the railway station, to recruiting for ISIS.[109] Wolfsburg is the youngest of the three cities: it was only founded in May 1938, when Adolf Hitler and Ferdinand Porsche celebrated the inauguration of Volkswagen's factory there. They called it 'the city of the KdF car' ('Stadt des'). It was only after the end of World War II that the city was named Wolfsburg.

The far right remains disproportionally active in Wolfsburg and its surroundings. In April 2013, the government banned members of the National Democratic Party of Germany (NPD) from 'marching against foreign domination'. On this occasion the city's mayor, Klaus Mohr, said: 'we have no space here for neo-Nazis'.[110] The NPD has capitalised on Islamist extremist arrests and scandals in Wolfsburg[111] and chose the city as the location for its kick-off event in the 2016 municipal elections.

Achim Buonafede, the founder and mastermind of the neo-Nazi group 'Berserker Deutschland – Division Wolfsburg', was also from Wolfsburg. He relaunched its Facebook page, posting statements such as: 'Multiculturalism is only a codeword for the white genocide' and 'National Socialism is the most powerful revelation of the soul of a race.'

In recent years, Lower Saxony has increasingly turned into a stronghold for German far-right movements, both populist and militant. 'We have to acknowledge that AfD is now a political factor in Lower Saxony,' said the leader of the Social Democratic Party, Stephan Weil, after Germany's regional elections in September

2016. In some cities, AfD achieved double-digit support, something unprecedented for far-right parties in post-war Germany. After experiencing several migration waves, Lower Saxony's population has almost doubled from 4.5 million to close to 8 million since the 1930s. In the 2016 municipal elections in Lower Saxony, the far-right AfD reached around 9 per cent in Braunschweig and Hildesheim, and over 10 per cent in Wolfsburg, making the cities far-right strongholds not just on a national level but also in comparison to most other cities in the state of Lower Saxony. Following the 2016 regional elections, the AfD was ironically given the chair of the committee for migration and integration in the Wolfsburg city council.[112]

BRAGIDA, the Braunschweig offshoot of PEGIDA, also enjoys considerable support from the local population. Although its leaders asserted that the movement had no links to the local militant far-right scene, its marches have in the past attracted neo-Nazis holding BRAGIDA banners. Braunschweig, which was dubbed 'the city of science', is the EU's most prominent hub for research and development. But the city also has darker sides. Between neo-Nazi bands that hold far-right concerts and far-right militants that put high-school students into hospital, the city's far-right scene appears at least as menacing as its hyper-radicalised Salafist network. It is home to a number of far-right hooligan groups such as Fette Schweine Braunschweig and Exzess Boys Braunschweig. The Braunschweig-based Marvin Vogelsang is considered one of the most influential neo-Nazis in the region. In July 2016, a handful of neo-Nazis from the neighbouring Salzgitter area founded the group National Resistance Lower Saxony East (NWNO) with the goal of 'stopping policies hostile to the German people and guiding youth towards a patriotic future'. One of their Facebook profiles has been removed because it was inciting hatred, and in July 2016 they were prohibited from returning to Braunschweig's city centre.

Northern Bavaria
In July 2016, many observers couldn't help but wonder what was going on in Germany. Within less than a week, the country suffered a series of four separate terrorist atrocities that included a gun, a bomb, an axe and a machete attack and killed a total of ten people. Three of those incidents took place in Bavaria, two were claimed by

ISIS's official Amaq news agency. Events were unfolding so quickly that Bavaria was propelled into the media spotlight all across the world and false alarms went off across Germany, as people started panicking.

It is hardly surprising that the media frenzy surrounding the first attacks gave rise to copycat attacks. When Johann Wolfgang Goethe's world classic *The Sorrows of the Young Werther* was published in 1774, young men who identified with the novel's protagonist's grievances began imitating the fictive character's actions, which resulted in a sharp rise in suicides across Germany. The incidents of July 2016 were a classic example of this Werther effect.

Media sensationalisation alone would not have sufficed to inspire other self-starter attacks in such a short time frame. The behavioural contagion effect would not have been possible had the region not been prone to extremism. For several years German intelligence services had warned of the rising radicalisation rates and growing extremist networks in the area. In the autumn of 2015 it was reported that Islamist extremists were trying to recruit alienated refugees in Bavaria.[113] The crime scenes of the 2016 ISIS-inspired attacks – Würzburg and Ansbach – the Islamist extremist stronghold Nuremberg and the neo-Nazi heartland Bamberg all lie within a radius of 60 kilometres.

Nuremberg enjoys an extraordinarily 'good reputation' among Salafists, according to regional newspapers.[114] In 2012, the Nuremberg mosque organised a secret conference with leading Islamist extremists from all across Europe. Currently, the Bavarian intelligence service is monitoring around 50 individuals considered extremists who could resort to violence, and three mosques in Nuremberg.[115]

Growing fears of Islamist terrorism have provided fuel for far-right parties and militants in the area. The existence of the National Socialist Underground only came to light in 2011; it had committed a total of ten lethal attacks against immigrants, six of which had taken place in Bavaria.[116]

If the Nuremberg area is Bavaria's Salafist hotspot, Bamberg is its centre of far-right activity. In October 2014, about 150 neo-Nazis were marching against immigration in Bamberg with the words 'Bamberg defends itself – asylum abuse, no thank you'.[117] Over recent years Bamberg has attracted increasing numbers of neo-Nazis, far-right militants and anti-Muslim activists. Its most prominent and dangerous one was the Bamberg Group. In 2015, the German Federal Criminal Police Office arrested 11 men and two women linked to the group, which had planned to stage large-scale attacks against refugees and asylum seekers in Bamberg. The police found several kilos of explosive materials and other weapons, mostly imported from Eastern Europe, together with far-right propaganda.[118]

United States: White Supremacism and Religious Wars

The stories do not change significantly after taking a trans-Atlantic flight: resentment fuses with fear and, when it meets boredom, translates into radicalisation.[119] But detecting cumulative extremism patterns in the US is trickier. According to the Soufan Group, there are no hotbeds for foreign fighter recruitment, and radicalisation happens mostly online, often through peer-to-peer social media interactions.[120] This section will therefore focus on the background to specific terrorist incidents rather than geographic areas.

In many ways, the relationship between racial and religious tensions is unique in the US. While many of the most obvious conflicts occur between racial identity groups, religious tenets are often linked to those. Christian identity movements have been closely intertwined with white supremacist groups and Islamist teachings have been tied to black pride movements. When the Afghan-born Wallace Fard co-founded the Nation of Islam in the 1930s he declared that Christianity was the white man's religion, which had been forced upon African Americans as a by-product of slavery. Members of the Nation of Islam and other 'Black Muslims' who followed his doctrines therefore thought that Islam was closer to their African identity.

The famous journey of Malcolm Little – better known as Malcolm X – started with his early experiences with white supremacism and far-right extremism. His autobiography begins with the chapter 'Nightmare', which recounts the night when Ku Klux Klan members set his family's house on fire. His mother, Louisa Little, was pregnant with him when Klan members shouted at her to 'better get out of town because "the good Christian white people" were not going to stand for my father's "spreading trouble" among the "good" Negroes of Omaha'.[121] Seven years later his father, Earl Little, was killed in a streetcar accident, but Malcolm X never doubted that what was officially declared an accident had in fact been an assassination by the KKK. The identity-based ideas that Muslim leaders like Malcolm X and Sayyid Qutb used as a means of resistance in the face of white supremacism served as a source of inspiration for many young Western-born Muslims who had endured similar experiences of discrimination and hatred. For example, Maajid Nawaz strongly identified with Malcolm X's and Qutb's struggles in his teenage years after falling victim to neo-Nazi aggression himself, before joining Hizb ut-Tahrir. It was the first step for him to embrace prejudice as a remedy against prejudice.

'A strange fetish exists between the hater and the hated', Maajid writes in his autobiography.[122] America is no exception to this. In fact, 'from the reverse racism of Malcolm X's early days in the Nation of Islam [...] to Qutb and Islamism, America has inadvertently bred her own worst enemies, her strongest co-dependents'.

'If there is more of an atmosphere of hostility and violence, there is more likely to be a reaction from Islamist extremists,' Richard Barrett, former Director of Global Counter Terrorism Operations for the British Secret Intelligence Service, tells me over hot chocolate in Victoria. Richard had just come back from New York, where he had spent his past few years working at the UN and as Senior Advisor to the Soufan Group. According to his observations, US society still breaks down into its different racial and religious groups. 'This violent racism that is deeply entrenched in American society is very much alive today. In many ways the civil war is still ongoing.'[123]

Like most people who work in security, Richard is concerned about the recent upsurge of far-right extremism in the US. 'I do think that there is going to be a bit of a dark period.' Although Islamist extremist attacks have been rare on US territory since 9/11, the country's population increasingly responds to perceived threats under the motto 'you don't want to wait until it's too late'. For Richard, reciprocal radicalisation often is the product of 'a reaction to perception rather than reality'.[124]

The Orlando Shootings
On 12 June 2016 Omar Mateen killed 49 people and injured 53 at the Pulse gay nightclub in Orlando, Florida. While most explanations

for Omar's radicalisation focused exclusively on his suppressed homosexuality, alleged cases of anti-Muslim hatred that he had repeatedly suffered at the hands of colleagues while working as an intern for St Lucie County Sherriff's Department may have played a role too. During his internship, Mateen had filed several complaints to the department regarding racial abuse from local deputies. A sheriff's deputy named John Roleau had asked him, 'Don't you Arabs sleep with goats?' even though Mateen was of Afghan descent (not Arab) and was born in the United States. A deputy and Gulf War veteran named Robert McNamara had praised former Republican Representative Allen West for urging the murder of 'all the fucking Muslims'. McNamara also allegedly taunted Mateen by clipping and unclipping his gun holster outside the courthouse.

Mateen claimed that someone had put Allen West campaign stickers on his car and deflated his front two tyres. Deputy Rusty Wright reportedly met Mateen in a courthouse hallway and, pointing to a mat on the floor, asked: 'Isn't it your prayer time? Take your magic carpet and pray to your Allah and make sure it's in the East.' Several deputies such as Sergeant Jeff Buchanan allegedly badgered Mateen on how Muslims have infiltrated American society with the aim of imposing Sharia. Deputy Bobby Dimarco would refer to Mateen as 'Aladdin' while Michael Robinson declared the beginning of a 'redneck spring'. Others mocked him as a backward primitive, offering him bacon and talking about slaughtering Muslims.

Mateen then went on to work for the private security firm G4S from 2007 until his death. David Torres, a colleague of Mateen's at the firm, reportedly urged the other deputies to be suspicious of him and once remarked, 'Muslims are similar to Jews [...] they rape the system and monopolize.' Another of his G4S colleagues, Hunter Dennis, claimed that Mateen resembled someone that he had killed in Iraq and threatened to shoot Mateen if he heard him say 'Allahu Akbar'. Mateen's subsequent outburst to his colleagues led to an FBI investigation concerning his claims to have links with the Boston marathon bombers and the Kenyan mall shooters. The FBI interviewers described him as pleasant and cooperative, while Mateen claimed that he was 100 per cent American and anti-terrorism, which is why he had chosen a career in security.

Alongside the reported cases of anti-Muslim hatred suffered by Mateen, there are other serious factors to consider as possible reasons for the shooting. For example, Mateen's official reason for the attack was the killing of ISIS commander Abu Wahib in Iraq weeks before. While Mateen had passed background checks in both 2007 and 2013, his former G4S colleague Daniel Gilroy claimed that Mateen was unstable and had talked about killing people. Furthermore, it was revealed after the shooting that Mateen had never received a psychological evaluation in 2007 for his firearms licence.

Mateen's ex-wife claimed that he had been mentally unstable, with a history of steroid use and domestic abuse towards her. Meanwhile Mateen's father (a member of the Afghan Taliban) claimed that, prior to the shooting, his son had become angered at the sight of two men kissing. Florida imam Syed Ur Rahman, who claimed that Mateen would come to pray at the local mosque four times a week, stated that the mosque's teachings were entirely peaceful. However, a few weeks before the attack, Sheikh Farrokh Sekaleshfar had given a talk outside Orlando calling for all homosexuals to be killed.

Some reports suggested that Mateen was a closet homosexual. Ty Smith, a regular at Pulse, told the *Orlando Sentinel* that Mateen would come to drink in the club, often becoming drunk and belligerent. Kevin West, another Pulse regular, claims that Mateen had messaged him on a gay dating app: Jack'd. Former classmates and teachers of Mateen said that he was an extremely aggressive and violent student, praising the 9/11 attacks and claiming that Osama bin Laden was his uncle. However, other students claimed that Mateen was bullied because of his weight and his Afghan descent.

A few cases of workplace anti-Muslim hatred can be found in the story of Syed Farook, who killed 14 people and injured 22 in a shooting in San Bernadino, California, on 2 December 2015. Farook suffered repeated harassment at the hands of right-wing, pro-NRA, anti-government, evangelical co-worker Nicholas Thalasinos. Thalasinos was among those colleagues targeted during the shooting. Farook had travelled to Pakistan to acquire a mail-order bride, who allegedly helped to radicalise him. Together they gathered 15 pipe bombs and 7,000 rounds of ammunition. Likewise, Major Nidal Hassan, who killed 13 and injured over 30 at Fort Hood on 5 November 2009, suffered Islamophobic harassment from colleagues for his opposition to the wars in Iraq and Afghanistan. Hassan was a devout Muslim who reportedly wrote 'Allah' on his door and had previously applied for an arranged marriage with an equally devout Muslim woman.

The #Texasattack

'We are here in defiance of Islam,' Dutch far-right politician Geert Wilders said at the Muhammad Cartoon Contest in Garland on 2 May 2015. 'Islam has declared war on us, on our Judeo-Christian civilization. Islam wants to rob us of the freedoms and liberties. Islam and freedom are totally incompatible.' The contest for drawings of the Prophet was organised by Pamela Geller's controversial American Freedom Defense Initiative (AFDI), also known under the name Stop Islamization of America.[125]

Most far-right keynote speakers had already given their speeches when a Twitter user called Sharia Is Light announced the #texasattack' at 6.35 p.m. Just minutes later, a shooting occurred outside of the Curtis Culwell Center where the event was being held. Police shot dead two gunmen who had targeted a security officer with assault rifles. Two days after the attack, ISIS claimed responsibility for the incident on Al Bayan radio, praising the two gunmen as 'soldiers of the caliphate'.

One year after the shootings in Garland, on 7 July 2016, army reservist Micah Xavier Johnson shot dead five police officers, wounded seven other officers and two civilians. The man, in his twenties, was wearing heavy body armour and kept saying that he wanted to kill white people, especially white police officers. On Facebook he had raged about racial discrimination, white supremacism and police violence, and had liked the pages of Nation of Islam, Black Riders Liberation Army and the New Black Panther Party. Although he had no formal links to militant groups, it took just hours before ISIS, Al Qaeda and far-right sympathisers hijacked the incident to customise it to their message. Breitbart quoted ISIS and Al Qaeda supporters who praised the attacks; Islamist extremists recited Breitbart readers' anti-Muslim messages that resulted from the media frenzy.

Inter-racial and inter-religious tensions in Texas appear to be especially high. According to the Southern Poverty Law Center's interactive hate map, Texas has more white supremacist organisations than any other state. Out of 892 active hate groups across all 50 US states, 84 are located in Texas – most of them are sub-groups of the KKK.[126] The country's two largest white supremacist prison gangs, the Aryan Brotherhood of Texas and the Aryan Circle, are also located in Texas. They comprise a total of 3,500 members across the US and committed over 33 racial murders in Texas between 2000 and 2015.[127]

These case studies demonstrate that the reciprocal radicalisation phenomenon occurs across different demographic, cultural and socio-economic settings. Country-specifics range from retaliation between British jihadists and counter-jihad groups, to French cultural identity wars, to German neo-Nazi–Salafi clashes, to American tensions between white supremacists and black identity groups. But the overall trend in these mutual breeding grounds remains the same: far-right and Islamist extremists react to each other's rhetoric and actions, creating a vicious circle of hate that often translates into violence.

8

Breaking the Vicious Circle

ON OUR TRIP INTO THE MINDS OF EXTREMIST SYMPATHISERS, FORMER extremists, terrorism victims and voters, we have found clear links between far-right and Islamist extremists' stories – the two strands of extremism feed off one another. In this sense, the conflict between far-right and Islamist extremists today mirrors that of communists and fascists in 1920s Italy – but on a much bigger scale. Rapidly changing economic, political and cultural environments have led to a global identity crisis that is further exacerbated by modern technology and the new media. Resulting grievances, uncertainty and a lack of perspective have formed a bitter cocktail of rage, which has been the elixir of life for extremists.

This book has demonstrated that far-right and Islamist extremist narratives ('The West is at war with Islam' and 'Muslims are at war with the West') complement and amplify each other, leading to a bizarre form of interdependency between the two. Far-right and Islamist extremists succeed in penetrating each other's echo chambers because their messages are mutually useful. This effectively makes the two extremes 'rhetorical allies'.

Far-right and Islamist extremist incidents correlate in terms of their timing, and areas with a strong far-right presence are more likely to breed Islamist extremists and vice versa. One side tends to provoke a retaliatory reaction from the other. The extremes thus escalate, resulting in a spiralling violence effect. With those on each side feeling the need to defend themselves from the offences of the other side, their predictions become a self-fulfilling prophecy: an increasing number of Muslims are lured into embracing Islamist views and a rising number of non-Muslims turn to far-right parties.

Our society's drift towards extremes is effectively validating the claim that we are facing a global cultural war between Muslims and non-Muslims, which extremists on both sides are propagating. This further strengthens extremists' credibility and appeal; we see that the war between far-right and Islamist extremists is increasingly turning into a war between the West and Islam. This is the vicious circle that we need to interrupt. Otherwise, we will not only live in an increasingly divided, polarised and extreme society, but we will also see more terrorist attacks, both from far-right and Islamist extremists.

Extremism is about grievances, identities and ideologies. Since the chief two opposing camps of today – far-right and Islamist extremists – reinforce each other's grievances, identities and ideologies, fighting one without simultaneously combating the other will be ineffective. We therefore need to reduce societies' overall vulnerability, to challenge both sides' binary worldviews and to create a stronger sense of collective identity that reunites rather than divides our societies. The Age of Rage has only just begun unless we tackle its underlying sources by adopting new, innovative approaches to politics, education, communication and activism.

By no means will I be able to offer *the* solution. What I can suggest is a collection of starting points and impulses for embarking on an arduous path that avoids bogeymen and total solutions. Just as there isn't one explanation for the rise of far-right and Islamist extremism, there isn't one answer to it. The underlying root causes are so complex, multidimensional and intertwined that the solution will have to be both multi-faceted and creative. The more diverse the problem solvers are, the more likely it is that we are up for the challenge. So let's look into ways to break the vicious circle, reshuffle the cards and move forward peacefully together.

What Next?

In July 2016, part-time Asda employee Ryan Ashley Counsell took a week off to go to the Philippines. His plan was not to go surfing on idyllic beaches but to join the ISIS-linked Abu Sayyaf group. Had the police not noticed his bizarre purchasing habits, he would have left behind his pregnant wife and three-year-old daughter. Post-Brexit tensions were the driving force behind Counsell's actions, according to his barrister John Kearney. '[A]fter the Brexit results [...] his feeling at the time was [that] there were divisions in his community in Nottingham and he was concerned at the way ordinary people were reacting to ordinary Muslims', Kearney said about Counsell's motives.[1] Counsell was sentenced to eight years in prison for preparing acts of terrorism.

If today's terrorism threat can indeed be seen as a vicious circle, in which far-right and Islamist extremist narratives amplify each other, this has major implications for prevention and counter-terrorism efforts: in a circle, the 'after' equals the 'before', meaning that reaction equals prevention. Reaction takes place on all levels: politics, the media and civil society all determine what 'after' looks like. They all shape the narrative. Political and societal reactions to terrorist attacks have allowed illegitimate players to dominate the debate and effectively rule the game.

Jack Buckby, press officer at Liberty GB, understands this dynamic. 'Exit polls suggest a left-wing coalition in the Netherlands. Horrible thing to think, but only terror attacks can save Netherlands now. Wake up,' he tweeted a few days before the Westminster attack. 'Fear of terrorist attacks and mass refugee flows are driving many Western governments to roll back human rights protections', the Director of Human Rights Watch, Kenneth Roth, wrote in the 'World Report 2016'.[2] Bombing Raqqa, curbing immigration, militarising streets, banning burkinis and voting for far-right parties will not only be ineffective but will also most likely be harmful. It further widens the rifts within our societies, validating extremists' narratives that know no grey zones between 'good and bad', 'innocent and guilty' and 'true and false'. By forgetting that preventing also means responding we might be turning extremists' binary worldviews that are based on identity creation through common victimhood into self-fulfilling prophecies.

Politicians, the media, voters have all been following the rules of the roulette that extremists want to play. In their attempt to stop them winning, they have ended up playing by the rules of extremists: terrorism itself does not pose an existential threat to Western countries, but inconsiderate and disproportionate reactions to it can. Today's widening divisions, between and within institutions as well as between and within communities, are driving both pull and push factors of violent extremism. They increase extremists' demand by fostering grievances and identity crises and feed extremists' supply by making their narratives more credible. They deprive communities of their resilience against violent extremism, and rob liberal, democratic pleas of their credibility.

How can the political centre refocus its attention on consistently applying its own rules – rules that are based on respect for fundamental human rights, democracy and pluralism and that have been created to ensure peace after the experience of two devastating world wars in the last century?

Mobilising the Middle

Everything I know about Seyran Ateş is exceptional. 'I want to become an imam,' is the first thing she tells me. Seyran is a bisexual Muslim lawyer. Her mother is Turkish, her father Kurdish, she is German. At the age of 18 she published her first autobiographical book. During her studies in Berlin, Seyran earned her money protecting Turkish and Kurdish women from domestic violence. In 1984, a contract killer linked to the Grey Wolves shot dead her client and severely injured Seyran. We meet in a rather unconventional place for a conversation about extremism: a hamam in the middle of Austria's countryside. 'Everyone should enjoy the freedom to explore their sexuality,' she tells me. Her work as a divorce lawyer and her controversial bestseller *Islam Needs a Sexual Revolution* resulted in multiple death threats.

When I talk to Seyran she is in the middle of registering Berlin's first liberal and inclusive mosque. 'The Ibn Rushd-Goethe Moschee will give the peaceful and kind Islam that I know a face.' It is a place where Muslim men and women can pray side by side and everyone is welcome – whether Alevite, Sunnite, Shiite or other schools. 'As a believing Muslim, it is unbearable to see people associate terror, hate and death with my religion. I find it just as insupportable to watch so many young people being lured into extremism by those who exploit my religion for their violent causes […] It is in our hands to show young people that there are alternative interpretations.' Seyran wants to give the silenced majority of Muslims, who do not support Islamist extremism, a platform. She is convinced that 'Islam can exist in a liberal, democratic and constitutional society. There is no contradiction.'

The former imam of the Central London Mosque, Sheikh Dr Salah Ansari, agrees that Islam and democracy are compatible. Salah devotes his life to challenging destructive misconceptions about Islam. He is a lecturer in Islamic studies at Muslim College London, as well as an inter-faith activist during the day and a tireless researcher at night. In 2017, he became the first theologian to challenge ISIS's handbook of violence commonly known as *Fiqh al-Dima* (the Jurisprudence of Blood), written by one of the organisation's key ideologues Abu 'Abdullah Al Muhajir. 'This book is not exactly the nicest bedtime read,' he says, laughing. Our table in Rabat is loaded with Moroccan food, as we listen to live music from his home country, Egypt. Salah seems to have kept his usual blithesome spirit. But reading 579 pages on beheadings, crucifixions and massacres was challenging even to him. 'I had a depression for three months,' he confesses to me.

'Islamic scriptures need careful attention in reconciling the relationship between various conflicts of evidences,' he explains. ISIS deals with this by using *naskh* (abrogation): verses 5 and 29 in Chapter 9 of the Qur'an become 'final commanding verses' that erase all the other verses on mercy, peace and pluralism. Both ISIS and the far right like to quote these two verses, which they claim prove that Islam is inherently violent and urges Muslims to kill non-Muslims. Additionally, both selectively quote medieval scholars and take verses out of the historical context that determined their meaning in the first place. Many then believe that this is real Islam. 'If I read this for the first time, I would buy it. That's why it's so important to fight this pseudo-knowledge of Islam, which suits both ISIS and the far right.'

There is little doubt that Salah will keep spending his nights tearing apart the foundations that underpin the misconceptions of both far-right and Islamist extremists. Most likely Seyran will keep exploring liberal, progressive interpretations of Islam. Concerted efforts of moderate Muslims such as Salah and Seyran can help extremists to reverse their journeys and prevent vulnerable individuals from going down that path.

Saving the Fringes

Maajid Nawaz was chasing a fly when a prison guard brought a new pile of Azhar University books to his cell in Egypt. By the end of his four-year prison term, the buzzing sound of the flies was so agonising, he could hardly stand it. Maajid was a political prisoner next to the assassins of the former Egyptian president Anwar Sadat: professional bomb-makers and Al Qaeda affiliates. Maajid's journey out of extremism began when Amnesty International adopted him as a prisoner of conscience: 'To see people fighting for me and giving me a second chance was an incredible source of inspiration and hope.' With every new encounter he had in prison – with ex-jihadists and political activists – he felt his binary understanding of 'good' and 'bad' mutate into a more multidimensional concept of identity. With every line he read, he felt his obsession with creating the caliphate fade. After reading George Orwell's book *Animal Farm* he realised how dangerous the desire to create a utopia could be. In 2007, a year after his release from prison, Maajid resigned from Hizb ut-Tahrir, leaving behind his extremist past, embracing liberal, democratic values and devoting his life to challenging extremism.

Ten years later, 'Trevor' was in danger of becoming a far-right extremist. 'And not one of these beer-swilling racist ranting EDL Britain First types; more a solitary figure with an undesirable skillset who would use that against the Muslim community in what I suppose would be an act of terrorism', he tells Maajid Nawaz in a personal Twitter message. 'No idea is above scrutiny, no people are beneath dignity' is Maajid's guiding principle. We can compete, debate, even clash, as long as we do not dehumanise and degrade those of other opinions. 'You brought me back from the brink of hate-filled extremist violent intent and planning against the Muslim community to a frustrated but peaceful place of relief and regret', the would-be far-right terrorist writes to the ex-Islamist extremist. 'Relief that I did not carry out my mission and regret that I somehow found myself there in the first place.'

My phone beeps with a message. 'Can we talk a bit later? I'm just in a cyber-security meeting with the police over a couple of trolls. Ivan.' Since his *Open Your Eyes to Hatred* campaign video had gone viral, the ex-EDL community manager was receiving threats and insults through various channels. 'They've been attacking me for five months now. I don't know who it is, what they know or what they are prepared to do.'

'I used to be a thug too,' he says about himself. Ivan was initially helping the EDL as a fan page administrator but he quickly became heavily involved, doing everything from fundraising to radicalisation.

He had lost many of his friends from home who disagreed with his racist views, but the EDL was a closed community that made it easy to make new friends. 'The EDL gave me back everything that I had lost.' His social media feed reinforced his views: 'I started seeing things online; it was like brainwashing – subconsciously, it affected my views but I didn't realise it. Thinking back now, I was radicalised.' When he joined the EDL, he didn't hate all Muslims, but six months in he hated everything about them. His philosophy was quite straightforward: 'Muslims are terrorists and they're going to take over, if we don't defend ourselves.'

Everything changed when Ivan met Manwar Ali, an imam and ex-jihadist who now heads the charity JIMAS. He had heard rumours that Manwar was planning to buy a church in Ipswich to turn it into a mosque and was expecting a heated debate with the imam. But Manwar surprised him with his warm, open-minded attitude: 'I've wanted to speak to you for ages', was the first thing he told Ivan. After hours of building trust and dispelling each other's fears, Ivan realised that he was quite similar to him. 'We may have had different journeys but our stories had the same basis. That's what people need to realise – even when we hate each other we're more alike.'

'A lot of people are blinded by their hatred and often they don't have the guts to talk to Muslims,' Ivan says. Many far-right organisations such as Britain First and the North West Infidels are craving for a way to justify their race wars. 'We are lucky in the UK,' according to the ex-EDL member; 'if we had more jihadist attacks, the far-right would go nuts.' But just labelling them as racists without trying to understand their grievances is pointless, according to him. 'As a nation we've become lazy.' To tackle the symbiosis of Islamist and far-right extremists we need to listen to the stories of both sides of the extremes, because the vicious circle of fear and hate can only be broken through dialogue.

Ivan's example shows that a 180-degree turn is possible. Today, most of his work is for Muslim communities and most of his interviews are with Muslim radio stations. 'Now no one would guess that I used to be an EDL member. I have an imam as a father figure and my daughter's best girlfriend is Muslim.' Although Ivan has neither converted to Islam nor become a Muslim spokesperson, his former EDL mates consider him a traitor. 'All I do is to support and highlight the valuable work done by many good Muslim men and women within their communities in tackling many of the issues I once thought were being unchallenged.'

For Ivan, creating save havens for people to talk openly to people whom they fear would be the first step in helping extremists to drop their hate. Since leaving the EDL, Ivan has tried to help others to widen their horizon by taking them to mosques and introducing them to Muslims. 'I may not be able to change the entire far right, or even the EDL, but at least I managed to change myself and maybe this will inspire others.' Most importantly, Ivan wants to be a positive role model. 'I don't want my kids to repeat my mistakes.' So he makes sure they develop positive relations with children of other racial and religious backgrounds. Much of this is about telling the right stories. 'I'm doing now what I did back when I was in the EDL. I'm telling stories.'

Critical Thinking, Courage and Creativity

'Stay safe as we are approaching the final battle. Against hate', the note in my bag now reads.

Since the turn of the millennium, extremists' stories have dictated our countries' political agendas and dominated our societies' behaviours. Now it is time for moderate voices to take back the online and offline space. How can we transcend the boundaries that extremists' binary stories have imposed on our worldviews? 'Freedom would be to not choose between black and white but to abjure such prescribed choices', according to the German philosopher Theodor Adorno. Equipping young people with curiosity, courage and critical thinking skills will be crucial to achieving this freedom: the critical thinking skills to identify manipulative language and distorted facts, the courage to question everyone and everything, and the creativity to go beyond one's own echo chambers and boundaries of imagination.

Countless studies have shown that education is the best remedy against extremism.[3] Europe produces more high-school and university graduates than ever: Eurostat statistics for 2015 reveal that more than 80 per cent of EU citizens between 20 and 24 gain at least an upper secondary level of education.[4]

But literacy rates and formal education levels are not the only metrics that matter. A-level jihadi brides, Oxford-graduate Hizb ut-Tahrir members and Ivy-League-educated white supremacists show that high formal education levels do not prevent individuals from falling prey to fake news, conspiracy theories and extremist propaganda. Re-energising democracy will mean tackling the proliferation of post-factualism and reviving the Enlightenment values. The 'Sapere aude' ('Dare to know') principle combined with digital literacy and critical consumption of new media might therefore allow for a global return from emotional to rational decision making, from fake-news-inspired to evidence-based thinking, from mythos to logos.

Returning to logos and telling alternative stories requires courage. We cannot always count on courageous, liberal Muslims being willing to sacrifice their personal safety to challenge extremism, and selfless imams to spend a year in depression and nightmares. What can one do, if moderate Muslims like Mohammed Chirani and liberal reformers like Seyran Ates continue receiving death threats from both ISIS sympathisers and far-right militants? The answer is: the louder moderate voices get, the harder it will become to intimidate and silence them.

Painting pictures using colours other than the black and white of far-right and Islamist extremists also takes creativity. How can we tell new stories that do not pit one identity group against another and divide societies into opposing camps? In binary stories with human opponents, the logical consequence of collective action is usually a war or a genocide. But what hinders us from telling stories with abstract antagonists instead of human ones? Could global challenges make for good common antagonists? We have more than enough common problems – climate change, environmental degradation, poverty, hunger, to name just a few – and they will all require internationally concerted efforts. Replacing human antagonists with abstract ones may be the biggest challenge but also the biggest opportunity of the twenty-first century.

Civil-society-led initiatives such as Families Against Terrorism and Extremism (FATE) and Extremely Together have made a good start: they have provided a platform for moderate voices and mobilised people across the world to counter extremism with innovative projects. The FATE network, for example, has brought together families of terrorists and families of terrorism victims, as well as former far-right extremists and former Islamist extremists. It has therefore enabled former adversaries to overcome their enmities to join forces in fighting their biggest common foes: fear, rage and hatred. It has catalysed their energy into a positive cause and fuelled the engine of unity and solidarity.

'Our strength is our unity of purpose',[5] Franklin D. Roosevelt declared on 6 January 1941. Roosevelt was one of modern history's most gifted storytellers: instead of emphasising the viciousness of the antagonists, thereby unintentionally reinforcing their narratives, he gave his people a positive vision, a cause that they could believe in and would be willing to fight for. We may have entered a new Age of Rage but history is not linear. We can always turn around and take a different direction. It is us who shape the narratives of our past, present and future, so let's believe in our ability to bring about positive change. Our only real enemy is hate; our best weapon is solidarity. Let's listen and learn rather than ban and bomb. Let's not shut the door to anyone; instead, let's remain open to dialogue and debate with all. What distinguishes the humanist from the anti-humanist is that the former would give everyone – even the person they hate most – a second chance.

Epilogue

In the Eye of a Hate Storm

WHILE I WAS PUTTING THE FINISHING TOUCHES TO THIS BOOK, I FOUND myself at the centre of an involuntary self-experiment: in a matter of minutes I became the target of a social media storm such as I had previously been researching. Joint efforts of far-right activists and alternative news outlets created an amplification effect across globally interconnected echo chambers, generating a self-sustaining campaign that attracted 20 million impressions on Twitter within a mere week.

The controversy was triggered by my opinion article on online and offline hate crimes, published in the *Guardian* on 1 May 2017. It argued that rhetorical provocations and political stagings of far-right activists were conducive to driving hatred against religious and ethnic minorities. Social media platforms, so goes the argument, often become nexus points that host and encourage various types of hate speech: anti-Muslim, anti-immigrant as well as racist. The lines that sparked outrage among 'counter-jihadists' were about Tommy Robinson's Twitter account. My article suggested that it demonstrates how the far right has moved from the fringe to the mainstream and how white supremacist movements have attracted massive support from digital natives.

Twenty-four hours after my article was released, Tommy Robinson raided Quilliam's office with a cameraman to confront me, livestreaming the entire spectacle as commissioned by the far-right news outlet *The Rebel*. Instead of giving me a call or suing the *Guardian* for libel, he used my article as a pretext for a more sensational form of redress. 'Julia, could you tell me how I am a white supremacist?' he kept repeating during his surprise visit.

The Rebel published edited footage of the ambush interview as the third edition of its 'Troll Watch' series.[1] In its previous episode, 'Troll Watch 2', Tommy is seen trespassing into WalesOnline's office to confront journalist Jack Pitts for labelling him 'far right'. Built on a skilful orchestration of victimhood, this systematic strategy of intimidation aims at attracting attention, manufacturing anger and instigating divisions. It succeeds in creating, reinforcing and exploiting widespread rage against mainstream politicians and 'the lying press'.

What followed was an excessive cyber-bullying campaign originating from the echo chambers of British and American 'counter-jihadists': unsurprisingly, its top influencers were Tommy Robinson and Robert Spencer of Jihad Watch. My analysis of all media outlets and social media accounts mobilised in this campaign confirmed the global interconnectedness of far-right echo chambers. The publication of 'Troll Watch 3: Tommy Robinson vs. Quilliam' led to a chain reaction within far-right media outlets: within a mere 24 hours, the story was reported by Gates of Vienna, Jihad Watch, PamelaGeller.com, Breitbart and others.

Gates of Vienna did an entire open-source intelligence investigation into my life, going as far as translating German interviews and deciphering Chinese documents. No wonder this rendered plenty of material for wild conspiracy theories: while some of Robinson's followers concluded I must be a naive Jewish journalist, others thought I was a Muslim convert working for a terrorist organisation. Most agreed that, in any case, I was a 'libtard' representing the rigged establishment and 'lying mainstream media'. Breitbart supported this narrative: 'Ebner, however, is your classic spoiled establishment type.'

Justified or not, being in the middle of a Twitter hate storm taught me a lot about the swiftness of far-right trolling and bullying activities. The combination of entertainment value, online anonymity and self-reinforcing group dynamics makes jumping on the bandwagon easy and appealing, even for users who would not usually self-identify as far-right supporters. It did not take long before the debate was carried into 4chan, where the alt-right split between neo-Nazis and counter-jihadists became visible again. To some, Tommy was 'a true legend and hero to Kekistan', the alt-right land; to others he was 'too moderate' as he was 'not explicitly anti-gay and anti-jew'.[2]

The 'Troll Watch' aftermath also exposed the connection between online trolling and real-life threats. Quilliam had to disband its office, as advised by the police. Colleagues visible in the video trying to protect me from the cameras and attempting to prevent Robinson from entering our premises received death threats from far-right sympathisers.

The far right uses trolling and bullying tactics as part of a larger guerrilla info war aimed at shutting up its opponents. The strategy does not only seek to intimidate any journalists, politicians and artists who voice criticism; it is also an attempt to undermine the legitimacy and credibility of 'mainstream media'. Efforts to pressure me into retracting my article were driven by *The Rebel* readers' desire to denounce the *Guardian* as 'fake news' and claim victory over 'mainstream media'.

A few days after my Twitter had calmed down, two things happened:

1. French presidential candidate Emmanuel Macron's campaign was leaked on the eve before the elections. The hashtag #MacronLeaks was soon trending worldwide; its first use was traced back to *The Rebel*'s Jack Posobiec. Posobiec's tweet included a link to the hacked documents, which WikiLeaks then spread more widely. These coordinated efforts by American far-right activists marked the climax of a months-long campaign to influence the elections in favour of Marine Le Pen.[3]
2. Robinson was arrested for breaking court rules when trying to livestream a trial in Canterbury Crown Court. In what he described as 'attempted journalism', he filmed 'Muslim paedophiles' outside the court.

These incidents show that guerrilla journalism and activism have moved to an entirely new level of creativity and imprudence. Both far-right and Islamist extremists have found innovative tools and tactics to denounce the mainstream, tell their own stories and create alternative news circles. Their strategies of intimidation, humiliation and terror should not prevent anybody from researching, reporting and countering extremism, whether Islamist, far right or far left.

However, their ability to mobilise thousands of individuals, not all of them extremists, should lead us to ask more questions. This includes self-scepticism. While I will not mince my words when speaking about extremism, this episode taught me to be more careful about associating individuals with labels. Listening to extremists without pandering to them and challenging thought leaders without dehumanising them is a difficult balance to strike. But it will be necessary to tackle the sources of extremism.

This book focused on the dynamics between far-right and Islamist extremists, but future research will need to explore the role of the centre ground in more depth: what is the responsibility of so-called establishment politicians, the mainstream media and counter-extremism activists? How can we build bridges between the middle ground and the extremes rather than exacerbating tensions? Extremists thrive in today's conditions, but it is the middle ground that has laid the groundwork for them to do so. The vicious circle of Islamist and far-right extremism did not come from nowhere. It was the establishment's action and inaction that gave birth to its main engine: The Rage.

Notes

Preface

1   Robert Booth, Vikram Dodd, Kevin Rawlinson and Nicola Slawson, 'Jox Cox murder suspect tells court his name is "death to traitors, freedom for Britain"', the *Guardian* (18 June 2016). Available at https://www.theguardian.com/uk-news/2016/jun/18/thomas-mair-charged-with-of-mp-jo-cox.

2   'Dewsbury in shock over its links to teenage suicide bomber', *Yorkshire Post* (15 June 2015). Available at http://www.yorkshirepost.co.uk/news/analysis/dewsbury-in-shock-over-its-links-to-teenage-suicide-bomber-1-7310887.

3   Mark Townsend, 'Why has the far right made West Yorkshire a home?', the *Guardian* (16 June 2016). Available at https://www.theguardian.com/uk-news/2016/jun/18/far-right-home-in-west-yorkshire-britain-first.

4   Nishaat Ismail, 'Anders Breivik, a mass murderer who did a Nazi salute in court, isn't being called a terrorist. Why? He's white', the *Independent* (15 March 2017). Available at http://www.independent.co.uk/voices/anders-breivik-a-mass-murderer-who-did-a-nazi-salute-in-court-isnt-being-called-a-terrorist-why-hes-a6932896.html.

5   More details based on the author's statistical analysis of GTDB data are provided in Chapter 6.

6   Jo Cox MP, 'Maiden speech in Parliament', 3 June 2015. Available at https://www.parliament.uk/business/news/2016/june/jo-cox-maiden-speech-in-the-house-of-commons/.

Introduction

1   Geraldine McKelvie, 'Horrific abuse scandal in town dubbed "child sex capital of Britain"', the *Mirror* (27 August 2016). Available at http://www.mirror.co.uk/news/uk-news/horrific-abuse-scandal-town-dubbed-8718139.

2   English Defence League, 'Telford demo 5 November: Media briefing' (16 October 2016). Available at http://www.englishdefenceleague.org.uk/wp-content/uploads/2016/10/16_10_23_Telford-demo-media-briefing.pdf.

3   Jamie Bartlett and Mark Littler, *Inside the EDL: Populist Politics in a Digital Age*, Demos (2011).

4   Salim Fredericks and Ahmer Feroze, *From Darkness into Light* (Al-Khilafah Publications, n.d.).

5   'The Murtadd Vote', Al Hayat Media Center (2016). Available at https://baytalmasadircom.files.wordpress.com/2016/11/is-text-the-murtadd-vote.pdf.

6   Jennifer Cole and Raffaelo Pantucci, 'Community Tensions: Evidence-Based Approaches to Understanding the Interplay between Hate Crimes and Reciprocal Radicalisation', STFC/RUSI Conference Series No. 3 (2014).

7   Roger Eatwell, 'Community Cohesion and Cumulative Extremism in Contemporary Britain', *The Political Quarterly* 77:2 (2006).

8   Matthew Feldman, 'Tit-for-tat extremism only fuels more hatred and violence', *The Conversation*, 24 May 2016. Available at http://theconversation.com/tit-for-tat-extremism-only-fuels-more-hatred-and-violence-14613.

9   Joel Busher and Graham Macklin, 'Interpreting "Cumulative Extremism": Six Proposals for Enhancing Conceptual Clarity', *Terrorism and Political Violence* 27 (2015), pp. 884–905.

10   See for example Ruth Manning and Courtney La Bau, 'In and Out of Extremism', Quilliam (2015). Available at https://www.quilliamfoundation.org/wp/wp-content/uploads/publications/free/in-and-out-of-extremism.pdf.

11   J. M. Berger, 'Nazis vs. ISIS on Twitter: A Comparative Study of White Nationalists and ISIS Online Social Media Networks', Program on Extremism (September 2016).

12   The most important contributions on this topic were made by Jamie Bartlett and Jonathan Birdwell, 'Cumulative Radicalisation Between the Far-Right and Islamist Groups in the UK: A Review of Evidence', Demos (2013), and Busher and Macklin, 'Interpreting "Cumulative Extremism"'.

13   Bartlett and Birdwell, 'Cumulative Radicalisation' and Busher and Macklin, 'Interpreting "Cumulative Extremism"'.

14   HM Government, 'The Prevent Duty: Departmental Advice for Schools and Childcare Providers', Department of Education (June 2015). Available at https://www.gov.uk/government/uploads/system/uploads/attachment_data/file/439598/prevent-duty-departmental-advice-v6.pdf.

1. The End of a Collective Illusion

1   'National Life Tables, UK: 2013–2015', UK Office for National Statistics, 2016 and Chris Belfield *et al.*, *Living Standards, Poverty and Inequality in the UK: 2015*, Institute for Fiscal Studies, 2015.

2   '2016 World Hunger and Poverty Facts and Statistics'. Available at http://www.worldhunger.org/2015-world-hunger-and-poverty-facts-and-statistics/#hunger-number, and World Health Organization, *World Health Statistics 2014*, World Health Organization, 2014.

3   'Inequality and the End of Extreme Poverty', Oxfam Media Briefing (2015). Available at https://www.oxfam.org/sites/www.oxfam.org/files/inequality_and_the_end_of_poverty_oi_media_brief_final.pdf.

4   United Nations, 'We Can End Poverty: Millennium Development Goals and Beyond 2015', Fact Sheet (2015). Available at http://www.un.org/millenniumgoals/pdf/Goal_1_fs.pdf.

5   http://www.who.int/gho/child_health/mortality/mortality_under_five_text/en/.

6   WHO, 'End in Sight' (2016). Available at http://apps.who.int/iris/bitstream/10665/249586/1/9789290225270-Eng.pdf.

7   Peter Apps, 'Commentary: How much worse could 2016 get?', Reuters (28 July 2016). Available at http://www.reuters.com/article/us-global-conflict-commentary-idUSKCN10527R.

8   Elena Holodny, 'Brexit is just one example of the political problems Europe is facing', *Business Insider Deutschland* (23 June 2016). Available at http://www.businessinsider.de/political-instability-in-europe-rising-2016-6?r=US&IR=T.

9   Elena Ulansky and William Witenberg, 'Is Nationalism on the Rise Globally?', the *Huffington Post* (n.d.). Available at http://www.huffingtonpost.com/elena-ulansky/is-nationalism-on-the-ris_b_10224712.html.

10 'EU referendum: Full results and analysis', the *Guardian* (2016). Available at https://www.theguardian.com/politics/ng-interactive/2016/jun/23/eu-referendum-live-results-and-analysis.

11 Demos, 'The Age of Fear: new polling reveals a gloomy, divided Europe' (October 2016). Available at http://www.demos.co.uk/press-release/the-age-of-fear-new-polling-reveals-a-gloomy-divided-europe/.

12 Stefan Zweig, *The World of Yesterday* (Pushkin Press, 2011).

13 Alasdair MacIntyre, *After Virtue: A Study in Moral Theory* (University of Notre Dame Press, 1984), p. 201.

14 Walter R. Fisher, 'The Narrative Paradigm: The Case of Public Moral Argument', *Journal of Communication* (pre-1986) 35:4 (Autumn 1985), p. 266.

15 Benedict Andersen, 'Imagined Communities: Reflections on the Origin and Spread of Nationalism (Verso, 1983) and Yuval Noah Harari, *Sapiens: A Brief History of Humankind* (Vintage Books, 2014).

16 Harari, *Sapiens*.

17 Ibid., p. 124.

18 Ibid., p. 131.

19 Ibid., p. 125.

20 Michael Wintle, 'Personifying the Past: National and European History in the Fine and Applied Arts in the Age of Nationalism', in Stefan Berger, Linas Eriksonas and Andrew Mycock (eds), *Narrating the Nation: Representations in History, Media and the Arts* (Berghahn, 2011).

21 PEN International, 'Day of the Imprisoned Writer & Day to End Impunity', Geneva (November 2015). Available at http://www.pen-international.org/centresnews/pen-suisse-romand-day-of-the-imprisoned-writer-and-the-day-to-end-impunity-for-crimes-against-journalists/?print=print.

22 Harari, *Sapiens*, p. 131.

23 Philip Zimbardo, 'On the Psychology of Evil', TED Talks (February 2008). Available at https://www.ted.com/talks/philip_zimbardo_on_the_psychology_of_evil.

24 Julia Ebner, 'The burkini is a sad symbol of Islam going backwards – and burkini bans are a sad symbol of France doing the same', the *Independent* (25 August 2016). Available at http://www.independent.co.uk/voices/burkini-ban-beach-france-islam-muslim-women-police-undressing-sad-symbol-backwards-french-right-wing-a7208831.html.

25 Markus Hametner and Gerald Gartner, 'Wer wen warum gewählt hat', *Der Standard* (24 April 2016). Available at http://derstandard.at/2000035556396/Wer-wen-warum-gewaehlt-hat.

26 'Islam in Germany', Euro-Islam Info. Available at http://www.euro-islam.info/country-profiles/germany/.

27 Spencer Ackermann, 'Foreign jihadists flocking to Iraq and Syria on "unprecedented scale" – UN', the *Guardian* (30 October 2014). Available at https://www.theguardian.com/world/2014/oct/30/foreign-jihadist-iraq-syria-unprecedented-un-isis.

28 'Break the Cross', *Dabiq Magazine*, Issue 15 (31 July 2016), Al Hayat Media Center, Clarion Project, p. 9. Available at http://www.clarionproject.org/factsheets-files/islamic-state-magazine-dabiq-fifteen-breaking-the-cross.pdf.

29 Jonah Berger, *Contagious: Why Things Catch On* (Simon & Schuster, 2013).

30 Edward Edinger, 'An Outline of Analytical Psychology' (Quadrant, 1968), pp. 1–11, quoted by Bettina Knapp, 'Women in the Twentieth Century Literature: A Jungian View' (Pennsylvania State University Press, 1987).

31 Jeffry R. Halverson, J. L. Goodall and Steven R. Corman, *Master Narratives of Islamist Extremism* (Palgrave Macmillan, 2011), pp. 21–3.

32 This will be explored and demonstrated further in Chapter 6.

33 Martina Stewart, 'Palin hits Obama for "terrorist connection"', CNN (10 April 2008). Available at http://edition.cnn.com/2008/POLITICS/10/04/palin.obama/.

34 Harry Cockburn, 'Donald Trump calls Barack Obama "founder of ISIS" and Hillary Clinton "co-founder"', the *Independent* (11 August 2016). Available at http://www.independent.co.uk/news/world/americas/us-elections/donald-trump-calls-hillary-clinton-founder-of-isis-world-terrorism-change-subject-rnc-campaign-a7170871.html.

35 Jonathan Russell and Haras Rafiq, 'Countering Islamist Extremist Narratives: A Strategic Briefing', The Quilliam Foundation (2016). Available at https://www.quilliamfoundation.org/wp/wp-content/uploads/publications/free/countering-islamist-extremist-narratives.pdf.

36 'A Call to Hijrah', *Dabiq Magazine*, Issue 3, Al Hayat Media Center, Clarion Project (September 2014), p. 16 and p. 19. Available at http://media.clarionproject.org/files/09-2014/isis-isil-islamic-state-magazine-Issue-3-the-call-to-hijrah.pdf.

37 Matern Boeselager, 'Ist die "Oldschool Society" die dümmste Terrorgruppe

Deutschlands?', VICE (6 May 2015). Available at https://www.vice.com/de/article/old-school-society-die-duemmste-terrorgruppe-deutschlands-882.

38 Kenneth Burke, *On Symbols and Society*, ed. Joseph Gusfield (University of Chicago Press, 1989).

39 Nathan C. Funk and Abdul Aziz Said, 'Islam and the West: Narratives of Conflict and Conflict Transformation', *International Journal of Peace Studies* 9:1 (Spring/Summer 2004). Available at http://www.gmu.edu/programs/icar/ijps/vol9_1/Funk&Said_91IJPS.pdf.

40 Adolf Hitler, *Mein Kampf* (Jaico Publishing House, 2007 edition), p. 82.

41 'A Call to Hijrah', *Dabiq Magazine* (September 2014).

42 Hizb ut-Tahrir, 'Ramadahn Kareem – from the West' (26 June 2016). Available at https://www.youtube.com/watch?v=tHkml7zOIqc&feature=youtu.be.

43 M. Goldberg, Theory and Narrative (Parthenon Press, 1982), p. 242.

44 Dr Ezz El Din Farag, د\ عزالدين فراج, Egyptian Education Ministry (2014), pp. 82–103. Available at http://elearning1.moe.gov.eg/prep/semester1/Grade2/pdf/kafah%20shab%20masr_2prep.pdf.

45 'History', AQA (2016). Available at http://www.aqa.org.uk/subjects/history.

46 Kate Connolly, 'Britain's view of its history "dangerous", says former museum director', the *Guardian* (7 October 2016). Available at https://www.theguardian.com/culture/2016/oct/07/britains-view-of-its-history-dangerous-says-former-museum-director.

47 'The Sunni–Shia Divide', Council on Foreign Relations (n.d.). Available at http://www.cfr.org/peace-conflict-and-human-rights/sunni-shia-divide/p33176#!/?cid=otr-marketing_url-sunni_shia_infoguide.

48 Muna Güvenç, 'Constructing Narratives of Kurdish Nationalism in the Urban Space of Diyarbakir, Turkey', *TDSR* 23:1 (2011). Available at http://iaste.berkeley.edu/iaste/wp-content/uploads/2012/07/23.1-Fall-11-Guvenc.pdf.

49 John Stephens and Robyn McCallum, *Retelling Stories, Framing Culture: Traditional Story and Metanarratives in Children's Literature* (Routledge, 1998).

50 Halverson, Goodall and Corman, *Master Narratives of Islamist Extremism*, p. 78.

51 Andrew Silke, 'Holy Warriors: Exploring the Psychological Processes of Jihadi Radicalization', *European Journal of Criminology* 5:1 (2008), pp. 99–123.

52 Later chapters will provide an in-depth analysis of these and other hashtags used by extremists.

53 Scott Anderson, 'Fractured Lands: How the Arab World Came Apart', *New York Times Magazine* (11 August 2016), Part I/3. Available at http://www.nytimes.com/interactive/2016/08/11/magazine/isis-middle-east-arab-spring-fractured-lands.html?_r=0.

54 Norman Cohn, *The Pursuit of the Millennium: Revolutionary Millenarians and Mystical Anarchists of the Middle Ages* (Oxford University Press, 1957).

55 For more information about the influence of Christianity on anti-communist politics and culture during the Cold War, see Dianne Kirby, *Religion and the Cold War* (Palgrave Macmillan, 2002) and Tony Shaw, 'Martyrs, Miracles and Martians: Religion and Cold War Cinema in the 1950s', *Journal of Cold War Studies* 4:2 (2002), pp. 3–22.

56 Christian Democratic parties lost their hegemonic influence in three European countries in rapid succession: Italy (1994), the Netherlands (1994) and Belgium (1999) – see Erik Jones, 'The Decline and Fall of Three Hegemonic Christian Democratic Parties in Europe' (Johns Hopkins School of Advanced International Studies, 30 November 2014).

57 From 1990 to 2000, the combined membership of all Protestant denominations in the USA declined by almost 5 million members (9.5 per cent), while the US population increased by 24 million (11 per cent). See http://www.churchleadership.org/apps/articles/default.asp?articleid=42346&columnid=4545.

2. The Global Jihadist Insurgency

1   President Obama on the death of Osama bin Laden. Available at https://www.youtube.com/watch?v=ZNYmK19-d0U and http://www.telegraph.co.uk/news/worldnews/asia/pakistan/8488792/Osama-bin-Laden-killed-cowering-behind-his-human-shield-wife.html.

2   Paul Rogers, *Irregular War: ISIS and the New Threat from the Margins* (I.B.Tauris, 2016), p. 141.

3   Frederick W. Kagan, Kimberly Kagan, Harleen Gambhir and Katherine Zimmerman, 'Al Qaeda and ISIS: Existential Threats to the US and Europe', AEI's Critical Threats Project and the Institute for the Study of War (January 2016). Available at http://www.aei.org/publication/al-qaeda-and-isis-existential-threats-to-the-us-and-europe.

4   Peter Neumann, *Radicalized: New Jihadists and the Threat to the West* (I.B.Tauris, 2016).

5   Janessa Gans Wilder, 'ISIS and Islamic Extremism: Where Did It Come From and How Do We Respond?', *Principia Purpose* (Winter 2016). Available at http://news.principia.edu/node/2240.

6   'The 9/11 Commission Report', National Commission on Terrorist Attacks upon the United States, 2004. Available at https://9-11commission.gov/report/911Report.pdf.

7   Ibn Taymiyya, *Enjoying Right and Forbidding Wrong* (n.p., n.d.), trans. Salim Morgan.

8   Yossef Rapoport and Shahab Ahmed (eds), *Ibn Taymiyya and His Times* (Oxford University Press, 2010).

9   Shiraz Mahler, *Salafi-Jihadism: The History of an Idea* (Hurst, 2016), p. 157.

10 Ibid.

11 WikiLeaks, 'Terrorist Finance: Action Request for Senior Level Engagement on Terrorism Finance', 30 December 2009. Available at https://wikileaks.org/plusd/cables/09STATE131801_a.html.

12 Claude Moniquet, 'The Involvement of Salafism/Wahabism in the Support and Supply of Arms to Rebel Groups Around the World', European Parliament. Available at http://www.europarl.europa.eu/RegData/etudes/etudes/join/2013/457137/EXPO-AFET_ET(2013)457137_EN.pdf.

13 Charlie Winter, 'ICSR Insight: Suicide Tactics in the Islamic State', International Centre for the Study of Radicalisation, 11 January 2017. Available at http://icsr.info/2017/01/icsr-insight-suicide-tactics-islamic-state/.

14 Hassan Al Banna, 'Our Invitation', in *Selected Writings of Hasan al-Banna Shaheed*, trans. S. A. Qureshi (Wajih Uddin, 1999), p. 103.

15 Philip Jenkins, 'Clerical Terror: The Roots of Jihad in India', *The New Republic* (24 December 2008).

16 John Esposito, *Voices of Resurgent Islam* (Oxford University Press, 1983).

17 Sayyid Qutb, *Milestones* (Islamic Book Service, 2001).

18 Gilles Kepel, *Jihad: The Trail of Political Islam* (Harvard University Press, 2002).

19 Ervand Abrahamian, *Khomeinism: Essays on the Islamic Republic* (University of California Press, 1993), p. 15.

20 Bruce Riedel, 'The 9/11 Attacks' Spiritual Father', Brookings (11 September 2011). Available at https://www.brookings.edu/opinions/the-911-attacks-spiritual-father.

21 Abdullah Azzam, *Defense of the Muslim Lands* (Maktabah Publications, 2nd edition, 2002).

22 Lawrence Wright, *The Looming Tower: Al-Qaeda's Road to 9/11* (Vintage Publishers, 2006).

23 Dominic Casciani, 'Barbar Ahmad: The Godfather of Internet Jihad?', BBC, 17 July 2014. Available at http://www.bbc.co.uk/news/magazine-28324222.

24 'Global Terrorism Index 2016: Measuring and Understanding the Impact of Terrorism', Institute for Economics and Peace (2016). Available at http://economicsandpeace.org/wp-content/uploads/2016/11/Global-Terrorism-Index-2016.2.pdf.

25 Neumann, *Radicalized*, p. 113.

26 https://twitter.com/AMDWaters/status/806451359138672640.

27 David Anderson QC, 'The Terrorism Acts in 2015', HM Government (December 2016). Available at https://www.gov.uk/government/uploads/system/uploads/attachment_data/file/573677/THE_TERRORISM_ACTS_IN_2015__web_.pdf.

28 Europol, 'Te-Sat 2016: European Union Terrorism Situation and Trend Report 2016', European Police Office (2016).

29 Europol, 'Te-Sat 2016'.

30 'Global Terrorism Index 2016: Measuring and Understanding the Impact of Terrorism', Institute for Economics and Peace (2016). Available at http://

economicsandpeace.org/wp-content/uploads/2016/11/Global-Terrorism-Index-2016.2.pdf.

31 Anderson, 'The Terrorism Acts in 2015'.

32 Europol, 'Te-Sat 2016'.

33 Europol, 'Te-Sat 2016'.

34 Anderson, 'The Terrorism Acts in 2015'.

35 The full list is available at http://www.state.gov/j/ct/rls/other/des/123085.htm.

36 The UN 1267 list is available at https://scsanctions.un.org/fop/fop?xml= htdocs/resources/xml/en/consolidated.xml&xslt=htdocs/resources/xsl/en/al-qaida-r.xsl.

37 'The Jihadi Threat: ISIS, Al Qaeda and Beyond'. Available at https://www.usip.org/sites/default/files/The-Jihadi-Threat-ISIS-Al-Qaeda-and-Beyond.pdf

38 Europol, 'Te-Sat 2016'.

39 Daniel L. Byman and Jennifer R. Williams, 'ISIS vs. Al Qaeda: Jihadism's Global Civil War', Brookings (24 February 2015). Available at https://www.brookings.edu/articles/isis-vs-al-qaeda-jihadisms-global-civil-war/.

40 Noman Benotman, 'An open letter to Osama bin Laden', *Foreign Policy* (10 September 2010). Available at http://foreignpolicy.com/2010/09/10/an-open-letter-to-osama-bin-laden/.

41 Lizzie Dearden, 'Al-Qaeda leader denounces Isis "madness and lies" as two terrorist groups compete for dominance', the *Independent* (13 January 2017). Available at http://www.independent.co.uk/news/world/middle-east/al-qaeda-leader-ayman-al-zawahiri-isis-madness-lies-extremism-islamic-state-terrorist-groups-compete-a7526271.html.

42 Maajid Nawaz, 'ISIS Wants a Global Civil War', *Daily Beast* (29 July 2016).

43 Abu Bakr Naji, 'Management of Savagery: The Most Critical Stage Through Which the Umma Will Pass', trans. William McCants (May 2006). Available at https://azelin.files.wordpress.com/2010/08/abu-bakr-naji-the-management-of-savagery-the-most-critical-stage-through-which-the-umma-will-pass.pdf.

44 Naji, 'Management of Savagery'.

45 William McCants, *The ISIS Apocalypse: The History, Strategy and Doomsday Vision of Islamic State* (St Martin's Press, 2015).

46 Yassin Musharbash, 'What al-Qaeda Really Wants', *Spiegel* (12 August 2005). Available at http://www.spiegel.de/international/the-future-of-terrorism-what-al-qaida-really-wants-a-369448.html.

47 Aaron Zelin, 'Jihad 2020: Assessing Al-Qaida's 20-Year Plan', *World Politics Review* (11 September 2013). Available at http://www.worldpoliticsreview.com/articles/13208/jihad-2020-assessing-al-qaida-s-20-year-plan.

48 Rukmini Callimachi, 'How a Secretive Branch of ISIS Built a Global Network of Killers', *New York Times* (3 August 2016). Available at http://www.nytimes.com/2016/08/04/world/middleeast/isis-german-recruit-interview.html.

49 Samira Shackle, 'The London Girls Lost to Isis: What Became of the "Jihadi Brides"?', *The New Statesman* (6 October 2016). Available at http://www.

newstatesman.com/culture/observations/2016/10/london-girls-lost-isis-what-became-jihadi-brides.

50 'Foreign Fighters: An Updated Assessment of the Flow of Foreign Fighters into Syria and Iraq', The Soufan Group (December 2015). Available at http://soufangroup.com/wp-content/uploads/2015/12/TSG_ForeignFightersUpdate3.pdf.

51 'Economic and Social Inclusion to Prevent Violent Extremism', World Bank Middle East and North Africa Region: MENA Economic Monitor, World Bank Group (October 2016).

52 Javier Lesaca, 'On Social Media, ISIS Uses Modern Cultural Images to Spread Anti-modern Values', Brookings (24 September 2014). Available at https://www.brookings.edu/blog/techtank/2015/09/24/on-social-media-isis-uses-modern-cultural-images-to-spread-anti-modern-values/.

53 Interview with an anonymous mother, 17 January 2017.

54 Michael A. Hogg and Janice Adelman, 'Uncertainty-Identity Theory: Extreme Groups, Radical Behavior, and Authoritarian Leadership', *Journal of Social Issues* 69:3 (2013), pp. 436–54. See also Arie Kruglanski, 'Psychology not Theology: Overcoming ISIS' Secret Appeal', *E-International Relations* (28 October 2014).

55 V. Ramalingam, 'What works in building common ground and shared values?', *Global Exchange Briefings* 9, Centre on Migration, Policy and Society, University of Oxford, 2014.

56 'A Call to Hijrah', *Dabiq Magazine* 2 (1435 Shawal), Al Hayat Media Center, p. 11.

57 Alex Schmid, 'Foreign (Terrorist) Fighter Estimates: Conceptual and Data Issues', ICCT Policy Brief (October 2015). Available at https://www.icct.nl/wp-content/uploads/2015/10/ICCT-Schmid-Foreign-Terrorist-Fighter-Estimates-Conceptual-and-Data-Issues-October20152.pdf.

58 Charlie Winter, 'Documenting the "Virtual Caliphate"', Quilliam (2015). Available at http://www.quilliaminternational.com/wp-content/uploads/2015/10/FINAL-documenting-the-virtual-caliphate.pdf.

59 Abuh Rumaysah al Britani, 'A Brief Guide to the Islamic State' (May 2015). Archived at https://archive.org/details/Khilafah2015.

60 Fyodor Dostoyevsky, *The Gambler* (Dover Publications, 1996), p. 29.

3. The Far-Right Renaissance

1 Daniel Köhler, 'Right-Wing Extremism and Terrorism in Europe: Current Developments and Issues for the Future', *Prism* 6:2 (2016), p. 86.

2 Ibid.

3 Ernest Gellner, *Thought and Change* (University of Chicago Press, 1978).

4 Roger Griffin and Matthew Feldman (eds), *Fascism: Critical Concepts – Volume 3: Fascism and Culture* (Taylor & Francis, 2004).

5 'A right menace: Nick Griffin', the *Independent*, 22 May 2009. Available at http://news.bbc.co.uk/1/hi/uk_politics/8320241.stm.

6   Ibid.

7   Caroline Mortimer, 'Holocaust denial and anti-Semitic books are being sold on Amazon', the *Independent* (12 February 2017). Available at http://www. independent.co.uk/news/uk/holocaust-denial-anti-semitism-amazon-books-sold-far-right-nazi-hitler-a7575841.html.

8   Matthew Feldman, 'From Radical-Right Islamophobia to "Cumulative Extremism": A Paper on the Shifting Focus of Hatred', *Faith Matters* (2012). Available at https://www.tellmamauk.org/wp-content/uploads/2013/02/islamophobia.pdf.

9   Joe Mullhall, 'The British Counter-Jihad Movement no longer really exists but its impact can still be felt', London School of Economics (20 December 2016). Available at http://blogs.lse.ac.uk/religionpublicsphere/2016/12/the-british-counter-jihad-movement-no-longer-really-exists-but-its-impact-can-still-be-felt/.

10   Chris Allen, 'The Rise of Europe's Far Right and the Anti-Islam Tide', *Huffington Post* (1 February 2017). Available at http://www.huffingtonpost. co.uk/dr-chris-allen/europe-far-right_b_9110004.html.

11   HM Government, 'Oral Evidence: Hate Crime and its Violent Consequences Inquiry', Home Affairs Committee (10 January 2017). Available at http://data.parliament.uk/writtenevidence/committeeevidence.svc/evidencedocument/home-affairs-committee/hate-crime-and-its-violent-consequences/oral/45063.pdf.

12   Peter Maxwill, 'Der Staat gegen den Fremdenhass', *Der Spiegel* (5 March 2017). Available at http://www.spiegel.de/panorama/justiz/gruppe-freital-prozess-in-dresden-staat-gegen-hass-a-1132879.html.

13   Bundesministerium des Innern, 'Verfassungsschutzbericht 2016'. Available at http://www.bmi.bund.de/SharedDocs/Downloads/DE/Broschueren/2017/vsb-2016.pdf?__blob=publicationFile.

14   Arie Perlinger, 'Challenges from the Sidelines: Understanding America's Far-Right', Combating Terrorism Center (January 2013). Available at https://www.ctc.usma.edu/posts/challengers-from-the-sidelines-understanding-americas-violent-far-right.

15   Perlinger, 'Challengers from the Sidelines'.

16   Kurt Eichenwald, 'Right Wing Extremists are a Bigger Threat to America than ISIS', *Newsweek* (2016). Available at http://europe.newsweek. com/right-wing-extremists-militants-bigger-threat-america-isis-jihadists-422743?rm=eu.

17   Eichenwald, 'Right Wing Extremists are a Bigger Threat to America than ISIS'.

18   'Far-right terrorism threat growing as forces face "broader range of dangerous ideologies"', *Police Professional* (29 November 2016). Available at http://www.policeprofessional.com/news.aspx?id=27875.

19   HM Government, 'Operation of police powers under the Terrorism Act 2000 and subsequent legislation: Arrests, outcomes, and stop and search, Great Britain, quarterly update to December 2016' (March 2017). Available

at https://www.gov.uk/government/uploads/system/uploads/attachment_data/file/597029/police-powers-terrorism-dec2016-hosb0417.pdf.

20 Peter Neumann, *Radicalized: New Jihadists and the Threat to the West* (I.B.Tauris, 2016), p. 29.

21 Pete Simi, Steven Windish and Karyn Sporer, 'Recruitment and Radicalization among US Far-Right Terrorists', National Consortium for the Study of Terrorism and Responses to Terrorism (College Park: START, November 2016). Available at https://www.start.umd.edu/pubs/START_RecruitmentRadicalizationAmongUSFarRightTerrorists_Nov2016.pdf.

22 Video report by ITV News Security Editor Rohit Kachroo. Available at http://www.itv.com/news/2017-03-20/exclusive-former-members-of-banned-terror-group-meet-at-far-right-training-camp.

23 Arun Kundnani, 'Blind Spot? Security Narratives and Far-Right Violence in Europe', ICCT Research Paper (June 2012).

24 Mark Townsend, 'Anti-Muslim prejudice "is moving to the mainstream"', the *Guardian* (5 December 2015). Available at https://www.theguardian.com/world/2015/dec/05/far-right-muslim-cultural-civil-war.

25 Benjamin Lee, 'Understanding the Counter-Jihad', Centre for Research and Evidence on Security Threats (3 November 2017). Available at https://crestresearch.ac.uk/comment/understanding-counter-jihad/.

26 Tommy Robinson, *Enemy of the State* (The Press News, 2015).

27 Edith Meinhart, 'Rechte Allianzen: Was hat Trump mit den Identitären zu tun?', *Profil* (8 September 2016). Available at https://www.profil.at/oesterreich/rechte-allianzen-was-trump-identitaeren-7557676.

28 Robert Midgley, 'Watch: How Nigel Farage became friends with Donald Trump', the *Telegraph* (22 November 2016). Available at http://www.telegraph.co.uk/news/2016/11/16/watch-how-nigel-farage-became-friends-with-donald-trump.

29 J. M. Berger, 'Nazis vs. ISIS on Twitter: A Comparative Study of White Nationalists and ISIS Online Social Media Networks', Program on Extremism (September 2016).

30 Clare Ellis, Raffaelo Pantucci, *et al.*, 'Lone Actor Terrorism: Final Report', Countering Lone-Actor Terrorism Series No. 11 (RUSI Publications, 2016). Available at https://rusi.org/projects/lone-actor-terrorism.

31 Andrew Anglin's fully recorded speech can be found at https://www.youtube.com/watch?v=v_4_XE2hQwc.

32 'Andrew Anglin in London', Daily Stormer (17 April 2014). Available at https://www.youtube.com/watch?v=D6vnT6Bt7go.

33 'Andrew Anglin in London', Daily Stormer.

34 Interview with Bjorn Ihler, 13 November 2016.

35 http://bjornih.co.uk/talks---consulting.html.

36 Simi and Futrell (2010), cited in Simi, Windish and Sporer, 'Recruitment and Radicalization among US Far-Right Terrorists'.

37 Kathleen Blee, 'Becoming a Racist Woman in Contemporary Ku Klux Klan and Neo-Nazi Groups', *Gender & Society* 10:6 (1996), pp. 680–702.

38 Andrew Anglin, 'A Normie's Guide to the Alt-Right', Daily Stormer (31 August 2016). Available at http://www.dailystormer.com/a-normies-guide-to-the-alt-right/.

39 Farid Hafez, 'Political Beats in the Alps: On Politics in the Early Stages of Austrian Hip Hop Music', *Journal of Black Studies* (June 2016). Available at http://journals.sagepub.com/doi/pdf/10.1177/0021934716653347.

40 The trailer is available at https://www.youtube.com/watch?v=qV3PhvCf_Jg.

41 Anglin, 'A Normie's Guide to the Alt-Right'.

4. Identity Politics

1 'Whites risk marginalization, mosque shooting suspect told friend a day before attack', CBC News (3 February 2017). Available at http://www.cbc.ca/news/canada/montreal/alexandre-bissonnette-trump-travel-ban-quebec-mosque-shooting-1.3966687.

2 Alex P. Schmid, 'Violent and Non-Violent Extremism: Two Sides of the Same Coin?', ICCT Research Paper (The Hague: ICCT, 2014). Available at https://www.icct.nl/download/file/ICCT-Schmid-Violent-Non-Violent-Extremism-May-2014.pdf.

3 Full speech manuscript available at https://www.gov.uk/government/speeches/extremism-pm-speech.

4 HM Government, 'Prevent: 2.44', CONTEST: The United Kingdom's Strategy for Countering Terrorism – Annual Report, Presented to Parliament by the Secretary of State for the Home Department (March 2013), p. 21. Available at https://www.gov.uk/government/uploads/system/uploads/attachment_data/file/170644/28307_Cm_8583_v0_20.pdf.

5 Schmid, 'Violent and Non-Violent Extremism', p. 2.

6 John Stapleton, *Terror in Australia: Workers' Paradise Lost* (A Sense of Place Publishing, 2015).

7 Aage Borchgrevink, *A Norwegian Tragedy: Anders Behring Breivik and the Massacre on Utøya*, translated from the Norwegian by Guy Puzey (Polity, 2013).

8 'Wealth: Having it all and wanting more', Oxfam Issue Briefing (January 2015). Available at https://www.oxfam.org/sites/www.oxfam.org/files/file_attachments/ib-wealth-having-all-wanting-more-190115-en.pdf?awc=5991_1480795508_5e7c723378337386e55e8d11f9de0c5f&cid=aff_affwd_donate.

9 Stephen Hawking, 'This is the most dangerous time for our planet', the *Guardian* (1 December). Available at https://www.theguardian.com/commentisfree/2016/dec/01/stephen-hawking-dangerous-time-planet-inequality.

10 Hannah Brock, 'Marginalisation of the Majority World: Drivers of Insecurity and the Global South', Oxford Research Group (1 February 2012). Available at http://www.oxfordresearchgroup.org.uk/publications/briefing_papers_and_reports/marginalisation_majority_world_drivers_insecurity_and_globa.

11 Manuel Funke, *et al.*, 'Politics in the Slump: Polarization and Extremism After Financial Crises, 1870–2014', European Commission (23 September 2015). Available at http://ec.europa.eu/economy_finance/events/2015/20151001_post_crisis_slump/documents/c._trebesch.pdf.

12 Henning Meyer and Ulrich Storck, 'The Three Drivers of European Populism', *Social Europe* (27 March 2017). Available at https://www.socialeurope.eu/2015/03/european-populism.

13 Julian Rappold, 'Time to Act – the Obligation of the European Mainstream to Respond to the Rise of Populism', Heinrich Böll Stiftung (22 May 2015). Available at https://eu.boell.org/en/2015/05/22/time-act-obligation-european-mainstream-respond-rise-populism.

14 Matt Philipps, 'Joseph Stiglitz on Brexit, Europe's Long Cycle of Crisis, and Why German Economics is Different', *Quartz* (16 August 2016). Available at http://qz.com/744854/joseph-stiglitz-euro-future-of-europe-book/.

15 'G20 Communiqué November 2010', Council on Foreign Relations (12 November 2010). Available at http://www.cfr.org/financial-crises/g20-global-plan-recovery-reform-april-2009/p19017.

16 Dan Merica, 'Bill Clinton on the rise of nationalism: "We are all having an identity crisis at once"', CNN (9 March 2017). Available at http://edition.cnn.com/2017/03/09/politics/bill-clinton-yitzhak-rabin-world/.

17 Max Weber, *Economy and Society* (University of California Press, 2013).

18 Hilarion G. Petzold, *Identität: Ein Kernthema moderner Psychotherapie – interdisziplinäre Perspektiven* (VS Verlag, 2012).

19 James E. Côté and Charles G. Levine, *Identity Formation, Agency, and Culture: A Social Psychological Synthesis* (Lawrence Erlbaum Associates, Inc., 2002), p. 1.

20 Jennifer Rankin, 'EU refugee crisis: asylum seeker numbers double to 1.2m in 2015', the *Guardian* (4 March 2016). Available at https://www.theguardian.com/world/2016/mar/04/eu-refugee-crisis-number-of-asylum-seekers-doubled-to-12-million-in-2015.

21 Phillip Connor, 'Number of Refugees to Europe Surges to Record 1.3 Million in 2015', Pew Research Center (2 August 2016). Available at http://www.pewglobal.org/2016/08/02/number-of-refugees-to-europe-surges-to-record-1-3-million-in-2015.

22 https://www.theguardian.com/commentisfree/2016/oct/31/refugees-problem-europe-identity-crisis-migration.

23 Kris Christmann, 'Preventing Religious Radicalisation and Violent Extremism: A Systematic Review of the Research Evidence', Youth Justice Board (2012). Available at https://www.gov.uk/government/uploads/system/uploads/attachment_data/file/396030/preventing-violent-extremism-systematic-review.pdf.

24 Katharina Mittelstaedt, 'FPÖ unterzeichnet Absichtserklärung mit Putin', *Der Standard* (19 December 2016). Available at http://derstandard.at/2000049497726/FPOe-fuehrt-mysterioese-Arbeitsgespraeche-in-Moskau.

25 Lizzie Dearden, 'Russia and Syria "weaponising" refugee crisis to destabilise Europe, NATO commander claims', the *Independent* (3 March 2016). Available at http://www.independent.co.uk/news/world/middle-east/russia-and-syria-weaponising-refugee-crisis-to-destabilise-europe-nato-commander-claims-a6909241.html.

26 Nigel Morris, 'Black people still far more likely to be stopped and searched by police than other ethnic groups', the *Independent* (6 August 2015). Available at http://www.independent.co.uk/news/uk/crime/black-people-still-far-more-likely-to-be-stopped-and-searched-by-police-than-other-ethnic-groups-10444436.html.

27 Interview with Rashad Ali, 16 November 2016.

28 S. Saggar and W. Somerville, 'Building a British Model of Integration in an Era of Immigration: Policy Lessons for Government' (University of Sussex and the Migration Policy Institute, 2012). Available at http://www.migrationpolicy.org/pubs/UK-countrystudy.pdf.

29 Joel Faulkner Rogers, 'The Majority of Voters Doubt that Islam is Compatible with British Values', YouGov (30 March 2015). Available at https://yougov.co.uk/news/2015/03/30/majority-voters-doubt-islam-compatible-british-val/.

30 Dame Louise Casey, DBE CB, 'The Casey Review: A Review into Opportunity and Integration' (December 2016), pp. 12–13. Available at https://www.gov.uk/government/publications/the-casey-review-a-review-into-opportunity-and-integration.

31 Cathy Gormley-Heenan and Roger Macginty, 'Ethnic Outbidding and Party Modernization: Understanding the Democratic Unionist Party's Electoral Success in the Post-Agreement Environment', *Ethnopolitics* 7:1 (2008), pp. 43–61.

32 Gavin Moore, *et al.*, 'Winning Peace Frames: Intra-ethnic Outbidding in Northern Ireland and Cyprus', *West European Politics* 37:1 (2014), pp. 159–81.

33 Shelina Janmohamed, *Generation M: Young Muslims Changing the World* (I.B.Tauris, 2016).

34 J. Dana Stuster, '9 Disturbingly Good Jihadi Raps' (29 April 2013). Available at http://foreignpolicy.com/2013/04/29/9-disturbingly-good-jihadi-raps.

35 The full song can be found at http://www.wired.com/images_blogs/dangerroom/2011/04/Make_Jihad_with_me.mp3.

36 Richard Smirke, 'Jihadi Rap: Understanding the Subculture', Billboard (10 October 2014). Available at http://www.billboard.com/articles/news/6273809/jihadi-rap-l-jinny-abdel-majed-abdel-bary.

37 Melisa Erkurt, 'Generation Haram', *Das Biber* (n.d.). Available at http://www.dasbiber.at/content/generation-haram.

38 Olivier Roy, *Globalised Islam: The Search for a New Ummah* (Columbia University Press, 2004).

39 Houriya Ahmed and Hannad Stuart, *Hizb ut-Tahrir*, Henry Jackson Society Publication (2009).

40 Taqiyuddin An-Nabahani, 'At-Takattul Al-Hizbi', *Hizb-ut-Tahrir*, 3rd edn (1372 hijri – 1953).

41 Dominic Casciani, 'Profile: Islam4UK', BBC News, 5 January 2010.

42 Achraf Ben Brahim, *L'Emprise: Enquête au Coeur de la Jihadosphère* (Lemieux, 2016), p. 62.

43 Schmid, 'Violent and Non-Violent Extremism'.

44 Charles Kimball, *When Religion Becomes Evil* (HarperCollins Canada, 2002).

45 Schmid, 'Violent and Non-Violent Extremism'.

46 'Gewalt gegen Migranten seit Pegida-Start gestiegen', Handelsblatt (27 January 2015). Available at http://app.handelsblatt.com/politik/deutschland/pegida-gewalt-gegen-migranten-seit-pegida-start-gestiegen/11290722.html.

47 Interview with a homeless person in Vienna, 30 October 2016.

48 Christina Schori Liang (ed.), *Europe for the Europeans: The Foreign and Security Policy of the Populist Radical Right* (Ashgate Publishing, 2007).

49 European Commission, 'Public Opinion in the European Union: Standard Eurobarometer 83' (July 2015). Available at http://ec.europa.eu/public_opinion/archives/eb/eb83/eb83_first_en.pdf.

50 Julian Coman, 'Party politics is slowly dying. So what will take its place?', the *Guardian* (8 September 2013). Available at https://www.theguardian.com/politics/2013/sep/08/party-politics-dying-anyone-care.

51 Mario Loyola, 'Behind America's Crisis of Confidence: Government Of, By, and For Special Interests' (2016). Available at http://www.nationalreview.com/article/430059/working-class-voters-distrust-government-restore-trust-restoring-constitution.

52 Roberto Stefan Foa and Yascha Mounk, 'The Democratic Disconnect', in *The Danger of Deconsolidation*, *Journal of Democracy* 27:3 (July 2016). Available at http://www.journalofdemocracy.org/sites/default/files/Foa%26Mounk-27-3.pdf.

53 Péter Krekó, 'Dangerous Harbours: Populism, Extremism and Young People', Policy Network (11 January 2013). Available at http://www.policy-network.net/pno_detail.aspx?ID=4312&title=+Dangerous+harbours%3a+Populism%2c+extremism+and+young+people.

54 Joe Twyman, 'Trump, Brexit, Front National, AfD: branches of the same tree', YouGov (16 November 2016). Available at https://yougov.co.uk/news/2016/11/16/trump-brexit-front-national-afd-branches-same-tree/.

55 Julian Rappold, 'Time to Act – the Obligation of the European Mainstream to Respond to the Rise of Populism', Heinrich Böll Stiftung (22 May 2015). Available at https://eu.boell.org/en/2015/05/22/time-act-obligation-european-mainstream-respond-rise-populism.

56 Ibid.

57 Henning Meyer and Ulrich Storck, 'The Three Drivers of European Populism', *Social Europe* (27 March 2015). Available at https://www.socialeurope.eu/2015/03/european-populism.

58 The video is available at https://www.youtube.com/watch?v=_3P8wI7OpWs.

59 David Smith, 'Fear and loathing in DC: Progressives dread Trump inauguration', the *Guardian*, 15 January 2017. Available at https://www.theguardian.com/world/2017/jan/15/donald-trump-inauguration-washington-progressives.

60 Interview with Rashad Ali, 16 November 2016.

61 Loyola, 'Behind America's Crisis of Confidence'.

62 Ipsos MORI, 'Immigration is now the top issue for voters in the EU referendum' (June 2016). Available at https://www.ipsos-mori.com/researchpublications/researcharchive/3746/immigration-is-now-the-top-issue-for-voters-in-the-eu-referendum.aspx.

63 Simon Tilford, 'Britain, Immigration and Brexit', Centre for European Reform (January 2016). Available at https://www.cer.org.uk/sites/default/files/bulletin_105_st_article1.pdf.

64 Ipsos MORI, 'Immigration is now the top issue for voters in the EU referendum'.

65 'Hate Speech After Brexit', Demos (July 2016). Available at https://www.demos.co.uk/project/hate-speech-after-brexit/.

66 'Zahl der Anzeigen wegen Verhetzung stark gestiegen', ORF (24 November 2016). Available at http://orf.at/stories/2368165/.

67 'Strache isst zehn Döhner im Jahr', Österreich (13 March 2014). Available at http://www.oe24.at/oesterreich/politik/biber-Interview-FPOe-Chef-Strache-isst-zehn-Doener-im-Jahr/135851117.

68 Tweet available at https://twitter.com/geertwilderspvv/status/842252283404554240?lang=en.

69 Pew Research Center, 'Election 2016'. Available at http://www.pewresearch.org/topics/2016-election.

70 Tweet available at https://twitter.com/GenFlynn/status/703387702998278144.

71 Anders Breivik, '2083: A European Declaration of Independence' (London, 2011). Available at https://info.publicintelligence.net/AndersBehringBreivikManifesto.pdf, p. 103.

72 Breivik, '2083: A European Declaration of Independence'.

73 Paul Watzlawick (ed.), *Die erfundene Wirklichkeit: Wie wissen wir, was wir zu wissen glauben* (Piper Verlag, 1981), pp. 192–3.

74 M. Smith (2016), 'Profiled for the first time: the UKIP Party membership', YouGov UK [Online], 22 October. Available from https://yougov.co.uk/news/2016/10/22/introduction-ukip-party-membership.

75 Imran Awan and Irene Zempi, 'The Affinity between Online and Offline Anti-Muslim Hate Crime: Dynamics and Impacts', *Aggression and Violent Behaviour* 27 (March–April 2016), pp. 1–8.

76 Jason Chan, Anindya Ghose and Robert Seamans, 'The Internet and Racial Hate Crime: Offline Spillovers from Online Access', *MIS Quarterly* 40:2 (2016), pp. 381–403.

77 Tom Dart, 'White Nationalist Richard Spencer fuels protest as he mocks critics in Texas', the *Guardian* (7 December 2016). Available at https://www.theguardian.com/us-news/2016/dec/07/white-nationalist-richard-spencer-texas-am.

78 Daniel Köhler, 'Right-Wing Extremism and Terrorism in Europe: Current Developments and Issues for the Future', *Prism* 6:2 (2016).

79 Paul Wilkinson, 'Violence and Terror and the Extreme Right', *Terrorism and Political Violence* 7:4 (1995).

5. The Media

1 'Newspapers: 400 Years Young!', World Association of Newspapers. Available at https://web.archive.org/web/20100310235015/http://www.wan-press.org/article6476.html.

2 Jason Ankeny, 'How These 10 Marketing Campaigns Became Viral Hits', *Entrepreneur* (23 April 2014). Available at https://www.entrepreneur.com/article/233207.

3 Stuart Jeffries, 'Viral videos: around the word in 18 seconds', the *Guardian* (7 June 2014). Available at https://www.theguardian.com/technology/2014/jun/07/viral-videos-around-world-in-18-seconds.

4 Uptin Saiidi, 'For someone who doesn't like social media, Erdogan used it effectively to put down coup', CNBC (18 July 2016). Available at http://www.cnbc.com/2016/07/18/for-someone-who-doesnt-like-social-media-erdogan-used-it-effectively-to-put-down-coup.html.

5 This is the number provided by *The Economist* (http://www.economist.com/blogs/economist-explains/2013/04/economist-explains-how-china-censors-internet). Yet hints received in my conversations with members of the CPC suggest that this is a very conservative estimate.

6 Jamie Bartlett, 'Why terrorists and far-right extremists will always be early adopters', the *Telegraph* (4 November 2014). Available at http://www.telegraph.co.uk/technology/11204744/Why-terrorists-and-far-Right-extremists-will-always-be-early-adopters.html.

7 Ibid.

8 Keegan Hankes, 'How the extremist right hijacked "Star Wars", Taylor Swift and the Mizzou student protests to promote racism', Southern Poverty Law Center (5 January 2016). Available at https://www.splcenter.org/hatewatch/2016/01/05/how-extremist-right-hijacked-%E2%80%98star-wars%E2%80%99-taylor-swift-and-mizzou-student-protests-promote.

9 'Terror's new headquarters', *The Economist* (14 June 2014). Available at http://www.economist.com/news/leaders/21604160-iraqs-second-city-has-fallen-group-wants-create-state-which-wage-jihad.

10 Interview conducted by Mike Giglio for BuzzFeed (June 2015). Available at https://www.buzzfeed.com/mikegiglio/fear-of-isis-drives-iraqi-soldiers-into-desertion-and-hiding?utm_term=.huOlDBL5Np#.teOo4Prby8.

11 J. M. Berger, 'How ISIS Games Twitter', *The Atlantic* (16 June 2016). Available at http://www.theatlantic.com/international/archive/2014/06/isis-iraq-twitter-social-media-strategy/372856/.

12 Ibid.

13 The primary source video with English subtitles is available at http://jihadology.net/2014/05/17/al-furqan-media-presents-a-new-video-message-from-the-islamic-state-of-iraq-and-al-sham-clanging-of-the-swords-part-4/.

14 The ISIS propaganda magazine is named after the Syrian city in reference to the final battle of Dabiq.

15 A detailed account of the presumed major and minor signs as well as the implications of the reappearance of the final Mahdi, the End Times prophecy and the Day of Judgement can be found in Harun Yahya, *Portents and Features of the Mahdi Coming* (Global Publishing, 2010).

16 'Muslim Americans: No Signs of Growth in Alienation or Support for Extremism', Pew Research Center (August 2011). Available at http://www.people-press.org/files/2011/08/muslim-american-report.pdf.

17 'The World's Muslims: Unity and Diversity', Pew Research Center (9 August 2012). Available at http://www.pewforum.org/2012/08/09/the-worlds-muslims-unity-and-diversity-3-articles-of-faith.

18 Interview with the *Guardian* (23 June 2014). Available at https://www.theguardian.com/world/2014/jun/23/who-behind-isis-propaganda-operation-iraq.

19 J. M. Berger and Jonathon Morgan, 'The ISIS Twitter census: Defining and describing the population of ISIS supporters on Twitter', Brookings, Analysis Paper No. 20 (March 2015). Available at https://www.brookings.edu/wp-content/uploads/2016/06/isis_twitter_census_berger_morgan.pdf.

20 Mike Isaac, 'Twitter Steps Up Efforts to Thwart Terrorists' Tweets', *New York Times* (5 February 2016). Available at http://www.nytimes.com/2016/02/06/technology/twitter-account-suspensions-terrorism.html?_r=1.

21 See, for example, http://www.dailymail.co.uk/video/news/video-1154530/ISIS-militants-behead-man-street-screams-help.html and http://www.dailymail.co.uk/video/news/video-1100813/Propaganda-video-purports-ISISs-workout-program.html.

22 Joshua Stewart, 'Isis has been trolled with mountains of porn – and it's been far more effective than imams telling young Muslims off', the *Independent* (8 June 2016). Available at http://www.independent.co.uk/voices/isis-has-been-trolled-with-mountains-of-porn-and-its-been-far-more-effective-than-imams-telling-a7070881.html.

23 For example, the live news French TV channel BFMTV had a measuring tool constantly updating the number of victims during the Paris terrorist attacks of November 2015.

24 Timothy Egan, 'The Eight-Second Attention Span', *New York Times*, 22 January 2016. Available at http://time.com/3858309/attention-spans-goldfish.

25 Katie Mansfield, 'Barbaric ISIS mangle 250 children in industrial dough kneader and cooks rest alive in oven', *Express*, 26 October 2016. Available at http://www.express.co.uk/news/world/723942/ISIS-kills-250-children-dough-kneader-burns-men-alive-oven-Syria-Open-Doors-report.

26 See, for example, http://www.mirror.co.uk/news/world-news/isis-monster-beheads-three-kurdish-7650871 and https://www.thesun.co.uk/archives/news/1105189/isis-monster-beheads-three-kurdish-prisoners-and-leaves-bloodied-bodies-in-the-middle-of-the-street.

27 Alex Matthews and Natalie Corner, 'They think they can get an AK and get forgiven by God at the same time: Channel 4's *Extremely British Muslims* reveals how young Asian men want to join ISIS because it's "the biggest most baddest gang in the world', *Daily Mail*, 9 March 2017. Available at http://www.dailymail.co.uk/news/article-4295196/Extremely-British-Muslims-reveals-men-join-ISIS.html.

28 Owen Jones, *The Establishment: And How They Get Away With It* (Penguin, 2014), p. 86.

29 The full open letter is available at https://www.theguardian.com/media/2011/mar/04/daily-star-reporter-letter-full.

30 Noah Yuval Harari, 'Noah Yuval Harari: the theatre of terror', the *Guardian* (31 January 2015). Available at https://www.theguardian.com/books/2015/jan/31/terrorism-spectacle-how-states-respond-yuval-noah-harari-sapiens.

31 'Trump says terror attacks "under-reported": Is that true?', BBC, 7 February 2017. Available at http://www.bbc.co.uk/news/world-us-canada-38890090.

32 Anders Breivik's manifesto can be found at https://info.publicintelligence.net/AndersBehringBreivikManifesto.pdf, p. 430.

33 Erin M. Kearns, Allison Betus and Anthony Lemieux, 'Why Do Some Terrorist Attacks Receive More Media Attention Than Others?', SSRN (5 March 2017). Available at https://ssrn.com/abstract=2928138.

34 Charles Kurzman and David Schanzer, 'The growing right-wing terror threat', *New York Times* (15 July 2015). Available at http://www.nytimes.com/2015/06/16/opinion/the-other-terror-threat.html.

35 William Parkin, Brent Klein, *et al.*, 'Threats of violent Islamist and far-right extremism: What does the research say?', START (22 February 2017). Available at http://start.umd.edu/news/threats-violent-islamist-and-far-right-extremism-what-does-research-say.

36 Clare Ellis, Raffaelo Pantucci, *et al.*, 'Lone Actor Terrorism: Final Report', *Countering Lone-Actor Terrorism Series* No. 11 (RUSI Publications, 2016). Available at https://rusi.org/projects/lone-actor-terrorism.

37 Ian Millhiser, 'You are More than 7 Times as Likely to be Killed by a Right-Wing Extremist than by Muslim Terrorists', ThinkProgress (2015).

38 Parkin, Klein, *et al.*, 'Threats of violent Islamist and far-right extremism'.

39 Ingrid Melle, 'The Breivik Case and What Psychiatrists Can Learn From It', *World Psychology* 12:1 (February 2013). Available at https://www.ncbi.nlm.nih.gov/pmc/articles/PMC3619172.

40 'A Créteil, un automobiliste tente renverser des fidèles à la sortie d'une mosquée', *Le Monde* (30 June 2017). Available at http://www.lemonde.fr/police-justice/article/2017/06/30/une-voiture-percute-les-barrieres-protegeant-la-mosquee-de-creteil_5153337_1653578.html.

41 'Fusillade devant une mosquée à Avignon: la piste du règlement de comptes privilégiées', *Le Parisien* (3 July 2017). Available at http://www. leparisien.fr/faits-divers/fusillade-devant-une-mosquee-a-avignon-huit-blesses-03-07-2017-7105506.php.

42 The press release is available at http://www.islamophobie.net/articles/ 2017/06/29/tentative-dattentat-devant-la-mosquee-de-creteil/.

43 See, for example, Mark S. Hamm, *American Skinheads: The Criminology and Control of Hate Crime* (Praeger, 1993), p. 8.

44 Ian Cobain, 'Jo Cox murder suspect collected far-right books, court hears', the *Guardian* (21 November 2016). Available at https://www.theguardian. com/uk-news/2016/nov/21/jo-cox-suspect-collected-far-right-books-court-hears.

45 Haras Rafiq and Douglas Hamilton, 'Thomas Mair is just as much a terrorist as the men who murdered Lee Rigby', the *Telegraph* (25 November 2016). Available at http://www.telegraph.co.uk/news/2016/11/25/thomas-mair-just-much-terrorist-men-killed-lee-rigby.

46 Juliet Samuel, 'It's time to call the killing of Jo Cox what it is: "an act of far-right terrorism"', the *Telegraph* (17 June 2016). Available at http://www. telegraph.co.uk/news/2016/06/17/its-time-to-call-the-killing-of-jo-cox-what-it-is-an-act-of-far.

47 Daniel Köhler, *Right Wing Terrorism in the 21st Century: The 'National Socialist Underground' and the History of Terror from the Far Right in Germany* (Routledge, 2017).

48 Daniel Köhler, 'Right-Wing Extremism and Terrorism in Europe: Current Developments and Issues for the Future', *Prism* 6:2 (2016).

49 Cas Mudde, *The Populist Radical Right: A Reader* (Routledge, 2012).

50 Peter Foster, 'The rise of far-right Europe is not a false alarm', the *Telegraph* (19 May 2016).

51 The conversations are available at http://boards.4chan.org/pol/thread/ 114500143/german-hostage-jurgen-kantner-beheading.

52 Rebecca Stewart, 'Creatives unveil "Alternative Facts" card game to troll Trump administration', *The Drum*, 7 February 2017. Available at http://www. thedrum.com/news/2017/02/07/creatives-unveil-alternative-facts-card-game-troll-trump-administration.

53 Aristotle, *Nichomachean Ethics* (Oxford University Press; rev. edn, 2009).

54 Darren Mulloy, *American Extremism: History, Politics and the Militia Movement* (Routledge, 2004), p. 178.

55 Tufyal Choudhury, 'The Role of Muslim Identity Politics in Radicalisation (a study in progress)', Department for Communities and Local Government (2007). Available at http://webarchive.nationalarchives.gov. uk/20120919132719/www.communities.gov.uk/documents/communities/ pdf/452628.pdf.

56 The video is available at https://www.youtube.com/watch?v=xGG23CarcQw.

57 Simon Shuster, 'Europe's Far-Right Leaders Unite at Dawn of Trump Era', *Time* (23 January 2017). Available at http://time.com/4643051/donald-trump-european-union-koblenz.

58 Al Muhajiroun, 'London Islamic Conference Review: The "Salafiyaa" Onslaught' (25 January 2004).

59 Peter Preston, 'Trust in the media is the first casualty of a post-factual war', the *Guardian* (25 September 2016). Available at https://www.theguardian.com/media/2016/sep/24/trust-in-media-first-casualty-post-factual-war-corbyn-trump.

60 The 'Ipsos MORI Veracity Index 2015: Trust in Professsions' is available at https://www.ipsos-mori.com/researchpublications/researcharchive/3685/Politicians-are-still-trusted-less-than-estate-agents-journalists-and-bankers.aspx.

61 Art Swift, 'Americans' Trust in Mass Media Sinks to New Low', Gallup (September 2016). Available at http://www.gallup.com/poll/195542/americans-trust-mass-media-sinks-new-low.aspx.

62 'Voters Don't Trust Media Fact-Checking', Rasmussen Reports (September 2016). Available at http://www.rasmussenreports.com/public_content/politics/general_politics/september_2016/voters_don_t_trust_media_fact_checking.

63 Ethan Epstein, 'Is Rush Limbaugh in Trouble?', *Politico Magazine* (May 2016). Available at http://www.politico.com/magazine/story/2016/05/is-rush-limbaugh-in-trouble-talk-radio-213914.

64 Rush Limbaugh on 28 September 2016 edition of Premiere Radio Networks' *The Rush Limbaugh Show*.

65 The full transcript of Rush Limbaugh's show is available at http://dailyrushbo.com/rush-limbaugh-gives-history-lesson-on-immigration.

66 Bruce Bartlett, 'It's not too late to fix Fox News', *New York Times* (19 September 2016). Available at http://www.nytimes.com/2016/09/19/opinion/its-not-too-late-to-fix-fox-news.html?_r=1.

67 Interview with Michael Fellner.

68 Ralph Keyes, *The Post-Truth Era: Dishonesty and Deception in Contemporary Life* (St Martin's Press, 2004).

69 Zeid Ra'ad Al Hussein's full speech is available at https://www.theguardian.com/law/video/2016/sep/06/atmosphere-thick-with-hate-un-human-rights-chief-rips-into-trump-and-wilders-video.

70 Adam Withnall, 'Tory minister Penny Mourdant "plain and simply lying" over Turkey joining the EU', the *Independent*, 22 May 2016. Available at http://www.independent.co.uk/news/uk/politics/penny-mordaunt-andrew-marr-uk-veto-tory-minister-accused-of-flat-out-lying-over-turkey-joining-the-a7041956.html.

71 Ben Wright, 'Reality check: How soon can Turkey join the EU?', BBC News, 17 March 2016. Available at http://www.bbc.co.uk/news/uk-politics-eu-referendum-35832035.

72 UK Statistics Authority, 'UK Statistics Authority Statement on the use of official statistics on contributions to the European Union' (2016). Available at https://www.statisticsauthority.gov.uk/news/uk-statistics-authority-statement-on-the-use-of-official-statistics-on-contributions-to-the-european-union.

73 Carl Emmerson, *et al.*, 'Brexit and the UK's Public Finances', Institute for Fiscal Studies, IFS Report 116 (2016). Available at https://www.ifs.org.uk/uploads/publications/comms/r116.pdf.

74 Jon Stone, 'Video evidence emerges of Nigel Farage pledging EU millions for NHS weeks before Brexit vote', the *Independent* (25 June 2016). Available at http://www.independent.co.uk/news/uk/politics/brexit-eu-referendum-nigel-farage-nhs-350-million-pounds-live-health-service-u-turn-a7102831.html.

75 'Donald Trump: "President Obama is the founder of Isis" – video', the *Guardian* (11 August 2016). Available at https://www.theguardian.com/us-news/video/2016/aug/11/donald-trump-president-obama-is-the-founder-of-isis-video.

76 Patrick Purcell, 'Boris admits there are no EU laws that ban people recycling tea bags', the *Mirror* (23 March 2016). Available at http://www.mirror.co.uk/news/video/boris-admits-no-eu-laws-7612442.

77 Nathan Heller, 'Trump, the University of Chicago and the Collapse of Public Language', *The New Yorker* (1 September 2016). Available at http://www.newyorker.com/culture/cultural-comment/trump-the-university-of-chicago-and-the-collapse-of-public-language.

78 According to German linguist Elisabeth Wehling; see https://www.welt.de/politik/ausland/article156089909/Trump-spricht-die-Sprache-eines-Viertklaesslers.html.

79 Interview with Lena Schmidtkunz, linguist and journalist, 31 October 2016.

80 Ibid.

81 George Orwell, 'Politics and the English Language', *Horizon* (April 1946). Available at http://www.orwell.ru/library/essays/politics/english/e_polit/.

82 'Unauthorized immigrant population stable for half a decade', Pew Research Center (September 2016): Available at http://www.pewresearch.org/fact-tank/2016/09/21/unauthorized-immigrant-population-stable-for-half-a-decade/.

83 Sam Harris, 'The Russia Connection: A Conversation with Anne Appelbaum' (23 March 2017). Available at https://www.samharris.org/podcast/item/the-russia-connection.

84 Sarah Pulliam Bailey, 'A startling number of Americans still believe President Obama is a Muslim', the *Washington Post* (14 September 2015). Available at https://www.washingtonpost.com/news/acts-of-faith/wp/2015/09/14/a-startling-number-of-americans-still-believe-president-obama-is-a-muslim/.

85 The discussion forum can be found at https://bbs.dailystormer.com/t/lets-try-two-new-terms-die-erbsunde-and-die-erbtuchtigkeit-in-learn-german-the-fun-and-easy-way-with-dr-goebbels/85663?page=6.

86 Andrew Anglin, 'Register NOW for the IRL Troll Army AKA the Stormer Book Club', Daily Stormer, 3 August 2016. Available at http://www.dailystormer.com/register-now-for-the-irl-troll-army-aka-the-stormer-book-club/.

87 Gabrielle Blanquart and David M. Cook, 'Twitter Influence and Cumulative Perceptions of Extremist Support: A Case Study of Geert Wilders',

Research Institute Conference (2013). Available at http://ro.ecu.edu.au/cgi/viewcontent.cgi?article=1021&context=act.

88 Articles available at http://yournewswire.com/new-911-evidence-cia-built-remote-controlled-passenger-jets/ and http://yournewswire.com/spy-assassination-russian-ambassador-turkey/.

89 Sean Adl-Tabatabai, 'DHS Insider: CIA and Mossad Behind DC Pedo Rink', YourNewsWire (19 February 2017). Available at http://yournewswire.com/dhs-cia-mossad-dc-pedo-ring/.

90 Baxter Dimitri, 'Queen Elizabeth Reveals She is Ready To Flee Britain', YourNewsWire (19 May 2016). Available at http://yournewswire.com/queen-elizabeth-reveals-she-is-ready-to-flee-britain/.

91 'Seriously?', *This American Life* 599 (21 October 2016). Available at http://www.thisamericanlife.org/radio-archives/episode/599/seriously.

92 Craig Silverman and Lawrence Alexander, 'How Teens in the Balkans are Duping Trump Supporters with Fake News', BuzzFeed (1 November 2016). Available at https://www.buzzfeed.com/craigsilverman/how-macedonia-became-a-global-hub-for-pro-trump-misinfo?utm_term=.yr54OzwXzz#.onYa12LP22.

93 See, for example, https://www.fakenewschecker.com/fake-news/bbc-covers-identitarian-movement.

94 'Memory and Attractor Dynamics', *Neuronal Dynamics*, section 17.1: 'Associations and Memory', École Polytechnique Fédérale de Lausanne. Available at http://neuronaldynamics.epfl.ch/online/Ch17.S1.html.

95 See Al Hayat Media Center's *Dabiq Magazine* issues available at http://www.clarionproject.org/news/islamic-state-isis-isil-propaganda-magazine-dabiq, and Noman Benotman and Nikita Malik, 'The Children of Islamic State', The Quilliam Foundation (March 2016).

96 Crofton Black and Abigail Fielding-Smith, 'Fake News and False Flags: How the Pentagon Paid a British PR Firm $500 Million for Top Secret Iraq Propaganda', The Bureau of Investigative Journalism (2 October 2016). Available at http://labs.thebureauinvestigates.com/fake-news-and-false-flags/.

97 Hankes, 'How the extremist right hijacked "Star Wars"'.

98 Eric Lipton, 'Man Motivated by "Pizzagate" Conspiracy Theory Arrested in Washington Gunfire', *New York Times* (5 December 2016). Available at https://www.nytimes.com/2016/12/05/us/pizzagate-comet-ping-pong-edgar-maddison-welch.html.

99 Russell Goldman, 'Reading Fake News, Pakistani Minister Directs Nuclear Threat at Israel', *New York Times* (24 December 2016). Available at https://www.nytimes.com/2016/12/24/world/asia/pakistan-israel-khawaja-asif-fake-news-nuclear.html.

100 The article of 70news is available at https://70news.wordpress.com/2016/11/12/final-election-2016-numbers-trump-won-both-popular-62-9-m-62-7-m-and-electoral-college-vote-306-232-hey-change-org-scrap-your-loony-petition-now/.

101 Olivia Solon, 'In firing human editors, Facebook has lost the fight against fake news', the *Guardian* (29 August 2016). Available at https://www.theguardian.com/technology/2016/aug/29/facebook-trending-news-editors-fake-news-stories.

102 Zeynep Tufekci, 'Mark Zuckerberg is in denial', *New York Times* (15 November 2016). Available at http://www.nytimes.com/2016/11/15/opinion/mark-zuckerberg-is-in-denial.html?_r=0.

103 'There is no such thing as the Denver Guardian, despite that Facebook post you saw', the *Denver Post* (5 November 2016). Available at http://www.denverpost.com/2016/11/05/there-is-no-such-thing-as-the-denver-guardian/.

104 Jeffrey Gottfried and Elsa Shearer, 'News Use Across Social Media Platforms 2016', Pew Research Center (May 2016). Available at http://www.journalism.org/2016/05/26/news-use-across-social-media-platforms-2016/.

105 Stuart Dredge, 'Facebook promises less hoax stories and spam posts in users' news feeds', the *Guardian* (21 January 2015). Available at https://www.theguardian.com/technology/2015/jan/21/facebook-news-feed-hoaxes-spam.

106 Jasper Jackson, 'Facebook and Twitter join coalition to improve social media newsgathering', the *Guardian* (13 September 2016). Available at https://www.theguardian.com/media/2016/sep/13/facebook-twitter-social-media-newsgathering.

107 Craig Silverman, Ellie Hall, *et al.*, 'Hyperpartisan Facebook Pages are Publishing False and Misleading Information at an Alarming Rate', BuzzFeed (20 October 2016). Available at https://www.buzzfeed.com/craigsilverman/partisan-fb-pages-analysis?utm_term=.xpy6Vbg0yG#.nvG1OWP06K.

108 Jonathan Albright, '"Fake News" Sites: Certified Organic?' *Medium* (15 November 2016). Available at https://medium.com/@d1gi/why-banning-fake-news-sites-from-ad-networks-wont-work-3995da452e70#.726tsoimy.

109 Ibid.

110 The archived forum is available at https://pastebin.com/n9vnF8pM and Google Doc is available at https://docs.google.com/document/d/1eogJtNsXkh6FsSvVuDMpe6dwZT_dehO33vgmDHiiEdA/edit

111 'Trump Supporters Online are Pretending to be French to Manipulate France's Election', BuzzFeed (24 January 2017). Available at https://www.buzzfeed.com/ryanhatesthis/inside-the-private-chat-rooms-trump-supporters-are-using-to?utm_term=.wrdZRz0jA#.orkPl4bwE.

112 Ralph Keyes, *The Post-Truth Era: Dishonesty and Deception in Contemporary Life* (St Martin's Press, 2004).

113 'Fake news is killing people's minds, says Apple boss', the *Guardian*, 11 February 2017. Available at https://www.theguardian.com/technology/2017/feb/11/fake-news-is-killing-peoples-minds-says-apple-boss-tim-cook.

114 Full documentary available at https://allgovernmentslie.com/film.

115 Haroon Siddique, 'Teach schoolchildren how to spot fake news, says OECD', the *Guardian* (18 March 2017). Available at https://www.theguardian.com/media/2017/mar/18/teach-schoolchildren-spot-fake-news-says-oecd.

116 Eytan Bakshy, Solomon Messing and Lada Adamic, 'Exposure to Ideologically Diverse News and Opinion on Facebook', *Science* (May 2015). Available at http://science.sciencemag.org/content/early/2015/05/06/science.aaa1160.

117 Bartlett, 'It's not too late to fix Fox News'.

118 Clark McCauley, *et al.*, 'Extremity Shifts, Risk Shifts and Attitude Shifts After Group Discussion', *European Journal of Social Psychology* 2:4 (1972), pp. 417–36.

119 Philip Zimbardo, https://www.ted.com/talks/philip_zimbardo_on_the_psychology_of_evil.

120 John Suler, 'The Online Disinhibition Effect', *Cyber Psychology & Behaviour* 7:3 (2014). Available at http://www.samblackman.org/Articles/Suler.pdf.

121 Benjamin Lee, 'Understanding the Counter-Jihad', Centre for Research and Evidence on Security Threats (3 November 2017). Available at https://crestresearch.ac.uk/comment/understanding-counter-jihad/.

122 Interview with Fiyaz Mughal, 7 November 2016.

123 At the time of writing in December 2016, the CDU Facebook page counts 123,035 likes.

124 At the time of writing in December 2016, Hollande's profile is at 987,732 likes and Valls's profile at 100,930 likes.

125 Melanie Smith and Chloe Colliver, 'Impact of Brexit on Far-Right Groups in the UK: Research Briefing', Institute for Strategic Dialogue (2016).

126 'Twitter shuts 235,000 more "extremist" accounts', BBC, 18 August 2016. Available at http://www.bbc.co.uk/news/technology-37120932.

127 Interview with Twitter employee, 9 November 2016.

128 Interview with Carl Miller, 26 October 2016.

129 Ibid.

130 Interview with Rashad Ali, 16 November 2016.

6. Escalating Extremes

1 Jörg Diel, 'Verhafteter Islamist war früher Neonazi', *Der Spiegel*, 24 February 2017. Available at http://www.spiegel.de/politik/deutschland/northeim-verhafteter-islamist-war-zuvor-neonazi-a-1136226.html.

2 Author's own translation.

3 'Neo-Nazi, radical feminist and violent jihadist – all at once', BBC, 21 September 2016. Available at http://www.bbc.co.uk/news/blogs-trending-34292809.

4 Ralph Ellis and Greg Botelho, 'Florida man accused of bomb plot at 9/11 memorial, FBI says', CNN, 11 September 2015. Available at http://

edition.cnn.com/2015/09/10/us/9-11-memorial-bomb-plot-kansas-city-missouri.

5   Georg Wilhelm Friedrich Hegel, *The Science of Logic*, trans. A. V. Miller (Prometheus Books, 1998).

6   Ibid.

7   The video is available at https://www.youtube.com/watch?v=pWZd088e2Lg.

8   https://twitter.com/TRobinsonNewEra?ref_src=twsrc%5Egoogle%7Ctwcamp%5Eserp%7Ctwgr%5Eauthor.

9   https://twitter.com/Tommy_Robinsons.

10 Tommy Robinson, *Enemy of the State* (The Press News, 2015).

11 Interview with Tommy Robinson, 12 December 2016.

12 'Giant Negro Disables 4 Policemen in Fight', *New York Times* (12 June 1927). Available in the *New York Times* archive at http://query.nytimes.com/mem/archive-free/pdf?res=9D06E6DC133FE03ABC4A52DFB066838C639EDE.

13 Author's translation of Julius Streicher (ed.), 'Die Mörder Deutschlands', *Der Stürmer* (Nürnberg, 1934), no. 38.

14 Tony Davies, *Humanism* (Routledge, 1997).

15 Heather Saul, '"Jihadi John": Mohammed Emwazi was "extremely kind, gentle, beautiful young man", says Cage director', the *Independent*, 26 February 2015. Available at http://www.independent.co.uk/news/uk/home-news/jihadi-john-mohammed-emwazi-was-an-extremely-kind-gentle-beautiful-young-man-says-cage-director-10073338.html.

15 Author's translation. The original article by Pierre Conesa is available at http://www.diploweb.com/Le-Salafisme-jihadiste-de-quoi-s.html.

16 Alexis Carrel, *L'Homme, cet inconnu* (Plon, 1999).

17 Anthony Black, *The History of Islamic Political Thought: From the Prophet to the Present* (Edinburgh University Press, 2nd edition, 2001), p. 309.

18 Interview with Götz Nordbruch, 25 October 2016.

19 Ibid.

20 'Shahida Marwa El-Sherbini – Berlin – Pierre Vogel' (August 2010). Available at https://www.youtube.com/watch?v=byllpOxS_FQ.

21 Author's translation. The original video is available at https://www.youtube.com/watch?v=C_GFcrkYur8.

22 Author's translation of Sven Lau, *Fremd Im Eigenen Land* (Al Madina Buch, 2015).

23 Ibid.

24 National Action, 'The Necessity of White Jihad' (8 November 2015). Available at http://national-action.info/news/2015/08/11/the-necessity-of-white-jihad/.

25 Interview with Götz Nordbruch, 25 October 2016.

26 Ḥarakat Al Shabāb Al Mujāhidīn, 'The Path to Paradise: From the Twin Cities to the Land of the Two Migrations #2' (January 2016).

27 Lizzie Dearden, 'Donald Trump featured in propaganda video praising Isis Brussels attacks and calling for more massacres in Europe', the *Independent* (25 March 2016). Available at http://www.independent.co.uk/news/people/

donald-trump-featured-in-propaganda-video-praising-isis-brussels-attacks-and-calling-for-more-a6951761.html.

28 For example, ISIS's Telegram channel Contestants of Jihad.

29 Juliette Harau, 'Marine Le Pen visée par la justice après avoir diffusé des photo de propagande jihadiste', *Le Monde* (16 November 2015). Available at http://www.lemonde.fr/politique/article/2015/12/16/pourquoi-marine-le-pen-a-publie-des-images-de-propagande-de-l-ei_4833263_823448.html.

30 Interview with Adam Deen, 28 October 2016.

31 Gilles Kepel, *Jihad: The Trail of Political Islam* (I.B.Tauris, 2009), pp. 208–9.

32 Interview with Adam Deen, 28 October 2016.

33 The original interview is available at http://edition.cnn.com/videos/politics/2016/03/10/donald-trump-islam-intv-ac-cooper-sot.cnn.

34 'Break the Cross', *Dabiq Magazine*, Issue 15 (31 July 2016), Al Hayat Media Center, Clarion Project, p. 9. Available at http://www.clarionproject.org/factsheets-files/islamic-state-magazine-dabiq-fifteen-breaking-the-cross.pdf.

35 'The Murtadd Vote', Al Hayat Media Center (2016). Available at https://baytalmasadircom.files.wordpress.com/2016/11/is-text-the-murtadd-vote.pdf.

36 'Break the Cross', *Dabiq Magazine*.

37 'ISIS details "Why We Hate You"' in new magazine', Fox News (1 August 2016). Available at http://www.foxnews.com/world/2016/08/01/isis-details-why-hate-in-new-magazine.html.

38 Interview with Usama Hasan, 7 November 2016.

39 Interview with Fiyaz Mughal, 7 November 2016.

40 Jamie Bartlett and Jonathan Birdwell, 'Cumulative Radicalisation Between Far-Right and Islamist Groups in the UK: A Review of Evidence', Demos (November 2013).

41 Bartlett and Birdwell, 'Cumulative Radicalisation'.

42 Interview with Fiyaz Mughal, 7 November 2016.

43 Author's translation of the rap song 'Dealer Pour Survivre' by the French hip hop group Expression Direkt featured in the movie *La Haine*.

44 'Forsane Alizza: neuf ans de prison pour le fondateur du grouuscule', *Le Figaro* (1 July 2015). Available at http://www.lefigaro.fr/actualite-france/2015/07/10/01016-20150710ARTFIG00190-forsane-alizza-neuf-ans-de-prison-pour-le-fondateur-du-groupuscule.php.

45 Maajid Nawaz, *Radical: My Journey from Islamist Extremism to Democratic Awakening* (W. H. Allen, 2012).

46 Interview with Abdelghani Merah, 19 December 2016.

47 Ibid.

48 Houria Bouteldja's speech 'Mohammed Merah and I' at '2012: Printemps des quartiers populaires' (Bagnolet, 31 March 2012).

49 The list of extremist accounts and Telegram channels was compiled with the aid of counter-terrorism and cyber security experts. It included members

of and sympathisers with both non-violent and violent Islamist extremist networks.

50 Interview with Omar, 9 November 2016.

51 'A Muslim Made Dua for Donald Trump at the Republican National Convention', Hizb ut-Tahrir America (n.d.). Available at https://hizb-america.org/a-muslim-made-dua-for-donald-trump-at-the-republican-national-convention.

52 Jonathan Martin, *et al.*, 'Voters express disgust over U.S. politics in new Times/CBS poll', *New York Times* (3 November 2016). Available at http://www.nytimes.com/2016/11/04/us/politics/hillary-clinton-donald-trump-poll.html?_r=0.

53 The post is available at https://www.facebook.com/abdulwahid.ht/posts/10154791895466869.

54 'The Murtadd Vote', Al Hayat Media Center (2016). Available at https://baytalmasadircom.files.wordpress.com/2016/11/is-text-the-murtadd-vote.pdf; spellings as seen.

55 Charlie Winter, '2016 Elections: ISIS Weighs In', *The Atlantic* (8 November 2016). Available at http://www.theatlantic.com/international/archive/2016/11/isis-2016-election/506924.

56 'The Murtadd Vote'.

57 Lizzie Dearden, 'Salman Abedi once called RE teacher an "Islamophobe" for asking his opinion of suicide bombers', the *Independent* (26 May 2017). Available at http://www.independent.co.uk/news/uk/home-news/salman-abedi-re-teacher-islamophobe-suicide-bombers-burnage-academy-for-boys-opinion-manchester-a7756611.html.

58 Martin Evans, Hannah Furness and Victoria Ward, 'Finsbury Park suspect "turned against Muslims" after London Bridge attack', the *Telegraph*, 20 June 2017 (http://www.telegraph.co.uk/news/2017/06/19/finsbury-park-suspect-had-abused-muslim-neighbour/).

59 A linear regression was conducted on the basis of data extracted from The Global Terrorism Database (GTD) for the US, Australia, the UK, France and Germany. All missing data for 2016 was completed manually in accordance with inclusion criteria used by GTD. The perpetrators of all incidents were examined for links to far-right and Islamist extremist groups on the basis of mainstream news articles.

60 Arie Perlinger, 'Challenges from the Sidelines: Understanding America's Far-Right', Combating Terrorism Center (January 2013), p. 87. Available at https://www.ctc.usma.edu/posts/challengers-from-the-sidelines-understanding-americas-violent-far-right.

61 Federal Bureau of Investigation, 'Uniform Crime Reports: Hate Crime' (2001).

62 Michelle Mark, 'Anti-Muslim hate crimes', *International Business Times* (18 November 2015).

63 Interview with Carl Miller, 26 October 2016.

64 Carl Miller, Jack Dale and Josh Smith, 'Islamophobia on Twitter: March to July 2016', Demos (2016).

65 Interview with Fiyaz Mughal, 7 November 2016.

66 Ibid.

67 Dominic Casciani, 'Six admit planning to bomb English Defence League rally', BBC, 30 April 2013. Available at http://www.bbc.co.uk/news/uk-22344054.

68 Interview with Fiyaz Mughal, 7 November 201.

69 Ibid.

7. Geography of Hate

1 Arie Perlinger and Daniel Milton, 'From Cradle to Grave: The Lifecycle of Foreign Fighters in Iraq and Syria', Combating Terrorism Center at West Point (November 2016). Available at https://www.ctc.usma.edu/v2/wp-content/uploads/2016/11/Cradle-to-Grave.pdf.

2 Jack Moore, 'London's ISIS Cell: Inside the East End Suburb of Barking Where Jihadis Meet Far-Right Nationalists', *Newsweek* (6 June 2017). Available at http://www.newsweek.com/barking-hometown-london-attackers-impoverished-suburb-where-extremism-bubbles-621259.

3 Jamie Bartlett and Jonathan Birdwell, 'Cumulative Radicalisation Between the Far-Right and Islamist Groups in the UK: A Review of Evidence', Demos (2013).

4 Matthew Goodwin, 'Woolwich attack and the far right: three points to consider when the dust settles', the *Guardian* (23 May 2013). Available at https://www.theguardian.com/commentisfree/2013/may/23/woolwich-attack-far-right-three-points.

5 Interview with Fiyaz Mughal, 7 November 2016.

6 Ollie Gillmann, 'How former mill town Dewsbury in West Yorkshire is linked to more than a dozen Islamist extremists and terrorists including Britain's youngest suicide bomber', the *Daily Mail* (15 June 2015). Available at http://www.dailymail.co.uk/news/article-3124673/Dewsbury-former-town-West-Yorkshire-home-Britain-s-youngest-suicide-bomber-links-Islamist-extremists.html.

7 A more detailed ethnicity breakdown can be found in the 2011 census: https://www.ons.gov.uk/census/2011census.

8 Sam Greenhill, 'Veil teacher link to 7/7 bomber', *Daily Mail* (21 October 2006). Available at http://www.dailymail.co.uk/news/article-411748/Veil-teacher-link-7-7-bomber.html.

9 Andrew Norfolk, 'Muslim group behind mega-mosque seeks to convert all Britain', *The Times* (10 September 2007). Available at http://www.thetimes.co.uk/tto/faith//.

10 Padraig Flanagan, 'Muslim courts are already here', the *Daily Express* (9 February 2008). Available at http://www.express.co.uk/news/uk/34373/Muslim-courts-are-here-already.

11 Gerard Tubb, 'Exposed: UK School Promoting Extreme Islam', Sky News (31 March 2016). Available at http://news.sky.com/story/exposed-uk-school-promoting-extreme-islam-10224616.

12 'Six admit planning to bomb English Defence League Rally', BBC News, 30 April 2013. Available at http://www.bbc.co.uk/news/uk-22344054.

13 Lauren Potts, 'Beleaguered town of Dewsbury back in spotlight', BBC, 15 June 2015. Available at http://www.bbc.co.uk/news/uk-england-leeds-33138398.

14 UK Online Census 2011, Office for National Statistics, Neighbourhood Statistics. Available at http://www.neighbourhood.statistics.gov.uk/dissemination/LeadTableView.do?a=7&b=6275157&c=luton&d=13&e=62&g=6394327&i=1001x1003x1032x1004&m=0&r=1&s=1361379856444&enc=1&dsFamilyId=2479.

15 Tommy Robinson, *Enemy of the State* (The Press News, 2015), p. 56.

16 Ibid.

17 Ibid., p. 261.

18 Neil Tweedie, 'The English Defence League – will the flames of hatred spread?', the *Telegraph* (10 October 2009). Available at http://www.telegraph.co.uk/news/6284184/The-English-Defence-League-will-the-flames-of-hatred-spread.html.

19 Nigel Copsey, 'The English Defence League: Challenging Our Country and Our Values of Social Inclusion, Fairness and Equality', *Faith Matters* (2010). Available at http://faith-matters.org/images/stories/fm-reports/english-defense-league-report.pdf.

20 Mark Townsend, 'After Paris, Luton wages its own battle for hearts and minds of homegrown radicals', the *Guardian* (28 November 2015). Available at https://www.theguardian.com/uk-news/2015/nov/28/why-luto-mosques-schools-battle-against-jihadi-propaganda.

21 Nick Lowles, 'The EDL marches into Luton today. Hold your breath', the *Guardian* (5 February 2011). Available at https://www.theguardian.com/commentisfree/2011/feb/05/edl-extremists-march-luton-interests.

22 Bartlett and Birdwell, 'Cumulative Radicalisation'.

23 Townsend, 'After Paris'.

24 The video is available at https://www.youtube.com/watch?v=fA6XcyXsxXU.

25 'How Christian Patrol inflames racial tension: Members of far-right group confront Muslim women and brand Mohammed a false prophet as they stage bizarre demonstration in Luton', the *Daily Mail* (31 January 2016). Available at http://www.dailymail.co.uk/news/article-3424680/How-Christian-patrol-inflames-racial-tension-Members-far-Right-group-confront-Muslim-women-brand-Mohammed-false-prophet-stage-bizarre-demonstration-Luton.html.

26 Chris Greenwood, '"Cell called for jihad" in Luton church hall: Police believe they have smashed network that encouraged people to support ISIS', *Daily Mail* (10 December 2015). Available at http://www.dailymail.co.uk/news/article-3353638/Cell-called-jihad-Luton-church-hall-Police-believe-smashed-network-encouraged-people-support-ISIS.html.

27 Liam Deacon, 'UK ISIS Cell Called for Terrorism Anniversary Bombing, Tried to Recruit Children', *Breitbart* (10 December 2015). Available at

http://www.breitbart.com/london/2015/12/10/luton-islamic-state-cell-called-for-77-anniversary-bombing-and-tried-to-recruit-children.

28 Mark Townsend, 'The Pompey Jihadis: How did one English city produce six young fighters for ISIS?', the *Guardian* (26 October 2014). Available at http://www.telegraph.co.uk/news/worldnews/middleeast/syria/11665456/How-Portsmouth-became-a-hotbed-of-radicalised-Muslims-and-far-right-thugs.html.

29 Joe Shute, 'How Portsmouth became a hotbed of radicalised Muslims and far right thugs', the *Telegraph* (13 June 2015). Available at http://www.telegraph.co.uk/news/worldnews/middleeast/syria/11665456/How-Portsmouth-became-a-hotbed-of-radicalised-Muslims-and-far-right-thugs.html.

30 Ibid.

31 'IERA linked to ISIS' (19 November 2014). Available at http://standforpeace.org.uk/iera-linked-to-isis-recruits.

32 Mark Townsend, 'The Pompey Jihadis: How did one English city produce six young fighters for ISIS?', the *Guardian* (26 October 2014). Available at https://www.theguardian.com/uk-news/2014/oct/26/portsmouth-jihadis-isis-islamic-state.

33 Shute, 'How Portsmouth became a hotbed'.

34 'Police to investigate mosque protest', *Portsmouth News* (13 November 2010). Available at http://www.portsmouth.co.uk/news/police-to-investigate-mosque-protest-1-2301213.

35 Ben Fishwick, 'EDL stage protest outside mosque', *Portsmouth News* (4 December 2013). Available at http://www.portsmouth.co.uk/news/edl-stage-protest-outside-mosque-1-5728995.

36 Ben Fishwick, 'Men arrested after pig's head cable-tied to Islamic school gates in Portsmouth', *Portsmouth News* (21 March 2016). Available at http://www.portsmouth.co.uk/news/crime/men-arrested-after-pig-s-head-cable-tied-to-islamic-school-gates-in-portsmouth-1-7293350.

37 Alice Ross, 'Westminster terrorist Khalid Masood wasn't an extremist, says ex-boss', the *Guardian* (28 March 2017). Available at https://www.theguardian.com/uk-news/2017/mar/28/westminster-terrorist-khalid-masood-wasnt-an-islamist-says-ex-boss.

38 Steven Swinford, 'Britain's terror hotspots: Raids focus on Birmingham, Luton and East London', the *Telegraph* (23 March 2017). Available at http://www.telegraph.co.uk/news/2017/03/23/britains-terror-hotspots-raids-focus-birmingham-luton-east-london.

39 The EDL Facebook post is available at https://www.facebook.com/EDLBournemouth/posts/701491876603324.

40 Joel Busher, *The Making of Anti-Muslim Protest: Grassroots Activism in the English Defence League* (Extremism and Democracy) (Routledge, 2015).

41 Peter Clarke, CVO, OBE, QPM, 'Birmingham Schools: Education Commissioner's Report, HM Government, Department for Education (22 July 2014). Available at https://www.gov.uk/government/uploads/system/uploads/attachment_data/file/340526/HC_576_accessible_-.pdf.

42 Mike Lockey, 'Far-right Combat 18 in "secret plan to recruit Birmingham teachers"', *Birmingham Mail* (2 July 2016). Available at http://www.birminghammail.co.uk/news/midlands-news/far-right-combat-18-secret-11557407.

43 The full video is available at https://www.youtube.com/watch?v=Z5gjFNc0Dgc.

44 'Monique Bousquet, 'i-Télé : Mohamed Chirani impose la langue arabe aux Français', *Riposte Laïque* (20 November 2015). Available at https://ripostelaique.com/arabe-texte-i-tele.html.

45 Ibid.

46 Gilles Kepel, *La Fracture* (Gallimard, 2016).

47 'Le Bloc Identitaire Devient Les Identitaires', Les Identitaires (13 July 2016). Available at http://www.les-identitaires.com/2016/07/le-bloc-identitaire-devient-les-identitaires/.

48 Achraf Ben Brahim, *L'Emprise: Enquête au Coeur de la Jihadosphère* (Lemieux, 2016), pp. 194–5.

49 Author's translation. The original interview with Causeur is available at http://www.causeur.fr/zemmour-guilluy-trump-mesguisch-40387.html.

50 The original iTélé debate is available at https://www.youtube.com/watch?v=Z5gjFNc0Dgc.

51 Rachid Benzine, in Pascal Blanchard, Nicolas Bancel and Dominic Thomas (eds), *Vers la Guerre des Identités : De la Fracture Coloniale à la Révolution Ultranationale* (La Découverte, 2016), p. 102.

52 Ibid.

53 Nicolas Bancel in Blanchard, Bancel and Thomas (eds), *Vers la Guerre des Identités*, p. 159.

54 Interview with Mohammed Chirani, 15 and 27 November 2016.

55 Kepel, *La Fracture*, p. 192.

56 Gavin Mortimer, 'Islamic State will want a landslide victory for Marine Le Pen', *The Spectator* (25 November 2016). Available at http://blogs.spectator.co.uk/2016/11/landslide-le-pen-perfect-election-outcome-islamic-state/

57 The article is available at http://laicart.org/sevran-devenu-khalifa-a-40-minutes-de-paris.

58 Raphaelle Besse Desmoulières, 'Molenbeek francais: le maire de Sevran se rebiffe', *Le Monde* (2 April 2016). Available at http://www.lemonde.fr/m-actu/article/2016/04/02/molenbeek-francais-le-maire-de-sevran-se-rebiffe_4894610_4497186.html.

59 Brahim, *L'Emprise* (2016).

60 Nawaz, *Radical*, p. 73.

61 Achaf Ben Brahim, *Encarté: Mon immersion dans les partis politiques* (Lemieux, 2015).

62 Brahim, *L'Emprise* (2016), p. 144.

63 'Réunion contre l'extrême droite à Sevran', *Le Parisien* (26 April 2002). Available at http://www.leparisien.fr/seine-saint-denis/reunion-contre-l-extreme-droite-a-sevran-26-04-2002-2003017274.php.

64 Interview with Mohammed Chirani, 15 and 27 November 2016.

65 Brahim, *L'Emprise* (2016), p. 133.

66 'Sevran, 'Le Molenbeek Français', *Français de Souche* (22 March 2016). Available at http://www.fdesouche.com/711803-sevran-93-le-molenbeek-francais.

67 Pierre Longeray, 'French Riviera has become a hotbed of jihadist recruitment', *Vice* (15 July 2016). Available at https://news.vice.com/article/the-french-riviera-has-become-a-hotbed-of-jihadist-recruitment.

68 'Djihad, les recruteurs', Complément d'enquête, *France* 2 (2 June 2016).

69 The web page of Les Identitaires is available at https://www.bloc-identitaire.com.

70 Interview with Mohammed Chirani, 15 and 27 November 2016.

71 Henri Astier, 'Why Jihadists stalk the French Riviera', BBC News, 16 July 2016. Available at https://news.vice.com/article/the-french-riviera-has-become-a-hotbed-of-jihadist-recruitment.

72 David Chazan, 'Muslim footballers on pitch risk suspension if they pray on the pitch', the *Telegraph* (30 April 2016). Available at http://www.telegraph.co.uk/news/2016/04/30/muslim-footballers-on-french-riviera-risk-suspension-if-they-pra/.

73 Romina McGuinness, 'As many as 70 Islamic terror attacks on French Riviera thwarted in just 12 weeks', the *Express* (28 September 2016). Available at http://www.express.co.uk/news/world/715397/70-Islamic-terror-attacks-French-Riviera-thwarted-12-weeks-Nice-Paris-terror-attacks.

74 Anne-Sylvaine Chassany, 'French town wrestles with extremes of Syrian war', *Financial Times* (15 April 2016). Available at https://www.ft.com/content/2146f434-fca9-11e5-b5f5-070dca6d0a0d.

75 Gilles Kepel, *Terreur dans l'Hexagone: Genèse du djihad français* (Gallimard, 2015).

76 Ysis Percq, 'Tahar Akermi, un engagement en faveur des jeunes à Lunel', *La Croix* (19 April 2016). Available at http://www.la-croix.com/France/Tahar-Akermi-engagement-faveur-jeunes-Lunel-2016-04-19-1200754412.

77 Interview with Tahar Akermi, 5 January 2017.

78 'Résultats des élections regionals 2015: Lunel (34400), Hérault'. Available at http://www.lexpress.fr/actualite/politique/elections/regionales-2015/resultats-elections/ville-lunel-34400_34145.html.

79 Christopher de Bellaigue, 'France's Clampdown on Radical Muslims Could be Storing Up Trouble', Pulitzer Center on Crisis Reporting (3 April 2016). Available at http://pulitzercenter.org/reporting/france-clampdown-radical-muslims-could-be-storing-trouble.

80 Brenna Daldorph, 'Jihadist arrests deepen divisions in French town', France24 (3 March 2015). Available at http://www.france24.com/en/France-Lunel-jihadist-town-divisions.

81 Interview with Alexander Ritzmann, 9 November 2016.

82 'Linke gegen rechte gegen Salafisten', *Osnabrücker Zeitung* (2 September 2016). Available at http://www.noz.de/deutschland-welt/politik/artikel/768781/linke-gegen-rechte-gegen-salafisten-1.

83 Interview with Alexander Ritzmann, 9 November 2016.

84 Interview with Daniel Köhler, 25 October 2016.

85 Ibid.

86 Ibid.

87 Verfasungsschutzbericht Niedersachsen.

88 'Ausländerfeindlicher Anschlag in Solingen: Das Brandmal', *Der Spriegel* (27 May 2013). Available at http://www.spiegel.de/panorama/gesellschaft/brandanschlag-in-solingen-was-taeter-und-opfer-heute-sagen-a-901431.html.

89 Günther Lachmann, 'Solingen, Türken und ein ewig brennendes Feuer', *Die Welt* (20 December 2012). Available at https://www.welt.de/politik/lachmann/article5581089/Solingen-Tuerken-und-ein-ewig-brennendes-Feuer.html.

90 The original footage is available at https://www.youtube.com/watch?v=f4WtoKG7eJ8.

91 'Graue Wölfe im Schafspelz: Türkische Faschisten in Deutschland', ZDF (26 May 2015). German manuscript available at https://www.zdf.de/ZDF/zdfportal/blob/38616008/1/data.pdf.

92 A summary of the background and activities of the Grey Wolves can be found at http://webstory.zdf.de/graue-woelfe/.

93 Florian Flade and Kristian Frigelj, 'Wie der Staat Salafisten aus Solingen verjagt', *Die Welt* (14 June 2012). Available at https://www.welt.de/politik/deutschland/article106594594/Wie-der-Staat-Salafisten-aus-Solingen-verjagt.html.

94 Justin Huggler, 'Islamist preacher in Germany arrested over terror links', the *Telegraph* (15 December 2015). Available at http://www.telegraph.co.uk/news/worldnews/europe/germany/12051721/Islamist-preacher-in-Germany-arrested-over-terror-links.html.

95 Soeren Kern, 'Germany vs. Radical Islamists', The Gatestone Institute (15 March 2013). Available at https://www.gatestoneinstitute.org/3625/germany-radical-islamists.

96 'Innenminister Friedrich fürchtet Gewalt in NRW', *Der Spiegel* (28 April 2012). Available at http://www.spiegel.de/politik/deutschland/bundesinnenminister-friedrich-warnt-vor-gewalt-im-nrw-wahlkampf-a-830400.html.

97 'Salafisten attackieren Polizisten nach Pro-NRW Kundgebung', *Der Spiegel* (1 May 2012). Available at http://www.spiegel.de/panorama/justiz/salafisten-attackieren-polizisten-nach-pro-nrw-kundgebung-a-830761.html.

98 'Salafisten stechen in NRW auf Polizisten ein', *Focus Online* (6 May 2012). Available at http://www.focus.de/politik/deutschland/29-polizisten-zum-teil-schwer-verletzt-salafisten-stechen-in-nrw-auf-polizisten-ein_aid_747917.html.

99 P. Beucker and W. Schmidt, 'Salafisten und Pro-NRW in Köln: Islamisten und Islamhasser getrennt', TAZ (8 May 2012). Available at http://www.taz.de/!5094334/.

100 Ibid.

101 'Salafisten bei Pro-NRW-Kundgebung: Radikale unter sich', *Der Spiegel* (5 May 2012). Available at http://www.spiegel.de/politik/deutschland/pro-nrw-anhaenger-und-salafisten-kundgebung-eskaliert-in-bonn-a-831570.html.

102 Lena Kampf and Andreas Spinrath, 'Verfahren mit Symbolcharakter', Tagesschau (6 September 2016). Available at http://www.tagesschau.de/inland/sven-lau-prozess-101.html.

103 Soeren Kern, 'Germany's Sharia Police', Gate Stone Institute (8 September 2014). Available at https://www.gatestoneinstitute.org/4681/germany-sharia-police.

104 Soeren Kern, 'Germany's Sharia Police', Gate Stone Institute (8 September 2014). Available at https://www.gatestoneinstitute.org/4681/germany-sharia-police.

105 'Hooligans against Salafists demo set to unfold', DW (26 October 2014). Available at http://www.dw.com/en/hooligans-against-salafists-demo-set-to-unfold/a-18021664.

106 Footage from the confrontations is available at https://www.youtube.com/watch?v=cs4O9pFzU6w.

107 'Georg Heil, Volkmar Kabisch and Georg Mascoli, 'Wichtiger Anwerber des IS in Deutschland verhaftet', *Die Süddeutsche* (8 November 2016). Available at http://www.sueddeutsche.de/politik/eil-wichtiger-anwerber-des-is-in-deutschland-verhaftet-1.3239523.

108 'In Wolfsburg leben bis zu 40 radikalisierte Salafisten', *Wolfsburger Allgemeine* (9 June 2016). Available at http://www.waz-online.de/Wolfsburg/Stadt-Wolfsburg/In-Wolfsburg-leben-bis-zu-40-radikalisierte-Salafisten.

109 Neumann, *Radicalized*, p. 118.

110 'Stadt Wolfsburg verbietet rechtsradikale Demo', *Wolfsburger Allgemeine* (3 April 2013). Available at http://www.waz-online.de/Wolfsburg/Stadt-Wolfsburg/Stadt-Wolfsburg-verbietet-rechtsradikale-Demo.

111 'IS Kämpfer in Wolfsburg festgenommen', *NPD Niedersachsen* (21 November 2014). Available at http://www.npd-niedersachsen.de/index.php/menue/58/thema/69/id/4214/anzeigemonat/11/akat/1/anzeigejahr/2014/infotext/IS_Kaempfer_in_Wolfsburg_festgenommen/Bundesweite_Nachrichten.html.

112 More information is available at https://www.afd-niedersachsen.de/index.php/afd1/2212-04-11-2016-wolfsburg-afd-uebernimmt-vorsitz-des-migrationsausschusses.

113 Beatrice Oßberger, 'Salafisten in Bayern woollen Flüchtlinge anwerben', *Die Welt* (11 September 2015). Available at https://www.welt.de/regionales/bayern/article146292193/Salafisten-in-Bayern-wollen-Fluechtlinge-anwerben.html.

114 'Verfassungsschutz: Nürnberg ist Salafisten-Hochburg', *Nordbayern* (17 September 2016). Available at http://www.nordbayern.de/region/nuernberg/verfassungsschutz-nuernberg-ist-salafisten-hochburg-1.5493098.

115 Ibid.

116 Daniel Köhler, *Right-Wing Terrorism in the 21st Century: 'The National Socialist Underground' and the History of Terror from the Far Right in Germany* (Routledge, 2017), p. 132.

117 Johannes Görz and Sebastian Martin, 'Die Rechte in Bamberg: Chronologie einer Radikalisierung', inFranken.de (25 October 2015). Available at http://www.infranken.de/regional/bamberg/Die-Rechte-in-Bamberg-Chronologie-einer-Radikalisierung;art212,1324124.

118 Köhler, *Right-Wing Terrorism*, p. 190.

119 Multiple studies found links between unemployment and radicalisation and suggested that boredom is a strong factor; see, for example, Moamen Gouda and Marcus Marktanner, 'Muslim Youth Unemployment and Expat Jihadism – Bored to Death?', SSRN (March 2017). Available at https://papers.ssrn.com/sol3/papers.cfm?abstract_id=2838796.

120 'Foreign Fighters: An Updated Assessment of the Flow of Foreign Fighters into Syria and Iraq', The Soufan Group (December 2015). Available at http://soufangroup.com/wp-content/uploads/2015/12/TSG_ForeignFightersUpdate3.pdf.

121 Alex Haley and Malcolm X, *The Autobiography of Malcolm X* (Ballantine Books, 1964). Available at http://nationalhumanitiescenter.org/ows/seminars/aahistory/MalcolmX.pdf.

122 Nawaz, *Radical*, Preface to the US edition.

123 Interview with Richard Barrett, CMG, OBE, 11 January 2017.

124 Ibid.

125 The full transcript of Geert Wilders' speech is available at http://pvv.nl/index.php/36-fj-related/geert-wilders/8337-speech-geert-wilde.

126 The Southern Poverty Law Centre's hate map is available at https://www.splcenter.org/hate-map.

127 'White Supremacist Prison Gangs in the United States: A Preliminary Inventory'. Available at http://www.adl.org/assets/pdf/combating-hate/CR_4499_WhiteSupremacist-Report_web_vff.pdf.

8. Breaking the Vicious Circle

1 'Asda shelf-stacker Ryan Ashley Counsell planned to join militants in post-Brexit low', Sky News, 3 March 2017. Available at http://news.sky.com/story/asda-shelf-stacker-ryan-ashley-counsell-planned-to-join-militants-in-post-brexit-low-10788720.

2 Human Rights Watch, 'World Report 2016'. Available at https://www.hrw.org/world-report/2016.

3 See, for example, studies by UNESCO, the British government and Hedayah.

4 The latest educational attainment statistics are available at http://ec.europa.eu/eurostat/statistics-explained/index.php/Educational_attainment_statistics.

5   Franklin D. Roosevelt delivered his speech, The Four Freedoms, on 6
     January 1941.

Epilogue

1   The footage is available here: https://www.therebel.media/troll_watch_3_
     tommy_robinson_vs_quilliam.
2   The discussions are available at http://boards.4chan.org/pol/thread/
     123867713/stupid-libtard-exposed and http://boards.4chan.org/pol/thread/
     125237285/is-tommy-robinson-ourguy.
3   Mark Scott, 'U.S. Far-Right Activists Promote Hacking Attack Against
     Macron', *New York Times* (6 May 2017). Available at https://www.nytimes.
     com/2017/05/06/world/europe/emmanuel-macron-hack-french-election-
     marine-le-pen.html?_r=0.

Further Reading

Andersen, Benedict, *Imagined Communities: Reflections on the Origin and Spread of Nationalism* (NY: Verso, 1983).

Ates, Seyran, *Selam, Frau Imamin* (Berlin: Ullstein, 2017).

Atwan, Abdel Bari, *Islamic State: The Digital Caliphate* (London: Saqi, 2015).

Bancel, Nicholas, Pascal Blanchard and Dominic Thomas, *Vers la Guerre des Identités? De la Fracture Coloniale à la Révolution Nationale* (Paris: La Découverte, 2005).

Bartlett, Jamie, *Radicals: Outsiders Changing the World* (London: Penguin Random House, 2017).

Bartlett, Jamie, Jonathan Birdwell and Mark Littler, *New Face of Digital Populism* (London: Demos, 2012).

Brahim, Achraf Ben, *L'Emprise: Enquête au Cœur de la Jihadosphère* (Paris: Lemieux, 2016).

Burke, Jason, *The New Threat from Islamic Militancy* (London: Bodley Head, 2015).

Busher, Joel, *The Making of Anti-Muslim Protest: Grassroots Activism in the English Defence League* (London: Routledge, 2015).

Camus, Jean-Yves and Nicolas Lebourg, *Far-Right Politics in Europe* (Cambridge: Harvard University Press, 2017).

Chirani, Mohammed, *Islam de France: La République en Échec* (Paris: Fayard, 2017).

Cockburn, Patrick, *The Rise of Islamic State: ISIS and the New Sunni Revolution* (London: Faber & Faber, 2015).

De Bellaigue, Christopher, *The Islamic Enlightenment: The Struggle Between Faith and Reason, 1798 to Modern Times* (NY: Liverlight, 2017).

Feldman, Matthew and Roger Griffin, *Fascism: Critical Concepts in Political Science* (London: Routledge, 2003).

Fishman, Brian M., *The Masterplan: ISIS, al-Qaeda and the Jihadi Strategy for Final Victory* (New Haven: Yale University Press, 2016).

Goodhart, David, *The Road to Somewhere: The Populist Revolt and the Future of Politics* (London: Hurst, 2017).

Goodwin, Matthew, *Right Response: Understanding and Countering Populist Extremism in Europe* (London: Chatham House Report, 2012).

Griffin, Michael, *Islamic State: Rewriting History* (London: Pluto Press, 2016).

Halverson, Jeffry R., J. L. Goodall and Steven R. Corman, *Master Narratives of Islamist Extremism* (NY: Palgrave Macmillan, 2011).

Harari, Yuval Noah, *Sapiens: A Brief History of Humankind* (NY: Vintage Books, 2014).

Harris, Sam and Maajid Nawaz, *Islam and the Future of Tolerance: A Dialogue* (NY: Harvard University Press, 2015).

Hassan, Hassan and Michael Weiss, *ISIS: Inside the Army of Terror* (NY: Regan Arts, 2015).

Husain, Ed, *The Islamist: Why I Joined Radical Islam in Britain, What I Saw Inside and Why I Left* (London: Penguin, 2007).

Jones, Owen, *The Establishment: And How They Get Away With It* (London: Penguin, 2015).

Kepel, Gilles, *Jihad: The Trail of Political Islam* (London: I.B.Tauris, 2009).

Keyes, Ralph, *The Post-Truth Era: Dishonesty and Deception in Contemporary Life* (NY: St Martin's Press, 2004).

Khan, Sarah, *The Battle for British Islam: Reclaiming Muslim Identity from Extremism* (London: Saqi Books, 2016).

Köhler, Daniel, *Right-Wing Terrorism in the 21st Century: The 'National Socialist Underground' and the History of Terror from the Far Right in Germany* (London: Taylor & Francis, 2017).

Kundani, Arun, *The Muslims Are Coming! Islamophobia, Extremism and the Domestic War on Terror* (NY: Verso Books, 2014).

Lister, Charles, *The Syrian Jihad: Al-Qaeda, the Islamic State and the Evolution of an Insurgency* (London: Hurst, 2015).

Maher, Shiraz, *Salafi-Jihadism: The History of an Idea* (London: Hurst, 2016).

Mansour, Ahmad, *Generation Allah: Warum wir im Kampf gegen den religiösen Extremismus umdenken müssen* (Berlin: S. Fischer, 2015).

Marzouki, Nadia, Duncan McDonnell and Oliver Roy, *Saving the People: How Populists Hijack Religion* (London: Hurst, 2016).

McCants, Will, *ISIS Apocalypse: The History, Strategy and Doomsday Vision of the Islamic State* (NY: St Martin's Press, 2015).

Mudde, Cas, *The Populist Radical Right: A Reader* (London Routledge, 2012).

Mudde, Cas, *On Extremism and Democracy in Europe* (London: Routledge, 2016).

Mulloy, Darren, *American Extremism: History, Politics and the Militia Movement* (NY: Routledge, 2004).

Nagle, Angela, *Kill All Normies: Online Culture Wars from 4chan and Tumblr to Trump and the Alt-right* (London: Zero Books, 2017).

Nance, Malcolm, *Defeating ISIS: Who They Are, How They Fight, What They Believe* (NY: Skyhorse Publishing, 2016).

Nance, Malcolm and Chris Sampson, *Hacking ISIS: How to Destroy the Cyber Jihad* (NY: Skyhorse Publishing, 2017).

Nawaz, Maajid, *Radical: My Journey from Islamist Extremism to a Democratic Awakening* (London: W.H. Allen, 2013).

Neumann, Peter, *Radicalized: New Jihadists and the Threat to the West* (London: I.B.Tauris, 2016).

Pantucci, Raffaello, *'We Love Death as You Love Life': Britain's Suburban Terrorists* (London: Hurst, 2015).

Rapoport, Yossef and Shahab Ahmed (eds), *Ibn Taymiyya and His Times* (Oxford: Oxford University Press, 2010).

Rogers, Paul, *Irregular War: ISIS and the New Threat from the Margins* (London: I.B.Tauris, 2016).

Soufan, Ali, *The Black Banners: Inside the Hunt for Al-Qaeda* (NY: Penguin, 2012).

Speckhard, Anne, *Talking to Terrorists: Understanding the Psycho-Social Motivations of Militant Jihadi Terrorists, Mass Hostage Takers, Suicide Bombers & 'Martyrs'* (McLean: Advances Press, 2012).

Warrick, Joby, *Black Flags: The Rise of ISIS* (London: Bantam Press, 2015).

Wright, Lawrence, *The Looming Tower: Al Qaeda's Road to 9/11* (London: Penguin, 2006).

Index